THEIR PROPER SPHERE

To my father, Gustav Ekeblad,
and the memory of my mother, Ingeborg Ekeblad

Their Proper Sphere

A STUDY OF THE BRONTË SISTERS AS EARLY-VICTORIAN FEMALE NOVELISTS

INGA-STINA EWBANK

Lecturer in English Literature in the University of Liverpool

HARVARD UNIVERSITY PRESS

Cambridge, Massachusetts

1966

This book is published in cooperation with Scandinavian
University Books/Akademiförlaget-Gumperts, Göteborg,
Sweden, and is not to be sold in Scandinavia

Printed in Great Britain by
The Camelot Press Ltd., London and Southampton

Contents

v

Preface

IN 1842, five years before the publication of *Jane Eyre*, *Wuthering Heights* and *Agnes Grey*, there appeared a book by Miss M. A. Stodart called *Female Writers: Thoughts on Their Proper Sphere, and on Their Powers of Usefulness*. In the same year Mrs. Sarah Ellis, in *The Daughters of England*, one in her series of manuals on womanhood, expressed her hope that

> the youthful reader of these pages has reflected seriously upon her position in society as a woman, has acknowledged her inferiority to man, has examined her own nature, and found there a capability of feeling, a quickness of perception, and a facility of adaptation, beyond what he possesses, and which, consequently, fit her for a distinct and separate sphere.

The novels of the Brontës appeared on a scene where it was assumed that woman occupies a sphere 'distinct and separate' from man's, and that when women take to writing, they should do so in terms of 'Their Proper Sphere'.

This book is an attempt to answer such questions as: what did the early Victorians see as the proper sphere of the woman novelist? how far is the work of each of the Brontës delimited by such a sphere? and, ultimately, what did each of the Brontë sisters see as her own proper sphere? In trying to provide answers I have concentrated on the novels of Charlotte, Emily and Anne Brontë *as novels*. The Brontës have been particularly subjected to the kind of 'literary' method that begins with biography, then searches the works for 'clues', only to return in the end to biography. My concern is with a critical appreciation of the art of the Brontës, and I have referred to their lives only when biography is an essential aspect of the quality of their works.

In the course of working on this book, I have contracted many debts. To those who have written on the Brontës and on social and literary issues of the period I have acknowledged specific debts in my text and in the notes; but I am conscious that much general indebtedness has been only partly, or not at all, accounted for. Throughout the writing, I have received invaluable stimulus from discussions with Professor G. K. Hunter. He, Mrs. Shelagh Hunter, Professor Kenneth Muir and Dr. Stanley Wells also took time to read chapters in typescript and provide constructive criticism. At proof stage I again received assistance from Professor Muir and Dr. Wells, and also from Dr. Ernest Schanzer. Needless to say, they are in no way responsible for the shortcomings of the book. I am grateful to Mr. Geoffrey Beard, who, during his curatorship of the Brontë Parsonage Museum in Haworth, let me use the facilities of the Parsonage Library. Miss Winifred Gérin (Mrs. John Lock) shared generously of her rich store of knowledge of the Brontës. The staff of the Liverpool University Library kindly allowed me to monopolise most of the Brontëana of the Harold Cohen Library, and Miss Eda Whelan of the Inter-Library Loan section valiantly coped with lists of unheard-of nineteenth-century novels. My neighbour, Mrs. Audrey Smith, swiftly reduced my foul papers to a fair typescript. By taking on much of the work of my domestic sphere, Mrs. Lilian Andison in her way helped me to explore the sphere of the Brontës. Mrs. Asta Ekenvall, in asking me in the first place to contribute to the *Kvinnohistoriskt arkiv* series, is probably the prime begetter of the book.

But, in the end, my greatest indebtedness is to my husband: without his positive and sustained encouragement, as well as his patient endurance of frozen fish-fingers and unmended socks, this book would never have been written.

Department of English Literature,   INGA-STINA EWBANK
The University, Liverpool.
September 1965.

A Brontë Chronology

This list does not aim at providing a history of the Brontë family, but only at pin-pointing the dates most immediately relevant to this book.

1812 December 29	The Rev. Patrick Brontë (b. 1777 in the parish of Drumballyroney, County Down, Ireland) marries Maria Branwell (b. 1783, at Penzance, Cornwall).
1814	First child, Maria, born.
1815	Elizabeth Brontë born.
1816 April 21	Charlotte Brontë born.
1817	Only son, Patrick Branwell, born.
1818 July 30	Emily Jane Brontë born.
1820 January 17	Anne Brontë born.
1820 April	The Brontës move to Haworth.
1821 September	Mrs. Brontë dies, after long illness. Her sister Miss Elizabeth Branwell, in charge of the parsonage household.
1824	Maria and Elizabeth go to the Clergy Daughters' School at Cowan Bridge in July, Charlotte in August and Emily in November.
1825	Maria leaves Cowan Bridge, ill, on February 14 and dies on May 6; Elizabeth leaves, ill, on May 31 and dies June 15; Charlotte and Emily withdrawn from the school on June 1.
1826 June	Mr. Brontë brings home a box of wooden soldiers for Branwell: from the games centred on these 'Young Men' grow the Brontës'

juvenile writings and the fantasy worlds of their adolescence and early maturity. By 1832 these have split into the Angrian world and literature of Charlotte and Branwell, on the one hand, and the Gondal saga of Emily and Anne, on the other.

1831 January   Charlotte goes to Miss Wooler's school at Roe Head, where she meets her friends and correspondents, Ellen Nussey and Mary Taylor.

1832 July   Charlotte leaves Roe Head, to teach her sisters at home.

1835 July   Charlotte returns to Roe Head as governess, accompanied by Emily as pupil. Emily, ill through home-sickness, leaves in October: Anne takes her place from January 1836 to December 1837. Charlotte leaves the school (by then removed to Dewsbury Moor) in May 1838.

1837 September   Emily becomes governess at Miss Patchett's school at Law Hill, near Halifax; she stays for a period variously estimated at six to eighteen months.

1839 April   Anne becomes governess in the Ingram family, Blake Hall, Mirfield; she leaves in December 1839.

1839 May   Charlotte becomes governess in the Sidgwick family, Stonegappe Hall, near Skipton; she leaves in July 1839.

1840   All three sisters at Haworth, where the Rev. William Weightman had become Mr. Brontë's curate the previous year; Weightman dies in September 1842.

1841 March   Anne becomes governess in the Robinson family, Thorp Green Hall, near York, where Branwell joins her as tutor in January 1843. Charlotte becomes governess in the White family, Upperwood House, Rawdon; she leaves in December 1841.

1841 Summer   School project takes shape: led by Charlotte, the sisters plan to start a school of their own.

1842 February	Charlotte and Emily go to Brussels, to study in the *Pensionnat* Héger. On the death of Miss Branwell, they return to Haworth in November 1842; Charlotte goes back alone to Brussels in January 1843 and stays until January 1844.
1844	Failure of school project: circulars advertising 'The Misses Brontë's Establishment for the Board and Education of a Limited Number of Young Ladies, The Parsonage, Haworth' fail to elicit even one inquiry.
1845 June	Anne leaves the Robinsons; Branwell is dismissed from Thorp Green in July 1845.
1845 Autumn	Charlotte comes across Emily's poems; plans for the publication of a selection from the poems of all three sisters.
1846 May	*Poems, by Currer, Ellis and Acton Bell* published by Aylott & Jones.
1846 Summer	*The Professor, Wuthering Heights* and *Agnes Grey* finished; the last two are eventually accepted by T. C. Newby, but *The Professor* continues to tour the publishing houses, until its rejection, accompanied by an encouraging note, by Smith, Elder & Co., in August 1847. Meanwhile, *Jane Eyre* is begun in August 1846; when submitted to Smith, Elder & Co., in August 1847, it is immediately accepted.
1847 October	*Jane Eyre* published by Smith, Elder & Co.
1847 December	*Wuthering Heights* and *Agnes Grey* published by T. C. Newby.
1848 Summer	*The Tenant of Wildfell Hall* published by T. C. Newby.
1848 July	To clear up the misunderstanding caused by T. C. Newby reporting *The Tenant* to be a new work of Currer Bell, Charlotte and Anne visit Smith, Elder & Co. in London and reveal the identity of the Bells.
1848 September 24	Branwell Brontë dies.
1848 December 19	Emily Brontë dies.

1849 May 28	Anne Brontë dies at Scarborough.
1849 October	*Shirley* published by Smith, Elder & Co.
1849 November/ December	Charlotte in London; first meeting with Thackeray and Harriet Martineau.
1850 June	Charlotte in London; first meeting with G. H. Lewes; dinner party at Thackeray's home.
1850 August	Charlotte's first meeting with Mrs. Gaskell.
1850 September/ December	Charlotte edits her sisters' work, writes the 'Biographical Notice of Ellis and Acton Bell' and a Preface to *Wuthering Heights*, which are published, together with a selection of poems from Emily's and Anne's MSS, in the new edition of *Agnes Grey* and *Wuthering Heights*, by Smith, Elder & Co.
1850 December	Charlotte visits Harriet Martineau at Ambleside.
1851 May–June	Charlotte visits London for Thackeray's lectures and the Great Exhibition.
1851 June	Charlotte's first visit to Mrs. Gaskell in Manchester; she pays a second visit in April 1853 and a third in May 1854; Mrs. Gaskell visits her at Haworth in September 1853.
1852 December	The Rev. A. B. Nicholls (b. 1818 at Crumlin, County Antrim, Ireland; curate of Haworth since 1845) proposes marriage to Charlotte, Mr. Brontë objects violently, and Nicholls is refused; he leaves Haworth in May 1853.
1853 January	*Villette* published by Smith, Elder & Co.
1854 April	Mr. Brontë's opposition gradually having broken down, Charlotte becomes engaged to Mr. Nicholls, who returns as curate to Haworth.
1854 June 29	Charlotte Brontë marries Arthur Bell Nicholls.
1855 March 31	Charlotte Brontë dies (expecting a child).
1857	*The Professor* (written 1845–6) published by Smith, Elder & Co., with a Preface by A. B. Nicholls, dated September 22, 1856.
1857 March	Mrs. Gaskell's *Life of Charlotte Brontë* published by Smith, Elder & Co.

1860	'Emma', a fragment of a story by Charlotte Brontë, published in *The Cornhill Magazine*, with an Introduction by Thackeray.
1861	The Rev. Patrick Brontë dies.
1906	The Rev. A. B. Nicholls dies.

Introduction

THIS is not a book about feminism, in the commonly accepted sense of the word. None of the Brontë sisters has left a mark on the history of female emancipation, in the same ways that such of their contemporaries as Harriet Martineau and Frances Power Cobbe did. The movement for Women's Rights was slowly beginning to gather force in the 1840s, but it received little support from the Haworth parsonage. Lacking any letters or other statements from Emily and Anne, we can only guess at their attitude; about Charlotte the documentation is, as usual, full and decisive. 'I often wish to say something about the "condition of women" question', she writes in May 1848; but what she has to say suggests *laissez-faire* rather than reform, duty and renunciation rather than vindication of rights:

> Many say that the professions now filled only by men should be open to women also; but are not their present occupants and candidates more than numerous enough to answer every demand? Is there any room for female lawyers, female doctors, female engravers, for more female artists, more authoresses? One can see where the evil lies, but who can point out the remedy? When a woman has a little family to rear and educate and a household to conduct, her hands are full, her vocation is evident; when her destiny isolates her, I suppose she must do what she can, live as she can, complain as little, bear as much, work as well as possible.[1]

Similarly, in a letter to Mrs. Gaskell in August 1850, she speaks of evils 'deep-rooted in the foundations of the social system'; but to her they are evils 'of which we cannot complain; of which it is advisable not too often to think'.[2] It is this kind of statement, no doubt, which has made a historian of the Victorian age call Charlotte Brontë a

'Custodian of the Standard'.[1] Seen in this light the Brontës were as Victorian as the Queen herself.

And yet the art of the Brontës was in the deepest sense feminist. In his *Victorian England* G. M. Young maintains that the fundamental issue of feminism, though 'often obscured by agitation for subordinate ends—the right to vote, to graduate, to dispose of her own property after marriage', was the entry of woman 'into the sexless sphere of disinterested intelligence, and . . . of autonomous personality'.[2] In this sense each of the Brontës is a feminist rejecting a collective classification as a 'female novelist', claiming an autonomous personality as a writer. In Charlotte and Anne this is deliberate and explicit. Charlotte formulates a reply to a critic of *Jane Eyre* who thinks that the author, if a woman, must be 'a woman unsexed':

> To you I am neither man nor woman—I come before you as an author only. It is the sole standard by which you have a right to judge me—the sole ground on which I accept your judgment.[3]

And Anne, in her one critical pronouncement—the Preface to the second edition of *The Tenant of Wildfell Hall*—resents questions of the author's sex:

> When I feel it my duty to speak an unpalatable truth, with the help of God, I *will* speak it. . . . All novels are or should be written for both men and women to read, and I am at a loss to conceive how a man should permit himself to write anything that would be really disgraceful to a woman, or why a woman should be censured for writing anything that would be proper and becoming for a man.

Emily Brontë has left us no comparable statement, but we know that to those around her she seemed 'a law unto herself, and a heroine in keeping to her law';[4] and that in her poetry she asserted the autonomy of the individual imagination. In the poem 'To Imagination' she finds her true identity within,

> Where thou and I and Liberty
> Have undisputed sovereignty.[5]

Thus the dutiful Victorian daughters, who did all the womanly tasks in the parsonage household so quietly and efficiently, wrote some of the most unwomanly novels of the Victorian period. Custodians of the standard, they yet also helped to undermine that standard.

All three Brontës were accused by contemporary reviewers of having written 'unwomanly' books—unwomanly as defined by the social and literary standards (and the two are inextricably tied up) of the time. All three met the social pressures and literary traditions of their age with a mixture of compliance, ignorance and defiance. The following chapters are an attempt to analyse some of those pressures and traditions and their relevance to the art of the Brontës; to see how three women, with the same heritage and background, each mapped out her own proper sphere—as moralist, as poet, as 'an author only'.

I

The Woman Writer

Averse to personal publicity, we veiled our names under those of
Currer, Ellis and Acton Bell; ... we did not like to declare ourselves
women, because—without at that time suspecting that our mode of
writing and thinking was not what is called 'feminine'—we had a
vague impression that authoresses are liable to be looked on with
prejudice; we had noticed how critics sometimes use for their
chastisement the weapon of personality, and for their reward, a
flattery which is not true praise.

(i)

THESE words of Charlotte Brontë's, from the 'Biographical Notice'
prefixed to the 1850 edition of *Wuthering Heights* and *Agnes Grey*,
refer in their immediate context to the publication of the little collection of *Poems* with which Currer, Ellis and Acton Bell first presented
themselves to an uninterested and unappreciative public. But they are
obviously also meant to explain why the incognito had been preserved (at least officially) up till that moment, and to state Charlotte
Brontë's quarrel with the conventional attitude of public and reviewer
to the woman author—attitudes with which, three years after the
publication of *Jane Eyre*, she was bitterly acquainted.

As modern readers we tend to forget that those familiar Victorian
pseudonyms—the Bells, Cotton Mather Mills,[1] George Eliot—were
initially adopted as desperate attempts at escaping prejudice. We tend
to forget how many novels by women were published anonymously,
and how reviewers delighted in the game of spotting the 'treble of a
fine melodious voice' or the 'delicate hand of a lady' in a work. As late
as 1865 Anthony Trollope, writing on 'Anonymous Literature', says
that, while it has become generally assumed that authors should

publish in their own name, women are an exception, because 'the nature of woman is such that we admire her timidity and do not even regret her weakness'.[1] Trollope no doubt means well, but the note of condescension and the suggestion of preferential treatment is just such as Charlotte Brontë objected to when she attacked the 'flattery which is not true praise'. Mrs. Gaskell tells us how Charlotte

> especially disliked the lowering of the standard by which to judge a work of fiction, if it proceeded from a feminine pen; and praise mingled with pseudo-gallant allusions to her sex, mortified her far more than actual blame.[2]

It may be an exaggeration to speak of the application of a double standard to literary works in the mid-nineteenth century; but it is true to say that all but the most enlightened of reviewers used one scale of merits for women writers and another for men. A woman was supposed to stay strictly within the limits of female delicacy in subject and style; in return she could expect from her reviewer the gallant treatment that a gentleman owes a lady: he would no more tell her that he disliked her novel than he would say that he could not stand the cut of her gown or the colour of her bonnet. Conversely, of course, she might be scolded for doing something which, had she been a man, would have been praised. To take just one example, one reviewer of *Jane Eyre* thinks that the book shows

> an intimate acquaintance with the worst parts of human nature, a practised sagacity in discovering the latent ulcer, and a ruthless rigour in exposing it, which must command our admiration, but are almost startling in one of the softer sex.[3]

The contrast between the two clauses separated by the crucial 'but' gives us a glimpse of the kind of prejudice under which the woman writer was labouring. Charlotte met the same double standard in the *Economist* review of *Jane Eyre*, which, in her own words, 'praised the book if written by a man, and pronounced it "odious" if the work of a woman'.[4]

That such prejudice did not merely annoy Charlotte Brontë, but actually hurt her to the quick and was seen by her as a potential danger to her work is shown by the urgency of the letter she wrote to G. H. Lewes soon after the publication of *Shirley*:

I wish you did not think me a woman. I wish all reviewers believed 'Currer Bell' to be a man; they would be more just to him. You will, I know, keep measuring me by some standard of what you deem becoming to my sex; where I am not what you consider graceful you will condemn me. . . . Come what will, I cannot, when I write, think always of myself and of what is elegant and charming in femininity; it is not on those terms, or with such ideas, I ever took pen in hand: and if it is only on such terms my writing will be tolerated, I shall pass away from the public and trouble it no more.[1]

Unfortunately this appeal misfired, and Lewes gave Currer Bell's secret away in a review of *Shirley*, which he opened with a survey of the female psyche and female literature generally and closed with a reproach to the author for trying to 'step out of her sex'.[2] Charlotte's one-sentence letter in reply was the bitterest she ever wrote:

I can be on guard against my enemies, but God deliver me from my friends! CURRER BELL.[3]

We no longer think of the Brontës, or of George Eliot, or even of Mrs. Gaskell at her best, as 'female writers', but as great individuals and major novelists. The perspective of their own age was different. It was natural for a *Blackwood's* reviewer in 1855 to refer to Charlotte Brontë as 'the most distinguished female writer of her time',[4] and for the *Athenaeum* to speak, somewhat guardedly, of *Wuthering Heights* and *Agnes Grey* as 'a more than usually interesting contribution to the history of female authorship in England'.[5]

To recover the perspective we should then, I think, before going any further, look at the state of female authorship in the 1840s. I deliberately refrain from saying 'in Victorian England', since such a generalisation would be so broad as to be meaningless. Historians of the period emphasise the flux and change within an era which we are only too apt to think of as one solid entity; and Professor Kathleen Tillotson, in her admirable study of *Novels of the Eighteen-Forties*, has shown how practically every decade of the reign had its own dominant moral tone, its own literary fashions, likes and dislikes.

(ii)

To put the 1840s in perspective, we might start by looking backwards forty years and forwards another forty. In 1882 Mrs. Oliphant

3

(herself a novelist and a reviewer) wrote a three-volume *Literary History of England in the End of the Eighteenth and Beginning of the Nineteenth Century*. In it she relates, with considerable amusement, an episode which she thinks throws light on the position of the female novelist around 1800. It refers to Matthew Gregory Lewis, who at the age of twenty had leapt into fame with a novel, *The Monk* (1796), which mixed fevered eroticism with the usual spectral and skeletal horror of the Gothic *genre*. Not long after this best-selling success, the young author finds out that his own mother has written a novel; and in a panic he implores her to suppress it. 'I do most earnestly and urgently supplicate you, whatever may be its merits, not to publish your novel', he writes, and continues:

'I cannot express to you in language sufficiently strong, how disagreeable and painful my sensations would be, were you to publish any work of any kind.'

In the darkest of colours he paints to her the disaster she is about to bring over her husband, her unmarried daughter (an end to matrimonial prospects), her married daughter (a writing mother would 'raise the greatest prejudice against her in her husband's family'); and, as for himself:

I really think I should go to the Continent immediately upon your taking such a step.

The exhortation ends with an exemplum:

'Be assured the trade of authoress is not an enviable one. In the last letter I had from poor Mrs. K——, she said that if she could but procure for her children the common necessaries of life by hard labour, she would prefer it to the odious task of writing.'

It is significant that Mrs. Oliphant, writing her *Literary History* eighty years after this family crisis, can find it merely ridiculous, commenting that:

the horror with which her son contemplates the mother's authorship is doubly amusing at the present moment, when to write novels has become so common an accomplishment.[1]

The 'odious task' has become 'so common an accomplishment'. The age of the unfortunate Mrs. Lewis still believed with Sir Charles

Grandison that a woman's writing is permissible if it is 'the easy production of a fine fancy'; but that she must under no circumstances make it the 'business of life, or its boast'.[1] Despite the popularity of Fanny Burney's domestic and society novels, and the ever-increasing crowd of ladies writing tales of Gothic horror, the general attitude around the turn of the century was not favourable to female novelists. Only two excuses for publishing were possible: moral zeal and financial distress. Literary ambition as such was anathema.[2]

But by the 1840s, mid-way between Mrs. Lewis and Mrs. Oliphant's *Literary History*, the position had changed. Mrs. Gaskell's husband may have pocketed the cheques which she received for her literary labours, but there is no indication that he felt her publishing to be a disgrace to him or a blight on the future of their children. It is true that when, in the late 1830s, Charlotte Brontë sent some of her poetry to Southey and asked for a verdict on it, she was warned that

> literature cannot be the business of a woman's life, and it ought not to be. The more she is engaged in her proper duties, the less leisure will she have for it, even as an accomplishment and a recreation.

Thinking, it would seem, that he is speaking to a daydreaming adolescent, he adds a patronising touch:

> To those duties you have not yet been called, and when you are you will be less eager for celebrity.[3]

Southey was, however, of an older generation; and even as he was advocating the 'proper duties' of a woman, more and more women were showing that literature can indeed be the business of a woman's life. The demand for fiction was greater than it had ever been before. Circulating libraries, the serialisation of novels in magazines and the introduction of cheap editions of novels were making fiction available not only to the very well-to-do, and a large and eager public were ready to devour what was published. In this situation, women were not content to remain readers only. *The Cambridge Bibliography of English Literature* lists at least forty women novelists, apart from the Brontës, publishing in the 1830s and '40s, accounting between them for at least three hundred new novels. This total does not include a large number of anonymously published novels; nor does it include the very large number of new editions of earlier novels (such as Jane

Austen's, or the earlier works of Maria Edgeworth); nor does it allow for the many further editions of new novels. There was also an influx of novels by women from abroad. George Sand enjoyed immense popularity; her works were reviewed in the leading English periodicals, as soon as they appeared in France; and by 1852 G. H. Lewes, discussing her in an article on 'Lady Novelists', sees her work as part of a larger phenomenon: 'the appearance of Woman in the field of literature'.[1] She was read both in the original and in translations (twelve at least of her novels were translated in the '40s), and so were such German novelists as the Countess Hahn-Hahn. In the case of another foreign best-seller, the Swedish spinster novelist Fredrika Bremer, the public had to rely entirely on translations. These were ably supplied by Mary Howitt, singly and in collected editions (one such in 1846). Miss Bremer's homely realism raised none of the problems of the more daring art of George Sand—according to one reviewer, there was a time when 'a discreet Englishwoman would have blushed to acknowledge acquaintance even with a chapter of George Sand'[2]—and there was no need to blush over the pages of an author whom the reviewers saw as a second (slightly inferior) Miss Edgeworth.[3]

Another large supply of fiction by women is connected with the numerous women's magazines, their editors and contributors largely women, which appeared in these decades. Practically all of them—from the more austere ones, like *The Christian Mother's Magazine*, to the more worldly ones, such as *The Ladies' Cabinet of Fashion, Music, and Romance*—contained tales or serialised stories. One of the best known, *La Belle Assemblée*, strove hard to avoid the stigma of being a mere fashion magazine, by mixing serious literary criticism with dress-patterns, moral tales with stories of romance. The tales in this type of magazine tend to read like compressed novels; they must have demanded deft handling of plot and alertness to current literary fashions. At a time, for example, when the question of governesses' position was much talked and written about, *La Belle Assemblée* would publish a story called 'The Young Governess', which reads very much like a short-hand version of the popular governess novel.[4]

There is no doubt, then, that by the 1840s publishers, editors and public welcomed the woman author. Through the sheer process of supply and demand she was rapidly making a place for herself. She did not so much appear because she had become recognised as become recognised because she had appeared. Her position here is, of course, very closely tied up with that of the novel as a whole. Throughout the first half of the nineteenth century the novel was rising in status, from being thought of as ephemeral entertainment to being regarded as a serious art form. In the essay 'On the Origin and Progress of Novel-writing' with which she introduces her edition of *The British Novelists*, Mrs. Barbauld, as early as 1810, does not find anything exceptional or objectionable in women writing novels; she also stresses that, apart from providing entertainment, novels 'have had a very strong effect in infusing principles and moral feelings'.[1] To a modern observer, the growth into respectability of the novel is most clearly reflected in the journals of the period, where the easy kind of reviewing, consisting mainly of long passages quoted from the novel under review, interspersed with a few rhapsodic remarks, is being replaced by general considerations of the art of the novel, with the individual novel, or novels, being used as touchstones. Professor Tillotson has drawn attention to the beginnings of serious novel criticism in the 1840s; but—though as late as 1864 a writer in *The Westminster Review* could say that 'it is only of recent days that critics have begun seriously to occupy themselves in the consideration of prose fiction'[2]—such criticism had been attempted much earlier. Walter Scott, reviewing *Emma* in *The Quarterly* in 1815, feels obliged to start with a strong assertion that the novel is *not* 'beneath the sober consideration of the critic'.[3] He then goes on to a famous analysis of Jane Austen as the outstanding example of a new kind of novelist who deals realistically with middle-class life. But only six years later Richard Whateley, in what claims only to be a review of *Northanger Abbey* and *Persuasion*, but is in fact a survey of Jane Austen's art and of the whole art of the novel (interestingly anticipating much later interest in novelists' handling of the point of view), thinks that 'the times seem to be past when an apology was requisite from reviewers for condescending to notice a novel'. This he sees as due 'not so much to an alteration in the public taste, as in the character of the productions in question'. The novel had made itself respectable by its subject-matter and technique; and Whateley is as moral as Mrs. Barbauld when he explains that 'a novel, which makes good its pretensions of giving a perfectly correct picture of common life, becomes a far more *instructive* work'.[4] Thus the novel at large preceded criticism rather than being an outcome of it

7

—though it must not be forgotten that some of the best novel critics, such as Scott and, later, G. H. Lewes, were also novelists; and that George Eliot wrote her essay for *The Westminster Review* on 'Silly Novels by Lady Novelists' in the very same month as she started to write her first work of fiction, the *Scenes of Clerical Life*. But it is true to say that by the 1840s, criticism had become more conscious of, sometimes also dogmatic about, the standards to be expected from novelists.

With the growing interest in the art of the novel it was impossible for reviewers not to notice how large a part women had come to play in this branch of literature. In 1849 the *Fraser* reviewer of 'New Novels' finds that the volumes which have accumulated on his desk are all by women (one is *Shirley*), and there is a slight note of resentment in his comment that 'the fairer portion of the creation seems to have made a monopoly of this art of novel-writing'.[1] In 1850 G. H. Lewes's weekly, *The Leader*, carries an article called 'A Gentle Hint to Writing-Women', which begins facetiously enough,

It will never do. We are overrun. Women carry all before them;

but leads on to a more serious consideration of recent female achievements:

It's a melancholy fact, and against all Political Economy, that the group of female authors is becoming every year more multitudinous and more successful. Women write the best novels, the best travels, the best reviews, the best leaders, the best cookery-books. . . .
[What can men do?] How many of us can write novels like Currer Bell, Mrs. Gaskell, Geraldine Jewsbury, Mrs. Marsh, Mrs. Crowe, and fifty others, with their shrewd and delicate observation of life? How many of us can place our prose beside the glowing rhetoric and daring utterance of social wrong in the learned romances and powerful articles of Eliza Lynn, or the cutting sarcasm and vigorous protest of Miss Rigby? What chance have we against Miss Martineau, so potent in so many directions?[2]

And by 1855 Mrs. Oliphant—without repeating this catalogue of female writers—can affirm that

this, which is the age of so many things—of enlightenment, of science, of progress—is quite as distinctly the age of female novelists.[3]

The 'arrival' of the female novelist, however, did not mean unqualified acceptance. It did not mean that Southey's worries over what was going to happen to women's 'proper duties' had been forgotten. The *Leader* writer obviously realises that the citadel has been stormed and is out to poke gentle fun at the conquerors when he ends on the following lament:

> This is the 'march of mind' but where, oh, where are the dumplings! Does it never strike these delightful creatures that their little fingers were made to be kissed not to be inked? . . . Woman's proper sphere of activity is elsewhere. Are there no husbands, lovers, brothers, friends to coddle and console? Are there no stockings to darn, no purses to make, no braces to embroider? *My* idea of a perfect woman is one who can write but won't.

This is really a valediction to the woman who could write books but prefers to make dumplings; but there are serious questions under the surface. Two years later G. H. Lewes takes these up in his article on 'The Lady Novelists'. He discusses at length his belief that the proper sphere of woman is home, husband and children. Inevitably the question follows: why, then, is she writing? In an age when genetics was a new and exciting science, it was brought in to explain the married woman writer (Mrs. Gaskell, for example):

> The happy wife and busy mothers are only forced into literature by some hereditary organic tendency, stronger than the domestic; and hence it is that the cleverest women are not always those who have written books.

Those who have written books have, according to Lewes, done so as a purely compensatory activity. Women turn to writing

> always to solace by some intellectual activity the sorrow that in silence wastes their lives, and by a withdrawal of the intellect from the contemplation of their pain, or by a transmutation of their secret anxieties into types, they escape from the pressure of that burden—[1]

the 'burden' being one of solitariness and thwarted affections. His life with George Eliot was undoubtedly to teach him that writing can be to a woman more than a substitute for domestic bliss and that the article just quoted had been sadly one-sided. On the other hand, his comments were less wide of the mark than they may seem to us. It is clear that Charlotte Brontë, at least in the year when she had lost two sisters in rapid succession, regarded her writing as a means of filling an emotional void. Where should she be without it, she asks:

> How should I be with youth past—sisters lost—a resident in a moorland parish where there is not a single educated family? In that case I should have no world at all;

and she ends with a pathetic: 'I wish every woman in England had also a hope and motive: Alas there are many old maids who have neither.'[1] We know that during her own tragically short marriage she wrote practically nothing; yet it is hard to believe that, had she lived, she would have devoted herself entirely to being 'the happy wife and busy mother'. Mrs. Gaskell may have taken up writing as a way of getting over the death of her baby son;[2] but the urge to write did not vanish once the immediate grief had worn off. She, perhaps better than anyone, knew that for most women novelists domestic duties and the urge to self-expression were not mutually exclusive. She also knew how difficult it might be to reconcile the two. Domestic cares rested heavily on the Victorian middle-class woman; and when Mrs. Gaskell speaks of Charlotte Brontë's position as daughter, housekeeper, and novelist, she does so with the quiet conviction of one who, even at the height of her fame as an author, did all her writing at the family dining-table— and was pleased that the dining-room had three doors, so that she could supervise housework in all directions. (Mr. Gaskell, of course, had his own study.) She, as much as any of her contemporaries, would have appreciated Virginia Woolf's *A Room of One's Own*. While to a man becoming an author merely means the exchange of one form of occupation for another, says Mrs. Gaskell,

> no other can take up the quiet, regular duties of the daughter, the wife, or the mother, as well as she whom God has appointed to fill that particular place.

A woman cannot

> drop the domestic charges devolving on her as an individual for the exercise of the most splendid talents that were ever bestowed.

But this divinely imposed duty does not mean an abnegation from the duty of developing one's intellectual gifts:

And yet she must not shrink from the extra responsibility implied by the very fact of her possessing such talents. She must not hide her gift in a napkin; it was meant for the use and service of others. In a humble and faithful spirit must she labour to do what is not impossible, or God would not have set her to do it.

The particular relevance of this austere generalisation becomes apparent when she adds: 'I put into words what Charlotte Brontë put into actions.'[1] The notion of literary ability as a talent, in the most literal and Biblical sense, is one which we meet frequently in discussions of female writing in the period; it was particularly alive, as we shall see in Chapter II, to Anne Brontë.

While some writers and reviewers saw serious emotional and moral reasons for the development of female literary talent, others had no illusions about why women wrote. In his essay on the 'False Morality of Lady Novelists', W. R. Greg maintains that 'there are vast numbers of lady novelists, for much the same reason that there are vast numbers of sempstresses'. Uneducated women who must earn their living take to sewing, educated women in the same position take to writing.

> Every educated lady can handle a pen *tant bien que mal*: all such, therefore, take to writing—and to novel-writing as the kind which requires the least special qualification and the least severe study, and also as the only kind which will sell.

Such authors (and they are often very young ladies) tend not only to be technically inept but also to produce novels which are intellectually and morally immature; and thus they are a menace, for

> it is not easy to over-estimate the importance of novels, whether we regard the influence they exercise upon an age, or the indications they afford of its characteristic tendencies and features.[2]

Greg is writing, it should be noted, at the end of the 1850s—a decade which had seen the flood-gates of female novel-writing open fully. Skimming through the mass of second- and third-rate literature of that decade, one is forced to agree with George Eliot's comment that writing novels had become 'a fatal seduction to incompetent women'. Her article on 'Silly Novels by Lady Novelists'[3] is in many ways symptomatic of the state of affairs. Although it was published anonymously (so that readers presumably thought it was by a man), it is wrong to think, as does one of her biographers, that she was hiding 'under a mask of masculinity and even hardness which was not her own', and that the whole essay is therefore artificial in tone.[1] She is not just a woman pretending to be a man pretending to be exasperated with women novelists; her tone has the genuine exasperation of one who does not suffer fools gladly, but who constantly sees fools rushing into print. Above all, the essay is permeated with a very real concern for *standards* in female writing: moral, intellectual and aesthetic. It was not a new concern with her; as early as 1853 she writes in a letter:

> How women have the courage to write and publishers the spirit to buy at a high price the false and feeble representations of life and character that most feminine novels give, is a constant marvel to me.[2]

By 1856 this has become:

> The foolish vanity of wishing to appear in print . . . seems to be encouraged by the extremely false impression that to write at all is a proof of superiority in a woman. On this ground, we believe that the average intellect of women is unfairly represented by the mass of feminine literature.[3]

Here is the real crux: insipid, unintelligent writing by women tends to confirm, rather than remove, popular prejudice against the female intellect. She is wickedly witty about a handful of novels which deserve all the abuse she gives them; but there is no doubt of her intention, which is to make a plea for women to take the art of writing seriously, with 'patient diligence, a sense of the responsibility involved in publication, and an appreciation of the sacredness of the writer's art', and for reviewers to take such women seriously:

> By a peculiar thermometric adjustment, when a woman's talent is at zero, journalistic approbation is at the boiling pitch . . . and if ever she reaches excellence, critical enthusiasm drops to the freezing point. Harriet Martineau, Currer Bell, and Mrs. Gaskell have been treated as cavalierly as if they had been men.[4]

We have reached, then, a position which is the exact reverse of that of 'Monk' Lewis and his mother. Mrs. Lewis was told not to publish her novel, '*whatever its merits*'; by the 1850s—after the experience of a little good and much bad female writing—it is taken for granted that a woman should publish, and the attention has been turned to the merits of what she has to publish. There is no suggestion from either male (Greg) or female (George Eliot) reviewer that woman should return to her proper sphere in the kitchen, nursery and drawing-room; instead there is a keen concern about the standards of her work. 'Should she write at all?' has had to yield, before a *fait accompli*, to 'why should she want to write?'; and this has led to the question: 'what, and how, should she write?'

At this point we must, I think, turn to a brief look at what women novelists were actually writing in the 1840s.

(iii)

The most efficient way of mapping a wilderness of writing is, I suppose, to divide it into *genres*. In doing so with the particular wilderness under survey, we soon find that it is impossible to draw clear-cut border-lines between *genres*, as one is nearly always shading into another. Gothic novels of gloom and terror have a surprising amount of serene domesticity about them (and *vice versa*); 'fashionable' novels get dangerously close to moralising on the evils of society; historical romances are used to embody political and social theories, and so on. But a rough division into kinds is in this case not only efficient, it is also illuminating. At first sight it would seem that women were writing much the same kinds of novels as men. There are female authors represented within every *genre* of the novel. Yet, any further examination reveals that the distribution of female authors is far from equal; and that the main body of female writing falls within two or three areas.

Here again it would be misleading to suggest too neat a pattern. For one thing, women who were driven to writing because of financial distress (and there were many of them) were inevitably anxious to 'give them what they want'. Mrs. Trollope, the mother of Anthony Trollope, and, though rarely read nowadays, herself the second most prolific woman writer in the 1840s, is a typical case. She gained fame at the age of fifty-two with her first work, *Domestic Manners of the Americans* (1832), at a moment when her neurotic and prematurely senile husband had proved definitely unable to be the head of the family in a financial, or in any other sense; and when her own financial projects—such as opening a bazaar in Cincinnati—had failed.[1] From then on she persisted for years in the profitable novel-market, running the house and nursing a family of more-or-less invalids in the daytime, and never failing to write her nightly stint of words. Her novels reveal a finger on the pulse of the public and an eye on the seller's market, rather than gifts or inclinations in any one particular literary direction. At the opening of the 'hungry '40s' she is one of the first to make fiction of industrial problems in her *Life and Adventures of Michael Armstrong, the Factory Boy* (1840); she realises the attraction of romance in *Young Love* (1844); she cashes in on the growing popularity of the religious novel, especially the rabidly anti-Jesuit variety, in *Father Eustace* (1847); and by the end of the decade she has caught on to the domestic-problem type of novel in *The Lottery of Marriage* (1849). On the other hand, writing because of lack of money did not always mean ranging through the whole gamut of popular *genres*: Miss Mitford supported her reckless and extravagant father, a physician without a practice, on the income from her tales of rural life in England and Scotland;[2] and Mrs. Gore maintained her family by consistently supplying the circulating libraries with novels of fashionable society. Conversely, an alertness to the changes in fashion was not always a matter of financial troubles. The literature of the 1840s as a whole shows a movement, however slow and gradual, away from the romantic and extravagant towards the everyday and homely; and this pattern is reflected in the output of many women novelists. To take one example, Mrs. Anna Eliza Bray had made her name as an author of romances of faraway places and distant times, and she was still true to her type when in 1844 she published a three-volume novel with the tellingly romantic title of *Courtenay of Wabreddon: A Romance of the West*. But four years later she has changed her line of attack; her 1848 novel is uncompromisingly called *Trials of Domestic Life*.

Allowing, then, for variations in public taste and literary fashion, the major kinds of female novels seem in the first half of the decade to have been, apart from the romance (often with Gothic or straight-forwardly historical content), the 'fashionable' novel of life in high society and the didactic novel of varied, but mainly middle-class background. Through various combinations and permutations there develop out of these, towards the second half of the decade, the religious novel and the social problem novel, the Novel with a Purpose.

The Gothic romance need not detain us long, though it is interesting to notice how attractive some of its features still were to the mid-nineteenth century. Initially, through its offer of escape to the remote and the long-ago, the mysterious and the supernatural, it had provided emotional release in a century dominated by reason; strangely enough, after the lead had been given by Horace Walpole's *Castle of Otranto* (1764), the chief practitioners of the form had been women—'ladies of fierce imagination living in Twickenham', as one critic describes them. The names of Miss Reeve and Mrs. Radcliffe, and many others, are for ever connected with ruined castles and subterranean passages, mysterious clangings of chains and mouldering family skeletons in the cupboard. Jane Austen's parody on the *genre*, *Northanger Abbey* (published, posthumously, in 1818; written about fifteen years earlier), had not laughed it out of existence; and some of the old guard were still writing in the 1830s. Mrs. Roche, who had written one of the most famous of the early Gothic novels, *The Children of the Abbey* (1796), offered her final piece of Gothicism, *The Nun's Picture*, in 1834; and twenty years after *Frankenstein* Mary Shelley, though she had largely abandoned the tale of horror for historical and social novels, still published her *Falkner* (1837) as 'by the Author of "Frankenstein"'. She also published a revised edition of that work in 1831, with a Preface explaining the genesis of what, with some pride, she calls 'my hideous progeny'; and most reviews of her later works start with a glance back to 'that promise of talent which so extraordinary a work, considered as the production of a young female under twenty years of age, held out'.[1] In their still-remembered awe at such a work from a female hand, these reviews are, incidentally, good examples of the double standard in reviewing: 'For a man it was excellent, but for a woman it was wonderful.'[2] By the '40s the Gothic novel as such had practically disappeared, but many of its components had been handed down via the historical romance and its greatest representative, Scott; many of them were used to add interest and suspense to plots of all kinds. Thus in *Consuelo* (1842), a best-selling novel at the middle of the decade and according to Charlotte Brontë the best of George Sand's works, Mrs. Radcliffe's technique is disclaimed:

If the ingenious and imaginative Anne Radcliffe had found herself in the place of the candid and unskilful narrator of this veracious history, she would not have allowed so good an opportunity to escape, of leading you, fair reader, through corridors, trap-doors, spiral staircases, and subterranean passages, for half a dozen flowery and attractive volumes, to reveal to you only at the seventh, all the arcana of her skilful labours. But the strong-minded reader, whom it is our duty to please, would not probably lend herself so willingly, at the present period, to the innocent stratagem of the romancer.[1]

But, although the novel as a whole is the story of an eighteenth-century Spanish-Italian singer and introduces authentic personages such as Joseph Haydn and the Empress Maria Theresa, and though her main intention is to show the obstacles that a lowly-born and talented woman must face in an aristocratic man's world, George Sand does not, when it comes to the point, reject Mrs. Radcliffe's devices. On the contrary, the second section of the rather disjointed novel takes place in Riesenburg, as Gothic a castle as was ever to be found in the Carpathian mountains; and here, to save the insane heir of the Rudolstadts, by whom she is beloved, Consuelo descends, through a fountain and via subterranean passages, into ghastly grottoes. No wonder that Charlotte Brontë thought this novel coupled 'strange extravagance with wondrous excellence'.

Some of the reviews of *Jane Eyre* show how alive the appeal of the Gothic was still felt to be. The *Athenaeum* reviewer, for example, places the whole emphasis on the book as a good story, one without any ulterior motives of social or religious propaganda:

> As exciting strong interest of its old-fashioned kind, 'Jane Eyre' deserves high praise, and commendation to the novel-reader who prefers story to philosophy, pedantry, or Puseyite controversy.[2]

By 'old-fashioned' here is meant Gothic. The reviewer does not find the mystery of Thornfield Hall at all disturbing, whereas Jane's later trials seem to him outrageous; and though 'obstacles fall down like the battlements of *Castle Melodrame* in the closing scene', that is in fact part of the melodramatic virtues which make the novel into a good story. This contrasts significantly with the opinions of many modern critics who praise the realism of *Jane Eyre* but find its Gothic elements hard to swallow.[3]

The historical novel, written as pure entertainment, or for didactic purposes, was popular among women writers. Miss Martineau's fictionalised biography of Toussaint L'Ouverture, the St. Domingo negro leader whom Wordsworth had celebrated in his sonnet on 'man's unconquerable mind', is a combination of both. *The Hour and the Man* (1841) glories in local colour and period references, but it never forgets its purpose of attacking white intolerance and prejudice.

The most popular kind of novel, however, did not claim a didactic purpose. The novel of the 'Silver-Fork School'[1] formed an unparalleled best-seller wave in the quarter-of-a-century between 1825 and 1850; and though the '40s saw the tail-end of the vogue, there was still vigour and sting in the tail. The appeal of the 'fashionable' novel was a simple one: it offered detailed records of life as lived in high society, often spiced by satirical observation of such life. To the middle-class reader it must have been rather like reading the gossip-column in one of the dailies. In her letter to Mrs. Gore, thanking her for the gift of a copy of *The Hamiltons*, Charlotte Brontë uses these telling terms of praise: 'I knew nothing of the circles you describe before I read "The Hamiltons", but I feel I do know something of them now.'[2] This type of novel confirmed the theory that the female novelist's special contribution lay in what G. H. Lewes called 'the peculiarly feminine quality of Observation'. In the writer it called for little constructional ability: the structure is usually picaresque, with one or more central figures moving through the social events of one or more seasons; characterisation is generally slight or stereotyped: the dandy, the match-making mother, the no-longer-so-young beauty with no dowry, ready to throw herself at anybody with a few thousand a year. Bulwer Lytton and the young Disraeli represent the male side of the *genre*, but it is only fair to say that it was perfected in the hands of women.

Two of these ladies, the Countess of Blessington (famous for her friendship with Byron) and Lady Charlotte Bury, each of whom published several novels in the 1840s, had the advantage of knowing intimately the society they were writing about; and there is the authenticity of actual experience in their glittering pictures of high life. But the most prolific of them all was Mrs. Gore, who was more of an outsider and therefore all the more able to lash the whip of satire over her lords and ladies. Mrs. Gore was, in fact, the most prolific of all women novelists in the decade: between 1840 and 1850 she published

twenty-five new novels, most of them in three volumes; and many
of her earlier works appeared in new editions. (When she finally
retired, quite blind, from writing, she had produced a total of some
two hundred volumes of novels, comedies and poems.) In her best
work the deft use of language for satirical portraiture is the greatest
attraction:

> Lady Maria Willingham was a person who, with indifferent
> features, had always managed to be called pretty; with very moderate
> abilities, had maintained the reputation of being extremely clever;
> and with a narrow selfish heart, was continually cited as the most
> excellent woman in the world. The tact which had thus universally
> enabled her to assume a virtue where she had it not, was of course a
> qualification of no feeble force. Early in her fashionable career it had
> been whispered to her, that a dress of the last new Parisian mode was
> an admirable mask for the body, an earnest, and deliberate, and
> mysterious tone of conversation, a most imposing cloak for the
> deficiencies of the mind: and she was well aware that *the heart* is
> usually taken upon the trust of these preceding and more ostensible
> endowments. She therefore confined the demonstrations of her
> virtue to a refraignment from all sins unrecognised as of the highest
> *ton*; and to a pathetic vibration of the head and elevation of the
> eyes, whenever the delinquencies of other people came under
> discussion.

Thus the opening of her novel *Mothers and Daughters* (1831). Clearly it
is the eighteenth-century qualities of balance, wit and elegance that
are being presented to Victorian (or near-Victorian) readers here, just
as the Gothic and historical novels carried on the Romantic interest in
intense emotion and in the remote and exotic. Clearly, too, Mrs. Gore
had learnt some of her art of observation from Jane Austen. Much has
been written on Thackeray's indebtedness to the 'fashionable' novel.[1]
Like Carlyle in *Sartor Resartus* before him, he ridiculed and attacked
the *genre*, but he also learnt a great deal from it. His *Vanity Fair* (1847),
its title significantly changed from the non-committal *Pen and Pencil
Sketches of English Society*, implies, as Gordon N. Ray has shown, a turn
towards a greater social consciousness and an awareness of the
novelist's responsibility. By the end of the decade the whole social
atmosphere was against the indifference, or even callousness, of the

fashionable novel. And yet it did not die unlamented; the nature and strength of its appeal are suggested in Mrs. Oliphant's comments in 1855:

> Mrs. Trollope is perhaps a clever woman, but we miss the silken rustle and ladylike pace of her contemporary, and find Mrs. Trollope a less agreeable companion than Mrs. Gore.[1]

It is an indication of the divided mind of the nation that parallel with the fashion for society non-committedly observed runs, all along, an equally strong fashion for society moralised. The novels of the two schools complement each other step by step. In Mrs. Gore's novels the young rake is essentially amusing and rarely receives worse punishments than bankruptcy and a commission in the Indian army. In Miss Edgeworth's *Vivian* (1812) he becomes a near-tragic figure and a warning example. It is the story of a young man whose great flaw of character is 'want of firmness', and we follow him from his coming down from college, through his political career and his contacts with the peerage, to his death in a senseless duel. The scheming mother who, like Jane Austen's Mrs. Bennet, causes more laughter than tears in Mrs. Gore's *Mothers and Daughters* is shown as a grave moral danger and is given a severe punishment at the end of Miss Edgeworth's *Manœuvring* (1809). It was left for the great mid-century novelists to fuse the two points of view: out of *Vivian* and *Pelham* comes *Pendennis*.

As the early dates of Miss Edgeworth's moral novels indicate, we are dealing here with a tradition of moral fiction firmly established long before Queen Victoria came to the throne. The foundations of Victorian didacticism had been laid in the Regency period and earlier. We do not always remember well enough that Mrs. Barbauld was of the same generation as the original Mrs. Grundy,[2] and that Dr. Bowdler's *Family Shakespeare* came out as early as 1818. The writer of the 'Sonnets Matrimonial' in *Fraser's Magazine* for December 1839, is sure that Prince Albert will chase from the royal palace

> Ladies of easy virtue, high and low,
> The fingering slave, the pander, or the scribe
> Of luscious novel, or the snuffling sage
> Who preaches "female liberty", or the peer
> Whose saint is Mary Magdalen . . .;

but it is worth remembering that the young Princess Victoria had been allowed to read no 'luscious novel', and indeed no fiction other than moral tales. The tone of much work within this popular branch of fiction was struck as early as 1793 by the title of Jane West's first published story: *The Advantages of Education; or, The History of Maria Williams. A Tale for Very Young Ladies. By Mrs. Prudentia Homespun.* Mrs. Opie, a Quaker lady, whose 'peculiarly pathetic powers' were praised by Mrs. Barbauld,[1] had warned against the *Dangers of Coquetry* in a two-volume novel in 1790; and her technique had altered little as, thirty-five years later, she wrote *Illustrations of Lying, in All Its Branches* (1825). Her real field, as with most of this type of fiction, is that of domestic, everyday, relationships; and it is the small change of day-to-day life that provides moral material for a novel like *Temper, or Domestic Scenes* (1812). Realistically detailed descriptions used for a moral end is the simple basis of her work. At the outset of *A Wife's Duty* she explains her method:

> I am only too painfully aware, my dear friend, that in my history of a 'Woman's Love' [the novel to which this forms a continuation], I have related none but very common occurrences and situations, and entered into minute, nay perhaps uninteresting details. Still, however common an event may be, it is susceptible of variety in description, because endlessly various is the manner in which the same event affects different persons.

Mrs. Opie's work is not chronologically of the '40s, but it is relevant to that period. Homely in content, realistic in technique, and moral in intention, it remained read and popular—as shown by the publication of a collected edition, twelve volumes of *Miscellaneous Tales*, in 1845–7.

Like Mrs. Prudentia Homespun's story, much of this type of fiction was not only generally edifying, but directly and specifically educational. In a society of large families, with few outside opportunities for female occupation, most women—married and single—were by necessity or choice educationalists; and in the novel they had early found a new pedagogic instrument. One of the most productive of such writers is Mrs. Hofland, who, next to Scott, was the best-represented novelist in the Keighley Mechanics' Institute where the Brontës borrowed books. She wrote a very large number of short novels, or 'Tales for Youth', stretching right across the '20s, '30s and '40s. They are stories mostly about young boys or girls who struggle along the straight and narrow path, achieving, as they do so, the most amazing victories over temptations, poverty and misfortune, inevitably ending up in economic prosperity and successful marriage. The appeal, akin to that of *Robinson Crusoe*, of seeing an individual persevere and prosper against impossible odds, raises them above the level of mere Sunday school tracts; and it is not difficult to imagine the young Brontës, severe literary critics as they were, being carried away by them. Without wishing to press the point I even think it possible that a story like *Ellen, The Teacher*, about a poor orphan girl who suffers miserably in a boarding school, eventually makes good as a governess and ultimately marries her cousin, Sir Charles Selby, might have been one of the germs from which *Jane Eyre* grew.

The prototype of educational fiction was no doubt Maria Edgeworth's *Parent's Assistant* (first published in 1796; many later editions). The aim of the exemplary stories which it contains is directly peda-gogical; and very close to these—indeed first planned as a sequel to the *Assistant*—are her *Moral Tales* (1801, many further editions). Miss Edgeworth's work shows how slender was the distinction between juvenile fiction and moral fiction intended for adults. The didactic basis on which the superstructure of fiction rested was the same, and so the transition from one to the other was easy. In the Preface to her *Tales of Fashionable Life* (1809-12), her father (who all his life was the proud supervisor and editor of her work) writes:

> Miss Edgeworth's former works consist of tales for children—of stories for young men and women—and of tales suited to that great mass which does not move in the circles of fashion. The present volumes are intended to point out some of those errors to which the higher classes are disposed.

As Maria Edgeworth has gone down into literary history primarily as the author of *Castle Rackrent* and other Irish stories, we tend to forget that by far the largest proportion of her output are tales or novels—early on she shuns the term 'novel', as under it 'so much folly, error and vice are disseminated'[1]—written to illustrate particular moral pre-cepts. Unswervingly she worked through the whole series of human weaknesses, starting with the young and the lower classes, and working

up to mature age and 'fashionable' life. There is no desire to make the
fiction hide the precept; and should the reader have missed the moral,
there is always a Preface to specify it, sometimes with a shade of self-
consciousness, as in *Ennui*:

> The causes, curses, and cure of this disease are exemplified, I hope,
> in such a manner as not to make the remedy worse than the
> disease;

but more commonly as a straight lesson:

> MADAME DE FLEURY points out some of the means which may be
> employed by the rich for the real advantages of the poor. This story
> shows that sowing gold does not always produce a golden harvest,
> but that knowledge and virtue, when early implanted in the human
> breast, seldom fail to make ample returns of prudence and felicity.

The greatest moral indignation is shown over the vices of high society;
indeed in most of the tales fashionable life stands for vice and middle-
class domesticity for virtue, while (as in *Almeria*) a season in London is
the surest way to moral wreck. For all this, one of her best novels is
the 'Moral Tale' *Belinda* (1801), where London society is observed as
keenly as the moral goodness of the heroine, who ends up by reform-
ing everybody within reach.

Miss Edgeworth's lasting popularity throughout the '40s—there was,
for example, a collected edition of her *Tales* in 1848—should remind
us that the public did not resent being told a very explicit lesson in
novel form. Mrs. Sarah Ellis no doubt aimed at much the same
readers in her moral-sociological survey, *Prevention Better than Cure,
or The Moral Wants of the World We Live In* (1847), and in her
didactic novel, *Social Distinctions* (1848–9). That readers had an appetite
for sugared pills, however thin the coating, is shown by the incredible popularity of Miss Martineau's series of instructive tales, her
Illustrations of Political Economy (1832–4), her *Illustrations of Taxation*
(1834); and her *Forest and Game Law Tales* (1845–6). Each story
illustrates a particular economic or social problem: shows conditions
as they are and suggests ways to improvement. Most of them also add a
'Summary of Principles illustrated in this volume', in case anyone has
become so engrossed in the story as to miss the problem. Thus, for
example, *Demerara* (1832) is an anti-slavery story, giving in a series of

episodes scenes of human misery on a West Indian plantation: one chapter shows how the slaves dare not marry for fear of husband and wife becoming separated by sale ('No haste to the wedding in Demerara'); another how they are treated worse than cattle ('Man worth less than beast in Demerara'); another how cruelly they are pursued if they try to escape ('Beasts hunt men in Demerara'), etc. The sum of this is to show that

> the slave system inflicts an incalculable amount of human suffering for the sake of making a wholesale waste of labour and capital;

and to suggest a remedy:

> A free trade in sugar would banish slavery altogether, since competition must induce an economy of labour and capital; i.e. a substitution of free labour for slave labour.

We can see the effectiveness of Miss Martineau's social and political agitation, but we miss the fuller human interest of a Harriet Beecher-Stowe; and we find it difficult to understand the taste for fiction like this. We need, I think, constantly to remind ourselves of the preference of the age for practical—moral, rather than aesthetic—merits in fiction: the kind of preference epitomised by a review of *Demerara*, in which the reviewer assures the author that

> we hold one of her little volumes to be a dearer and more tangible boon to all social humanity, than an *Iliad* or a *Paradise Lost*.[1]

There is another side to the picture, too. The existence of so much didactic fiction by women suggests that to many women didacticism had become the justification for art. The feeling that women are, as it were, working off a guilt-complex (about writing at all) is voiced by Crabb Robinson in 1834:

> How strange it is, that while we men are modestly content to amuse by our writings, women must be didactic! Miss Baillie writes plays to illustrate the passions, Miss Martineau teaches political economy by tales . . . and Miss Edgeworth is a schoolmistress in her tales.[2]

Even earlier the moral-precept novel had been questioned. Bulwer Lytton's *Pelham* (1828) is a 'fashionable' novel, but it has also learned a great deal from the German *Bildungsroman*; above all, it has borrowed from *Wilhelm Meister* the device of long discussions of philosophy and literature which hold up the action as such. At one point in it, in Chapter LII, a group of people are discussing the art of the novel:

'Speaking of morals', said Lady Roseville, 'do you not think every novel should have its distinct object, and inculcate, throughout, some one particular moral, such as many of Marmontel's and Miss Edgeworth's?'

To this, Lord Vincent, who is apparently the author's spokesman here, replies:

'No! . . . every good novel has one great end—the same in all—viz. the increasing our knowledge of the heart. . . . Whoever succeeds in showing us more accurately the nature of ourselves and species, has done science, and, consequently, virtue, the most important benefit; *for every truth is a moral. This* great and universal end, I am led to imagine, is rather crippled than extended by the rigorous attention to the *one* isolated moral you mention.'

But Bulwer Lytton was in this case ahead of his times. Didacticism had become too firmly entrenched a mode of writing, too popular with the reading public, and too unimpeachable a *raison d'être* for the female novelist, to be easily shaken off. In 1851 we find a reviewer in *Fraser's Magazine*, writing on recent English novels, complaining:

We are too didactic. Thinking too much of the moral, and too little of the story through which it is enforced, we suffer the end to overwhelm the means.

The didactic bent of much fiction in the 1840s has put the intelligent reviewer in a dilemma:

If we are to make a choice between prosy decent books, and vicious books that are written with sprightliness and skill, we are, of course, bound to prefer the former. There is no room or excuse for hesitation. But we cannot help regretting, at the same time, that our English novelists, who, for the most part, write unexceptionable morality, should not be able to make it a little more amusing. It is a pity that morality should be rendered so excessively stupid on this side of the Channel, while on the other, all the social vices are tricked out with irresistible attractions.[1]

His words reflect, however regretfully, a sense—widespread in the period, and particularly among its women writers—of literature being under a moral obligation.

Part of a critic's task had become to fit a book into the right moral category; and thus *Jane Eyre* was by some praised for qualities which would seem more appropriately attributed to Miss Edgeworth. *La Belle Assemblée* sees it as a kind of new Parent's Assistant: most of its review of the book consists of a long extract from the episode where Jane is punished by being shut in the red room, and this is praised

> as warning to all placed in authority over the young, whether in the capacity of parent, teacher or nurse . . . as warning against leaving the young and impressible to the charge of uneducated and lax-principled servants.[2]

Wuthering Heights, on the other hand, would not yield an easy lesson; and so it was condemned by *Tait's Edinburgh Magazine* for lacking a moral or social aim: it neither teaches 'mankind to avoid one course and take another', nor does it dissect 'any portion of existing society, exhibiting together its weak and strong points', the reviewer complains.[3] On this score *Agnes Grey* was preferred to *Wuthering Heights* as being more open to a didactic interpretation:

> It has an advantage over its predecessor [*Wuthering Heights*], that while its language is less ambitious and less repulsive, it fills the mind with a lasting picture of love and happiness succeeding to scorn and affliction, and teaches us to put every trust in a supreme wisdom and goodness.[4]

The inclusion in the list of criteria which *Wuthering Heights* fails to fulfil of the dissection of 'any portion of existing society' reminds us that, especially during the second half of the decade, didacticism had been finding new channels. Industrial unrest and a growing realisation of the conditions of the working classes had opened up a new field for the novel with a purpose. We have already seen that Mrs. Trollope was quick to exploit it in her *Michael Armstrong*. Her aims in this novel, she says in her Preface, were, first 'to drag into the light of day, and place before the eyes of Englishmen, the hideous mass of injustice and suffering to which thousands of infant labourers are subjected, who toil in our monster spinning-mills', and, secondly, to show her hero 'embarked in those perfectly constitutional struggles for the ameliora-tion of the sufferings of his class, in which many of the more enlight-ened operatives have been for some years engaged'. But frightened by actual industrial action—'scenes of outrage and lawless violence' and workers 'uniting themselves with individuals whose doctrines are sub-versive of every species of social order'—she shuns her second aim, and what remains of the first are some scenes, both lurid and sentimentalised, of children suffering in the factories of Sir Matthew Dowling and in the concentration-camp establishment of Deep Valley Mill. The main character is not so much Michael Armstrong, the factory boy, as the incredibly rich and benevolent Miss Brotherton; and the novel dis-solves into a fantastic romance where Michael, having escaped from the mill and been fortified by some years of shepherding 'in one of the most romantic spots of Westmorland', joins Miss Brotherton abroad, has his 'richly teeming eager mind' further educated by two years at a German university and finally settles in a 'château upon the Rhine'—in a *ménage à quatre* with his childhood love from the Deep Valley Mill and with Miss Brotherton who marries his brother, also a former factory boy. As Mrs. Trollope's novel shows, not many women had enough experience of the other nation in Disraeli's *Sybil, or The Two Nations* (1845) to deal convincingly with the facts of a new society. But life as a minister's wife in industrial Manchester had equipped Mrs. Gaskell for the writing of what Raymond Williams has called 'the most moving response in literature to the industrial suffering of the 1840s'.[1] In subject matter *Mary Barton* (1848) had been anticipated by Harriet Martineau's tale, *A Manchester Strike* (1832; no. 7 of her *Illustrations of Political Economy*); and, unlike Mrs. Trollope, Miss Martineau had done her homework thoroughly, providing detailed information about the Lancashire cotton industry and the state of labour in various parts of England as well as in other parts of the world. In dealing with the hardships of a strike, she also has realistic and moving touches, such as the description of the children who, out of work, do not know what to do with themselves, because they have forgotten how to play. But her characters are nothing but mouthpieces for various economic theories, and the action nothing but an illustration of the 'Summary of Principles' given at the end of the tale. Where Miss Martineau begins and ends with the theoretical problem, Mrs. Gaskell gives us the concrete human suffering: the starving family in the damp cellar, the woman driven on to the streets, the weaver forced, by the miseries around him and by allegiance to his trade union, to commit a murder. Poverty to her is not, as it is to Miss Martineau, an aspect of the 'Administration of Labour' or of the failure to discourage 'imprudent, early marriages'; it is filth and squalor and humiliation beyond endurance. She is artistically superior because she realises that individuals are more important material than a social thesis: and her effect on 'the conscience—not to mention the downright factual ignorance—of the middle class' (Arnold Kettle)[1] was correspondingly greater.

The distress of the industrial workers was outside the sphere of knowledge of most women writers; but they were not short of social problems nearer home. One of these, and one to which many novelists turned their attention, was the position of the governess. The decade which saw the founding of the Governesses' Benevolent Institution (1841) and an ever-growing movement towards an improvement of governesses' conditions, also saw a number of novels dealing with the sufferings of the governess, often underpaid, overworked and suffering various forms of humiliation from having to earn her living with people who were her social equals or inferiors. The chief novels on this theme will be dealt with in Chapter II, in connection with Anne Brontë's governess novel, *Agnes Grey*; here it may be sufficient to point out that the subject attracted novelists from the most different *genres*. Lady Blessington placed her governess in a 'fashionable' novel (*The Governess*, 1839), and Mrs. Sherwood set hers in a religious tale for the young (*Caroline Mordaunt*, 1835). Between the two extremes, governesses of all descriptions enter fiction; and as late as 1850 we find Miss Martineau writing a story of an old governess who, her employer and his family having emigrated to Canada, dies in utter destitution in the work-house—but not before she has written a cheerful letter to her former employer, assuring him that the time will come when 'a greater variety of employment should be opened to women'.[2]

While moralising within the domestic sphere was thus expanding into moralising on the evils and injustices of society, the moral-precept tale was simultaneously growing into the fully fledged religious novel. In the hands of novelists like Miss Sewell and Mrs. Marsh domestic scenes are made the settings of religious debates, and characters are analysed in order to show the ordeals, sufferings and rewards of a Christian life. These ladies are writing for much the same audience as Mrs. Hofland and Mrs. Opie before them—as described by Mrs. Oliphant, writing on Mrs. Marsh:

> a little circle of young ladies emancipated from the schoolroom, but scarcely entered upon the world, sitting in one of her own pretty orderly morning rooms. . . .
>
> 'My dear children, here is the good and here is the evil, and you see what they lead to; and here again you perceive how the evil is overcome by the good', is the burden of her tale. [1]

Many of the listening young ladies soon turned their hands to novels of their own; and it is against the resulting 'mind-and-millinery species' that George Eliot cries out in her article on 'Silly Novels by Lady Novelists'. It had become too easy to be didactic in fiction:

> Take a woman's head, stuff it with a smattering of philosophy and literature chopped small, and with false notions of society baked hard, let it hang over a desk a few hours every day, and serve up hot in feeble English, when not required. [2]

Under the facetiousness of this, there lies a serious regret that women, by finding their *raison d'être* as novelists in easy and unthinking didacticism, were neglecting the unique contribution they could make to literature: 'a precious speciality', she says in her last paragraph, 'lying quite apart from masculine aptitudes and experience'. Just wherein this 'speciality' lies, she does not say; she could only prove it, fortunately, by writing her own novels. A few years earlier, in his essay on 'The Lady Novelists', G. H. Lewes had tried a theoretical definition:

> Woman, by her greater affectionateness, her greater range and depth of emotional experience, is well fitted to give expression to the emotional facts of life, and demands a place in literature corresponding with that she occupies in society.

28

'A place in literature corresponding with that she occupies in society':
we are back here with the ambivalence in attitudes to woman in the
mid-nineteenth century, well expressed by G. M. Young when he
shows how strong champions spoke for her, while simultaneously

> at the base, no doubt, we shall find unchanged a solid block of what
> some may call convention, some instinct, and some prejudice; a
> dislike of disturbance, a real care for the finer qualities of women,
> and a genuine fear of the consequences if they are led out of their
> proper sphere into a world where, if they are unsuited to it, they
> will be wasted; if suited, they may undersell the men.[1]

For all the empirical proof that the woman writer had established
herself firmly in several branches of fiction, we are back to an underlying query of what her proper sphere ought to be. We must turn to
consider that query.

(iv)

We might expect to find an answer in a book published in 1842,
with the promising title: *Female Writers: Thoughts on Their Proper
Sphere, and on Their Powers of Usefulness*. The author is Miss M. A.
Stodart, a learned lady who knew Latin and Greek, and wrote books on
female education and on how to lead a good Christian life.[2] This book
turns out to be, in its attitude to female writing, both typical and
a-typical of the period. Miss Stodart's notion that fiction, *qua* fiction,
is evil was shared only by the strictest Evangelicals; and even they,
during this decade, were discovering the enormous possibilities of
fiction as a handmaid of religion. 'Novels are not objected to as they
were', said a writer in *Blackwood's* in 1848,

> now that every sect in politics and religion have found their
> efficacy as a means, the form is adopted by all.[3]

In an earlier work, *Hints on Reading: Addressed to a Young Lady* (1839),
Miss Stodart had warned her hypothetical Young Lady that 'a Christian novel-reader is a contradiction in terms; a thing, which, like the
gryphon, dragon, unicorn, etc., may be imagined, but which like
them, has not, and never had any real existence'; and in *Female
Writers* she elaborates the point. Having recognised that many of the
novelists of the day are women, she exclaims:

This is exceedingly to be regretted. If the evils to women from novel-reading are not small, those which arise from novel-writing, are alarming [*sic*] great. (p. 134)

If this extremist attitude were all, *Female Writers* would not have much to offer. But when Miss Stodart leaves her general objections to the novel as novel and comes to her particular objections to female novelists, she is tapping a much more vital vein. Her arguments here reflect widespread feelings, conventions and prejudices.

As we see Miss Stodart work her way to her proposed subject via lengthy chapters on 'Mental Faculties of Woman', 'Disadvantages of Education', 'Women of Ancient Times' and 'Considerations on Learning in Women', we are reminded that to most minds of the period the question of the female writer could never be properly considered apart from that favourite question of the intellectual differences between the sexes. G. H. Lewes is typical when he introduces his review of *Shirley* with a couple of pages on the 'mental equality of the sexes'. To us it may seem irrelevant to the literary merits of Charlotte Brontë's novel to ask:

What should we do with a leader of opposition in the seventh month of her pregnancy? or a general in chief who at the opening of a campaign was 'doing as well as could be expected'? or a chief justice with twins?[1]

But to Lewes and his contemporaries, these questions were all part of the same general problem: a chief justice with twins and a woman writing novels would both be doing less than justice to 'the grand function of woman . . . Maternity' in order to claim intellectual equality with man. Similarly, Miss Stodart's discussion of the peculiar qualities of the female mind reveals many of the assumptions underlying the attitude of reviewers to the female writer. The foremost characteristic of woman's mind, she thinks, is 'the extreme delicacy and sensitiveness of its organisation'; and in contemplating this organisation she becomes quite lyrical: the mimosa, which shies away from every rude touch, and the 'Aeolian harp which trembles and vibrates at every breath of wind' are only 'faint emblems of a sensitive and refined woman'. Intellectually, woman has intuition rather than reasoning power; there is less separation between the 'moral' and the 'mental' faculties, between heart and head: she excels in 'quickness of sympathy'. On the other hand, she has less power of application and patient research, less strength of will, than man. When it comes to the aesthetic qualities that may be expected from her work, she is good at close observation, at noticing and reproducing details; she has what Coleridge would call fancy rather than imagination: is 'endowed with polished taste, but destitute in general of the creative power of high imagination'. Throughout this there goes a firm belief in the essential inferiority of the female mind. To agree with Mary Wollstonecraft's belief in the intellectual equality of the sexes would mean

> aiming a presumptuous blow at that wisdom which assigned to man to rule, to woman to obey. (p. 14)

The crucial word here is, of course, 'presumptuous'. Each sex has been perfectly endowed for its particular sphere of action; to try to break out of that sphere would mean a challenge to the whole order of creation:

> This fitness of means to an end, this beautiful adaptation to circum-stances, must carefully be borne in mind, or else each will be dis-posed to say to the Supreme Ruler of the universe, 'Why hast thou made me thus?' (p. 15)

Such a heretical question would be tantamount to questioning that whatever is, is right. Despite her apocalyptical tone, we have not moved very far from Pope's *Essay on Man* in Miss Stodart's affirmation of the Chain of Being:

> The same wisdom that taught the lion to prowl in the midnight forest, and the little birds to sing among the branches, that taught the fishes to glide in deep waters, and the mole to burrow under-ground, has assigned to woman her post, and richly, most richly endowed her for fulfilling its duties. (p. 15)

Obviously she is arguing here from a central conservative principle, that which, with all its ramifications, proved the basic obstacle to female emancipationists, and also that which Charlotte Brontë, because of the contents and the nature of her first novel, came up against in the bitterest review she ever had: Miss Rigby's article on '*Vanity Fair, Jane Eyre* and *Governesses' Benevolent Institution—Report for 1847*' in the

Quarterly Review for December 1848. *The Quarterly* was known as the champion of the Established Church and the established social order, and Miss Rigby (later Lady Eastlake) was known as one of the most relentless supporters of this policy. Her review, coming fourteen months after the appearance of *Jane Eyre*, was written in reaction against the popular acclamation of the novel (and also for love of scandal; there are in it mysterious hints at some connection between Currer Bell and Thackeray). For all this, which—as Professor Tillotson points out[1]—does not make it fully representative of public opinion of Charlotte Brontë's book, it shows the nature and the deep-rootedness of the worst kind of prejudice—prejudice which by those who held it was thought of as both religious and political dogma—which the woman breaking out of her proper sphere had to fight. Jane Eyre is seen as 'the personification of an unregenerate and undisciplined spirit', one which shows no signs of Christian grace; above all she is guilty of 'the sin of pride'. Jane's alleged pride is the same 'presumptuousness' that Miss Stodart attacks. Not only is her wish for, and achievement of, independence a revolt against the order of the world, but she, an orphan, also upsets the social order by marrying her master:

> Altogether the auto-biography of Jane Eyre is pre-eminently an anti-Christian composition. There is throughout it a murmuring against the comforts of the rich and against the privations of the poor, which, as far as each individual is concerned, is a murmuring against God's appointment—there is a proud and perpetual assertion of the rights of man, for which we find no authority either in God's word or in God's providence—there is that pervading tone of ungodly discontent which is at once the most prominent and the most subtle evil which the law and the pulpit, which all civilised society in fact has at the present day to contend with.[2]

We are reminded how closely the rights of woman were tied up with the rights of man. Jane's self-assertion, which the reviewer implicitly transfers to her creator, is seen as in kind one with the revolutionary movements of the decade. When we remember that 1848 was also the year of the February revolution in France and the last Chartist demonstration in England, we can more easily place the note of urgency behind Miss Rigby's lines,

We do not hesitate to say that the tone of mind and thought which has overthrown authority and violated every code human and divine abroad, and fostered Chartism and rebellion at home, is the same which has also written Jane Eyre.

While an English ultra-conservative critic attacks *Jane Eyre* for having the revolutionary spirit of 1848, a French critic praises the book for not having it. Eugène Forçade, writing in the *Revue des Deux Mondes*, makes exactly the opposite point from Miss Rigby's: this novel is *not* an outcry against the established order; its spirit is *not* that of rebellion but of patience and endurance:

> . . . ce qui m'a surtout charmé, c'est que l'auteur . . . n'a pas un instant songé à fulminer une apocalypse contre la société dans un drame où pourtant la société joue à peu près le rôle tyrannique et cruel de la fatalité antique.[1]

So relative are points of view. Yet we must not think Miss Rigby alone and totally unrepresentative in her reaction. In 1855 another reviewer—again a woman—looks back on the novel and finds it 'but a wild declaration of the "Rights of Women" in a new aspect'; she then goes on to relate it to the general social and political situation:

> Yes, it is but a mere vulgar boiling over of the political cauldron, which tosses your French monarch into chaos, and makes a new one in his stead.

Indeed this upheaval is far more dangerous, for

> here is your true revolution. France is but one of the Western Powers; woman is the half of the world.[2]

Male reviewers tended to be less excited about the ideas in *Jane Eyre*, even when reading them in the same terms. Thus in his sympathetic essay on her works to date (including *Wuthering Heights*, which he believes to be hers) Sydney Dobell in *The Palladium* of September 1850, sees Currer Bell as a great revolutionary. When he speaks of how she exhibits 'the conventional rank of outward circumstance bowing before the absolute rank of intrinsic superiority',[3] he puts in a nutshell the implications which both the Jane–Rochester relationship and the story of Louis Moore and Shirley Keeldar must have had for many of Charlotte Brontë's early readers.

That *Jane Eyre* could possibly be seen as subversive took Charlotte Brontë by utter surprise. As a Preface to her next novel, *Shirley*, she prepared a 'Word to the *Quarterly*', and it was only to please her publishers that she finally agreed to leave it out. Her letters about it show that she thought she had treated the *Quarterly* 'with the lightest satire', but some of the real sting of that reply may be inferred from the way she puts into the mouth of one of the characters of the novel, Mrs. Pryor, long snatches of direct quotations from Miss Rigby's article. Miss Rigby's words are divided between Mrs. and Miss Hardman, respectively mother and eldest daughter in a family 'of considerable pretensions to good birth and mental superiority', where Mrs. Pryor has served as governess—an experience she is now relating in order to dissuade Caroline Helstone from becoming a governess. Like Miss Rigby to Currer Bell, Mrs. Hardman had told Mrs. Pryor to quell her 'ungodly discontent' and to cease 'murmuring against God's appointment'; and into the mouth of Miss Hardman—'a very strong-minded young lady, of most distinguished talents: the aristocracy are decidedly a very superior class, you know—both physically and morally and mentally'—are put those callous words with which Miss Rigby had welcomed the state of affairs that supplied the more fortunate classes with suitable governesses. Nor can Charlotte Brontë refrain from letting Caroline Helstone comment that 'Miss Hardman must have thought herself something better than her fellow-creatures . . . her religion must have been that of the Pharisee, who thanked God that he was not as other men are' (*Shirley*, Chapter XXI).

Charlotte Brontë's handling of her governess-heroine in *Jane Eyre* had meant that in that novel the love theme, the woman question and the larger social, or class, theme were united into one. With her interest so firmly fixed on Jane and her love, it is hardly likely that she was even aware of the social implications of her novel. In *Shirley*, which is much more self-consciously a social novel, the themes are, at least partly, separated. In the early stages of writing the novel, before the *Quarterly* article had appeared, she wrote to W. S. Williams of her new work:

I have not therein so far treated of governesses, as I do not wish it to resemble its predecessor. I often wish to say something about the 'condition of women' question, but it is one respecting which so much 'cant' has been talked, that one feels a sort of repugnance to approach it.

The letter shows the same kind of moderation—recognising the problem but also the difficulty of doing anything about it—that one finds in *Shirley* as a whole, both as regards the women and the working classes. Her thinking on this point, and the fact that these two social problems are interrelated in her mind, can be seen from her concluding sentence:

> I conceive that when patience has done its utmost and industry its best, whether in the case of women or operatives, and when both are baffled, and pain and want triumph, the sufferer is free, is entitled, at last to send up to Heaven any piercing cry for relief, if by that cry he can hope to obtain succour.[1]

This 'cry' is the Yorkshire 'yell' of the weavers in *Shirley*, as well as Jane Eyre's, 'Do you think, because I am poor, obscure, plain and little, I am soulless and heartless?' and, later, Lucy Snowe's 'My heart will break!' This is the cry that marked Charlotte Brontë as a rebel.

While Shirley Keeldar, by fortune and character, is, throughout the novel, until she is tamed by love, a representative of the independent woman, there are, in those parts of *Shirley* which must have been written after the appearance of Miss Rigby's article, several set-pieces of discussion of the woman question. In the somewhat awkward device of an interior monologue the meek and mild Caroline Helstone is made to argue out the position of the single woman, in terms which suggest how little Charlotte Brontë conceived of her position as subversive:

> Nobody in particular is to blame, that I can see, for the state in which things are; and I cannot tell . . . how they are to be altered for the better; but I feel there is something wrong somewhere. I believe single women should have more to do—better chances of interesting and profitable occupation than they possess now. And when I speak thus, I have no impression that I displease God by my words; that I am either impious or impatient, irreligious or sacrilegious. (Chapter XXII)

These are also very much the terms in which Charlotte Brontë repeatedly in her letters deals with the woman question.

But willy-nilly, then, the reception of *Jane Eyre* had been conditioned by its date of publication. The year 1847 was a milestone in the history of woman's intellectual development. One of the outstanding features of the 1840s is the growing interest in the subject of female intelligence and female education; the insistence from strong-minded women and their male champions that, given equal education, woman would prove to have equal intellect. In 1847 this interest was beginning to achieve tangible results. John Stuart Mill's *Subjection of Women* (1869) was still a long way off, and what G. M. Young calls the true 'collision of the two Spheres' was not to come till late Victorian times; but 1847 is marked by a series of victories for female educationalists: Queen's College for Women was founded (and in a letter to Williams, while she was writing *Shirley*, Charlotte Brontë advises him to let his daughter accept a place there, as education is 'a step towards independency'), and within a short space of time King's College started classes for governesses, and Bedford College began classes in a private house. Humble enough at the beginning, these were to form the foundation of higher education for women in England. While women's hopes ran high, the air was tense with prejudice. Perhaps the best reflection of this tension is Tennyson's 'medley', *The Princess*, published in 1847. The poem is known nowadays chiefly for the lyrics interspersed in it, but its narrative sections show a characteristically Tennysonian alertness to the thoughts and problems of the day. Its subject is female intellect and female education. Various attitudes are played off against each other; there is the old King, who puts the conservative view:

> Man for the field and woman for the hearth:
> Man for the sword and for the needle she:
> Man with the head and woman with the heart:
> Man to command and woman to obey:
> All else confusion.

The other extreme is represented by the Princess and the Female Academy she has founded:

> Maintaining that with equal husbandry
> The woman were an equal to the man.

And there is the resolution of opposites, in the lover of the Princess, who shows her that equality is a meaningless word:

Not like to like, but like in difference.

The real solution lies in marriage:

> . . . seeing that either sex alone
> Is half itself, and in true marriage lies
> Nor equal, nor unequal: each fulfils
> Defect in each, and always thought in thought,
> Purpose in purpose, will in will, they grow,
> The single pure and perfect animal.

The work was hailed because it treated, in the words of the *Fraser* reviewer, 'an essentially modern theme'; it came to be used, as in an article in the *Oxford and Cambridge Magazine*, as a text-book showing 'the truest conception of woman's duty and position'.[1] Its resolution is certainly very much closer to the fate of all of Charlotte Brontë's (and Anne's) heroines than the idea of the rebel would suggest. It is close also to Charlotte's comments to Mrs. Gaskell on a *Westminster Review* article about the woman question, the tenor of which she has found cold and hard: 'To many women, affection is sweet, and power conquered indifferent.'[2] When the *Fraser* reviewer of *The Princess* sees it as an attack on woman's 'self-willed and proud longing . . . to unsex herself', and adds

> in *The Princess* Mr. Tennyson has embodied the ideal of that nobler, wider, purer, yet equally fallacious, because equally unnatural analogue, which we may meet too often up and down England now,[3]

he brings us at last back to Miss Stodart again, to the 'unnatural' quality she saw in woman's wish to usurp the 'masculine ground of intellect'. For by pursuing her attitude of distrust of the female intellect and her strongly emotional, quasi-philosophical and -religious, reaction to anything which challenges that distrust, we have seen, I think, some basic factors in the climate which any female novelist would have to face in the 1840s.

Miss Stodart's objective is, after all, to discuss the proper sphere of the female writer; and however inauspicious a beginning she makes with her assertion that 'nothing can alter the position assigned to [woman] in Scripture', she takes off from there via another Biblical imperative: the duty of every individual to develop his or her given talent:

> Let it be conceded, for the sake of argument, that women often have, compared with the nobler sex, but one intellectual talent; it is the more incumbent upon them to cultivate it. (p. 67)

The main concern of her book, then, is to trace the proper direction of such development. We do not have to take very seriously her advice to the poetess that she should let the male poet watch the eagle, while she herself watches the turtle-dove and gives 'with responsive readiness . . . meaning to its tender cooing'; but, in view of the didactic tendencies of the great mass of female writing which we looked at in the previous section of this chapter, it is interesting that she sees the function of women prose-writers to be that of 'popularising instruction'. More important still is her dread of specious emotional excitement; this makes her condemn the social-problem novel, and in her advice against reading (let alone writing) something like 'Mrs. Trollope's Factory Boy' she states that its unhealthy effect on the mind is an evil outweighing any possible good done by the social message of the novel.

Here we are, I think, brought up against a concern for the qualities of womanliness which more than anything helped to delimit the proper sphere of the female novelist. When we look into Miss Stodart's specific objections to female novel-writing, we find that she bases them, first, on the fact that all writing of fiction is to some extent self-revelatory and, secondly, on her own assumptions (common enough in the period) that, as woman's sphere of observation is so much more limited than man's, and as she is dependent on the mode of memory rather than creative imagination, she is all the more prone to such revelation. She is only articulating here what most reviewers seemed tacitly to take for granted: as Charlotte Brontë learnt, to her embarrassment, there was a particularly strong tendency to read autobiographically a novel known to be by a woman and to identify her with her own characters. Even Whateley, writing on *Mansfield Park*, and praising Jane Austen for the way she describes Fanny's love 'with a vividness and a detail of which we can scarcely conceive anyone but a female . . . capable', had not been able to refrain from the rider: 'and we should almost add, a female writing from recollection'.[1] Miss Stodart's phraseology may be exceptionally coy, but she is typical in her assumption that the woman writer wilfully exposes her most intimate self to the public:

> Now in this laying bare of the workings of the inward heart, there is a peculiar inconvenience for delicate and sensitive woman. It is like proclaiming to the public that which passes within her own breast. It is more—it is placing a glass window in her bosom, that every passer-by may look in and see the workings of her heart.

If authorship, then, means something almost like prostitution of one's self, then

> it is needless to point out the obvious inconveniences; every woman of ordinary delicacy of feelings instinctively perceives them, and, like the mimosa plant, shrinks away from the danger. (pp. 134–5)

We are reminded here that the despiser of female intellect was perhaps a less embarrassing enemy to female writing than the worshipper of female sensibility. (The two were, of course, often united in one person.) Just as many—and many intelligent women, including George Eliot, among them—feared that emancipation of woman might mean a coarsening of the feminine nature itself, so female authorship was seen as a potential danger to female delicacy. To see the full implications of this, we must remember one very widespread conception of womanhood in the period: the idea that woman, destined by her delicateness and sensitivity, finds her true identity in being a moral influence on man.[2] A writer in the liberal *Westminster Review* for January 1850, puts the typical point of view:

> The woman evenly developed, unfolded after her own type, the one God struck approvingly when she was created, differs from man in this—in possessing a greater capacity—a greater genius to influence.

And though he feels in conscience bound to urge that woman should be brought up independent of man for subsistence, he ends with a vision of the millennium when woman's true function as influence, rather than an independent agent, is realised:

... the Garden of Eden is once more around us, and in the evening-hour do men, as Adam of yore, converse with archangels in the sunny glades.[1]

One presumes that, as in Milton's prototype of this situation, Eve is getting supper in the background. It is surprising how often the Miltonic vision of a prelapsarian Eve crops up as the ideal image of womanhood in writings of the first half of the nineteenth century. In novels by women I have found it from Susan Ferrier's *Marriage* (1818) onwards; it took the boldness of a Shirley Keeldar to react against it: 'Milton tried to see the first woman ... but ... it was his cook that he saw' (*Shirley*, Chapter XVIII). The emotionalism with which this image of womanhood was surrounded often leads to such sentimental imagery as Tennyson's, in *The Princess*:

> Not learned, save in gracious household ways,
> Not perfect, nay, but full of tender wants,
> No Angel, but a dearer being, all dipt
> In Angel instincts, breathing Paradise,
> Interpreter between the Gods and men,
> Who look'd all native to her place, and yet
> On tiptoe seem'd to touch upon a sphere
> Too gross to tread, and all male minds perforce
> Sway'd to her from their orbits as they moved,
> And girdled her with music.

The Romantics' worship of the child had been replaced by the mid-Victorians' worship of the woman.

In less high-flown and more practical terms, this—the belief in woman as the source and maintainer of moral idealism—was the ideal preached by many women authors themselves. It was made explicit in the series of manuals on womanhood by Mrs. Sarah Ellis: *The Women of England* (1839), *The Daughters of England* (1842), *The Wives of England* (1843), and implicit (though often barely so) in the mass of domestic novels, some of them written by the same Mrs. Ellis. In fact the step from treatise to novel is often very short: Mrs. Ellis's book on *The Women of England: their Social Duties and Domestic Habits* reads like a blueprint, or rather a number of blueprints, for a set of novels on woman, home and family. The only difference is that where the domestic novelist starts with the concrete situation and draws the moral out of it, Mrs. Ellis starts with the precept and proceeds to suggest a fictitious situation which illustrates it. Thus her section on how not to receive a guest reads like a paraphrase of Fanny Price's visit to her Portsmouth home, and the one on how people tend to treat their poor relations, like a sketch of Fanny's position at Mansfield Park. All this may seem to have little to do with Mrs. Ellis's proposed subject, 'the moral worth of the women of England', but in the course of her book it becomes clear that for the women of England, morality dwells but in minute particulars—or, as she says, 'those minor parts of domestic and social intercourse, which strengthen into habit'. Morality dwells above all in kindness and consideration within family relationships; the identity of woman lies in her moral function as daughter, sister, wife, and mother. Mrs. Ellis again helps us to see how easily the mid-century domestic novel had developed out of the more obviously didactic fiction of earlier decades. At this stage, the openly directive titles (such as Mrs. Opie's *A Wife's Duty*) were becoming rarer and were being replaced, very often, by a woman's name. In *Amy Herbert* (Miss Sewell, 1844), *Ellen Middleton* (Lady Fullerton, 1844), *Emilia Wyndham* (Mrs. Marsh, 1846), *Margaret Maitland* (Mrs. Oliphant, 1849), and scores of others, plot-concerns differ but the central preoccupation in all is with the woman as an influence on others within her domestic and social circle. It was in this preoccupation that the typical woman novelist of the 1840s found her proper sphere: in using the novel to demonstrate (by assumption rather than exploration of standards of womanliness) *woman's* proper sphere. And it is here that the Brontës are most a-typical, just as the greatest woman novelist before them had been a-typical.

For all the apparent domesticity of her novels (which makes parts of them read like anticipations of Mrs. Ellis's precepts), Jane Austen is not—not even in *Mansfield Park*—a forerunner of this kind of fiction: her vision of the good life is so much more inclusive and far-reaching than the domestic-social issues she uses to project it. And when Charlotte Brontë writes of Jane Eyre, it is Jane asserting her own identity as an individual, rather than Jane existing in terms of her influence within a domestic context, that matters. (Jane's being an orphan may be both cause and effect of this.) Agnes Grey and Helen Huntingdon in Anne Brontë's two novels exist as moral individuals, not as images of womanly morality. But *Emilia Wyndham* (which novel was sometimes reviewed together with *Jane Eyre*) is a typical domestic study of ideal womanhood. Dedicated to Wordsworth and bearing as a motto those lines from 'She was a Phantom of Delight' which define 'a perfect woman, nobly planned', it shows how Emilia learns to love the man she has married (in order to be able to provide for her ailing father), and how her loving-kindness conquers all. The authoress frequently pauses to reflect on such deformities of nature as bad mothers and coquettish wives; and Mrs. Danby, Emilia's mother-in-law is used as a particularly dark foil to the heroine:

> It tends very much to harden and blight a man's character, when the mother whom he loves and trusts is such a being as Mrs. Danby. There has no sense of moral beauty, there has none of the divine influence of gentle tenderness, none of the high adoration of what appear to him angelic virtues—none of all this has flowed into his soul;—the very fountain from which the finer feelings and the higher tendencies are to be drawn has been changed and petrified at its source.
>
> (Chapter XVII)

It is this kind of semi-religious worship of pure, delicate womanhood which often underlies and defines the adjective 'unwomanly' when applied to a novel by a woman. What Miss Stodart means by the 'obvious inconveniences of writing' which 'every woman of ordinary delicacy of feeling instinctively perceives' and shrinks away from, may best be illustrated by Mrs. Oliphant's review of Mrs. Gaskell's *Ruth* (1853)—the story of an unmarried mother who is given a home and refuge in a dissenting minister's family and who expiates her sin by an almost saintly life and a sacrificial death. To us the novel seems harmless and even a little cowardly in that it lets the heroine die as a concession to conventional morality. Charlotte Brontë thought so, too.[1] But to Mrs. Oliphant, *Ruth* is 'a great blunder in art': Mrs. Gaskell was wrong in choosing such a subject and such a heroine at all. As a woman she should not know of, but shy away from such a sin:

> Every pure feminine mind, we suppose, holds the faith of Desdemona—'I do not believe there is any such woman.'[2]

It is worth noticing that in the same review Mrs. Oliphant's objections to Hawthorne are purely aesthetic and psychological; she dislikes his method of using a 'spiritual dissecting-knife'. *The Scarlet Letter* may be about an adulteress who has an illegitimate child, but it is written by a man.

Measured against a criterion of womanliness which states that the pure feminine mind must, even theoretically or imaginatively, know no sin, no evil, no sexual passion, all the three Brontës could not but seem unwomanly. Not for them the *noli me tangere* of the mimosa or the wilful ignorance of a bowdlerised Desdemona, when it came to treating of the mutual passion between Jane and Rochester, or Helen Huntingdon's struggles with a drunken and adulterous husband, or the love and hatred of Heathcliff. In innocence, rather than bold defiance, did they write, and nowhere is this more obvious than in Charlotte Brontë's treatment of love in *Jane Eyre*. The scenes of mutually declared love between Jane and Rochester (and he a married man)—shocking enough as breaches against the 'she never told her love' convention which most novelists religiously observed; and positively scandalous if actually by the hand of a woman—provoked the *Quarterly*'s Miss Rigby into saying that if the novel was by a woman, it must be by 'one who has, for some sufficient reason, long forfeited the society of her own sex'; her insinuations suggesting the truth of Miss Stodart's belief that 'a gifted female has most to fear from her own sex'. Mrs. Oliphant, when the sex of the author was officially known, could be openly catty about it:

> The grossness of the book was such grossness as only could be perpetrated by a woman. . . . There is a degree of refined indelicacy possible to a woman, which no man can reach.[1]

Clearly Charlotte Brontë had had little idea that there was anything improper about her handling of love in *Jane Eyre*, and she was disturbed not so much by the *Quarterly* article, which was openly malicious (and which in any case reached her at a time when Emily was just dead and Anne dying), but by such early comments as that of *The Christian Remembrancer* where she was told that 'the love-scenes glow with a fire as fierce as that of Sappho, and somewhat more fuliginous'.[2] Somewhat pathetically puzzled by this reaction, she consulted Miss Martineau who, Mrs. Gaskell tells us, explained to her that in *Jane*

Eyre 'love was treated with unusual breadth, and that the kind of intercourse was uncommon, and uncommonly described'.[1] It must have irked Miss Martineau to find, when *Villette* appeared, that Charlotte had learned so little from her explanation of the facts of love in fiction. She wrote a sharp letter to Charlotte and an equally sharp review of the novel in the *Daily News*, in which she complained that *Villette* made love too general and too absorbing a factor in women's lives. (She does not say what no doubt was in her mind: that she herself had taken care duly to dilute the double love-plot in her novel *Deerbrook* by philosophical disquisitions on subjects like 'What is Poverty?', and by such social events as the mobbing of the house of a doctor suspected of body-snatching.) Miss Martineau's strictures on what she takes to be the novel's assumption, 'that events and characters are to be regarded through the medium of one passion only', recall Miss Stodart's fear that the female novelist will become too engrossed with 'the tender passions', which she sees as 'the breach in the wall by which the enemy often enters into the city'. Again Miss Stodart only says in a more general and dogmatic form what many reviewers were to say specifically about Charlotte Brontë.

Professor Tillotson is right in warning us against confusing attitudes to modesty and propriety in the 1840s with the strictness of the Evangelicals earlier in the century and with the prudishness of the '60s, '70s and '80s. But I think she underplays the reaction to Charlotte Brontë's novels, for the complaints about an unwomanly treatment of passion seem to grow more, rather than less, ardent as *Jane Eyre* is followed by *Shirley* and, above all, by *Villette*. Thus the *Athenaeum* gives a long and serious review to *Villette*, which discusses the similarity of love relationships in all Charlotte Brontë's novels, finds her treatment of love excessively passionate, sees this as symptomatic of female writing in the period and Charlotte's own influence as dangerous:

> Her books will drive many minds out among the breakers,—they will guide few to sure havens.[2]

The Christian Remembrancer speaks at greater length and with more sharpness on very similar lines. It begins by recalling

> the outrages on decorum, the moral perversity, the toleration of, nay, indifference to vice which deform her first powerful picture of

a desolate woman's trials and sufferings—faults which make Jane
Eyre a dangerous book, and which must leave a permanent mistrust
of the author on all thoughtful and scrupulous minds.

It then goes on to point to a 'faulty morality' in details (such as letting
lovers carry on clandestine correspondence) and mounts to a grand
climax, which must be quoted at length, because it brings together all
the fundamental reasons for Charlotte Brontë's alleged lack of womanliness:

> We want a woman at our hearth; and her impersonations are
> without the feminine element, infringers of modest restraints, despisers
> of bashful fears, self-reliant, contemptuous of prescriptive decorum;
> their own unaided reason, their individual opinion of right and
> wrong, discreet or imprudent, sole guides of conduct and rules of
> manners,—the whole hedge of immemorial scruple and habit broken
> down and trampled upon.

Such heroines as hers may inspire passion, but—writes the female
reviewer—never affection, 'that one important, we may say, indis-
pensable element of man's true love':

> A restless heart and vagrant imagination, though owned by woman,
> can have no sympathy or true insight into the really feminine nature.
> Such cannot appreciate the hold which a daily round of simple
> duties and pure pleasures has on those who are content to practise
> and enjoy them.[1]

The same journal which, after the appearance of *Villette*, saw in
Charlotte Brontë's works an ignorance of what womanhood means
and a betrayal of some of its most cherished values, had some years
earlier used the word 'masculine' as a measuring-rod for *Jane Eyre*:

> A book more unfeminine, both in its excellences and defects, it
> would be hard to find in the annals of female authorship. Through-
> out there is masculine power, breadth and shrewdness, combined
> with masculine hardness, coarseness, and freedom of expression.[2]

Masculinity means praise where it stands for imaginative qualities:
invention, style (other reviewers praised the style of the novel for being
'nervous and manly'); but it means blame where it stands for insights

into the human mind which a lady ought not to have, and uses of language which a lady ought not to permit herself. *The Edinburgh Review* strikes much the same note:

> A more masculine book, in the sense of vigour, was never written. Indeed that vigour often amounts to coarseness—and is certainly the very antipode to 'ladylike.'[1]

'Coarse' was a word used at one time or another about all the Brontë novels. It seems to have been a word applicable to a whole range of unfeminine sins: to what we would now call 'realism' of action and characterisation (the brutal fights in *Wuthering Heights*, the nasty children in *Agnes Grey* or the unpleasant young ladies in the *Villette pensionnat*, the drunken brawl in *The Tenant of Wildfell Hall*); to lack of prudishness in language (in her Preface to *Wuthering Heights* Charlotte Brontë defends the practice of giving oaths in full); to the use of scriptural quotations and images for profane purposes (*The Christian Remembrancer* is particularly worried about this practice in *Jane Eyre*, and *Fraser's Magazine* on this ground finds *The Tenant of Wildfell Hall* superior to *Jane Eyre* in religious tone, albeit it shows a 'low moral tone' throughout); but above all to the insight into human passion and human evil.

It was on this last count that *The Tenant of Wildfell Hall* was especially reviled. It is interesting to see some of the abusive criticism anticipated and replied to by the discerning reviewer in *Fraser's*: drawing a parallel with Juvenal's exposure of vice, he points out that the coarseness is part of the moral aim of the book; but he also knows that 'the world will revile Acton Bell'.[2] Charlotte Brontë's second novel confirmed many people's ideas of the coarseness of the author. Charles Kingsley—who makes the curious statement that he had hardly looked into *Jane Eyre*, as he very seldom read a work of fiction—found that

> *Shirley* disgusted me at the opening, and I gave up the writer and her books with a notion that she was a person who liked coarseness.[3]

And when *The Professor* was unearthed after Charlotte Brontë's death, it struck even Mrs. Gaskell as 'disfigured by more coarseness and profanity in quoting texts of scripture disagreeably than in [*sic*] any of her other works'.[1]

And yet it was Mrs. Gaskell's *Life of Charlotte Brontë* which was most instrumental in changing people's ideas about the supposed coarseness of the Brontës; and it is in reviews of her biography that we first see the very terms of abuse turned into praise. Perhaps the reaction which set in is best summed up in the words of the *Fraser* reviewer of Mrs. Gaskell's *Life*, when he points out how unthinkingly some have called *Jane Eyre* a story of 'an immoral tendency':

> For it speaks freely of many questionable matters on which our sanctimonious society closes its eyes or passes by on the other side; and it exhibits a freedom and latitude in discussing difficult questions which have struck many pious souls with consternation. Wiser critics there are, however, who may judge more leniently. They may hold that rudeness, indelicacy, masculine directness, are words that have been somewhat loosely applied to describe a fine and peculiar insight into the heart of man.[2]

One of these 'wiser critics' writes in the *Westminster Review* of July 1864, on the falseness with which relationships between men and women are treated in the English novel: the girls are always totally innocent and never experience a ripple of passion; even Dickens's Nancy 'talks delightful sentiments, and melts away into refreshing Sunday-school piety and pathos'. But, he goes on,

> Women have especial need, as the world goes, to be shrewd, self-reliant and strong; and we do all we can in our literature to render them helpless, imbecile and idiotic.

Charlotte Brontë is held up as the great defier of such convention:

> When Charlotte Brontë endeavoured to do otherwise, we can all recollect that a prudish scream was raised against her, and genteel virtue affected to be horrified with the authoress who drew women and girls endowed with human passion.[3]

We see here some of the earliest formulations of the late nineteenth-century view of the Brontës as romantic rebels. Even that stalwart Mrs. Oliphant was in 1897, looking back over *Women Novelists of Queen Victoria's Reign*, ready to see *Shirley* as a 'revolution as well as revelation'.[1] To us, either view may seem equally dated, not to say irrelevant, and the modern reader may feel with Richard Chase, in his essay on 'The Brontës, or, Myth Domesticated',[2] that the Brontës embraced and affirmed the social and moral codes of their own time.

But, ultimately, there is in the Brontës' unwomanliness something more at stake than period conventions. What it is, is hinted at in the letter which Charles Kingsley wrote to Mrs. Gaskell after reading her *Life of Charlotte Brontë*:

> Be sure that the book will do good. It will shame literary people into some stronger belief that a simple, virtuous, practical home life is consistent with high imaginative genius; and it will shame, too, the prudery of a not over cleanly though carefully whitewashed age, into believing that purity is now (as in all ages till now) quite compatible with the knowledge of evil.[3]

Thus, if we may believe with Mr. T. S. Eliot that the mind of England is a mind which changes but abandons nothing *en route*, and that each individual work of literature modifies that mind—then this is one way of measuring the importance of the individual talent of each of the Brontës to the English literary tradition. The awareness that 'purity is compatible with the knowledge of evil' characterised the Elizabethans; it was obscured for the later Romantics; it was in danger of getting lost to the Victorians. It was salvaged by the Brontës, each in her own way as an unwomanly woman writer.

II

Anne Brontë: The Woman Writer
as Moralist

Of him, to whom less is given, less will be required; but our utmost exertions are required of us all.

(The Tenant of Wildfell Hall)

(i)

No one would deny that of the Brontë sisters Anne was the one to whom least talent had been given, if by talent we mean the power of imaginative, artistic, creation. On the other hand, none of the Brontës was more concerned about the idea of talents in its biblical connotation. None had a greater sense of the imperative duty of the individual to develop, to the utmost, whatever talents he or she does possess; none would have been more prepared to agree with Miss Stodart's belief that 'talent, where it exists in man or in woman, is a precious gift of God, for the improvement as well as employment of which the possessor is accountable'.[1] To be thus accountable means a moral responsibility which is a very different matter from the modern notion of 'self-fulfilment'; it means that one's powers are to be exercised, not for their own sake, or for one's own sake, but for the good of one's fellow men. Anne Brontë, then, puts into one sentence the whole basis of her literary theory when, defending the moral intention of *The Tenant of Wildfell Hall*, she writes in the Preface to the second edition of that novel: 'Such humble talents as God has given me I will endeavour to put to their greatest use.'

Conscience, as the force which impels one to do one's duty at any cost, is a key-word in all Anne's writings. Since Charlotte, in publishing *Selections from the Poems of Acton Bell*, spoke of Anne as having been under the 'tyranny of too tender a conscience', it has been generally thought that 'religious feeling had been to her but too much like what it was to Cowper'.[1] It is true that, for all the artlessness of their hymn form, most of her religious poems go far beyond any expression of simple piety. They reveal anguished struggle:

> My sins increase, my love grows cold,
>   And Hope within me dies;
> And Faith itself is wavering now;
>   Oh, how shall I arise?
>
> ('Despondency')

The consciousness of sin is ever-present:

> Not only for the past I grieve,
>   The future fills me with dismay;
> Unless Thou hasten to relieve,
>   Thy suppliant is a castaway;
>
> ('A Prayer')

and there is something of the tension of Donne's 'Batter my heart' (though without metaphysical paradox) in lines like 'Oh, take the heart I cannot give'. That Anne had read Cowper is shown by the image of the castaway in the poem just quoted and by the poem included in the volume of *Poems, by Currer, Ellis and Acton Bell* entitled 'To Cowper'. There were depths of melancholy in all the Brontës— whether we explain it by the double Celtic ancestry of an Irish father and a Cornish mother, by the bleakness of the Haworth parsonage, or by some other psychological theory. But it is in Anne alone that melancholy takes the form of religious brooding and, at its worst, turns into the spiritual torments of one who fears for her own damnation. Certainly her religious troubles are like Cowper's in kind, but they differ in intensity. Her poem 'To Cowper' shows this, for, while she points the kinship:

> The language of my inmost heart
>   I traced in every line;
> *My* sins, *my* sorrows, hopes, and fears,
>   Were there—and only mine,

she also indicates the difference:

> I little knew what wilder woe
> Had filled the Poet's heart.

> I did not know the nights of gloom,
>   The days of misery;
> The long, long years of dark despair,
>   That crushed and tortured thee.

Cowper was indeed crushed under the burden of believing himself predestined to damnation, but in even the most agonised poems of Anne Brontë there enters a gleam of hope. It is not hope of a vague emotional kind; it is a matter not of escapism but of facing life squarely, and

> Knowing that earthly joys decay,
> But hoping through the darkest day.
>   ('*Vanitas Vanitatum, Omnia Vanitas*')

It is hope wrought out of a keen awareness of the hopelessness of life—as she writes in a poem from June 1845, 'Views of Life':

> Though hope may promise joys, that still
> Unkindly time will ne'er fulfil;
> Or, if they come at all,
> We never find them unalloyed,—
> Hurtful perchance, or soon destroyed,
> They vanish or they pall;

> Yet hope *itself* a brightness throws
> O'er all our labours and our woes;—

and so it is not a Romantic power of hoping 'till Hope creates from its own wreck the thing it contemplates'. Rather, it is a drive to persevere, a kind of moral passion

> To labour and to love
>   To pardon and endure,
> To lift thy heart to God above,
>   And keep thy conscience pure.
>   ('The Narrow Way')

One might call this commonplace didacticism—and much of her poetry is didactic—but that would be less than the truth. It is didacticism of a strangely passionate kind, for its chief function is to control and counteract the doubts of religious despair. Her poems are nearly all autobiographical: they take their subject-matter from her own experience of life; their intention is to find a meaning in that experience. And the meaning, when found, is a moral imperative, as expressed in her last poem, written four months before her death:

> That secret labour to sustain
> With humble patience every blow;
> To gather fortitude from pain
> And hope and holiness from woe.
>
> ('Last Lines')

It is, I think, this kind of moral passion which determines the peculiar qualities of her two novels, *Agnes Grey* and *The Tenant of Wildfell Hall*.

Like her poems, the novels of Anne Brontë are constructed out of the stuff of her own life. Yet there is an important difference here. While the poems were primarily self-expression, the novels were written with a public in view. *Agnes Grey* may, it is true, have grown out of the 'Passages in the Life of an Individual' which we hear of in her birthday note of 1845,[1] but it is sure to have been given its final form with publication in mind. After the ill-fated poems of the Bells had appeared in 1846, Charlotte says, 'we each set to work on a prose tale'. It would seem that in working on this prose tale, Anne came to feel about her own experiences as she did about her talents: they became a moral responsibility, a fund of material to be put to use for the moral benefit of others. This is not to say, as Naomi Lewis does in an article on *The Tenant of Wildfell Hall*, that 'her books are most interesting for their revelation of herself'.[2] The tendency of much work on the Brontës has been to use the novels as material for biography, and the road to Thrushcross Grange, or to the *Villette pensionnat*, is as well trodden as that to Xanadu. To say that Anne drew on her own life for the material of her novels is not to replace criticism with biography; it is to emphasise her pragmatic and moral approach to the art of writing fiction. For much longer periods than either of her sisters, Anne had had, in Charlotte's words, 'to taste the cup of life as it is mixed for the class termed "Governesses"'. It is the bitter mixture of that cup which fills *Agnes Grey*. Anne, too, had had to witness more directly the breakdown of Branwell, who joined her as a tutor in the Robinson family at Thorp Green, where Anne held her longest governess's appointment. Whatever the truth of the relationship between Mrs. Robinson and Branwell Brontë,[1] it hastened his moral and physical collapse, made Anne give up her post and caused her to write in the 1845 birthday note words which hide a wealth of meaning: 'during my stay I have had some very unpleasant and undreamt-of experiences of human nature'. Out of these experiences, and out of the sight of Branwell at home, killing himself with drink and drugs, grew *The Tenant of Wildfell Hall*. 'She brooded over it', says Charlotte in her 'Biographical Notice', 'till she believed it to be a duty to reproduce every detail (of course with fictitious characters, incidents, and situations), as a warning to others.'

(ii)

'All true histories contain instruction.' Thus the first sentence of *Agnes Grey*, and here we have the link between the intention of the novel and the technique Anne Brontë used in writing it. There is no attempt to make the sugar hide the pill: in the first paragraph we are told that the book 'might prove useful to some, and entertaining to others'. A few chapters later, the purpose is whetted, as we are reminded that 'my design, in writing the last few pages, was not to amuse, but to benefit those whom it might concern'. Those concerned are further defined:

> if a parent has, therefrom, gathered any useful hint, or an unfortunate governess received thereby the slightest benefit, I am well rewarded for my pains.

From these statements of what would seem to be a narrowly didactic, even pedagogic intention, *Agnes Grey* would appear to belong in that tradition of instructive fiction which includes books like Miss Edgeworth's *Parent's Assistant* or Mrs. Hofland's *Ellen, The Teacher*. It does certainly owe something to that tradition, but very far from everything. To Anne Brontë, being a governess had been, in Keats's phrase, a kind of soul-making; and so the 'instruction' in *Agnes Grey* goes much further than merely telling parents how to manage their children and governesses how to handle their pupils and make the best of their lot. The 'instruction' lies in the 'true history' of *Agnes Grey* as a whole.

There is no reason to suspect that Anne shared Miss Stodart's suspicion of fiction *qua* fiction. We know that she contributed to the Gondal legends and that she found pleasure in reading novels. Yet, for the purposes of instruction, truth is more impressive than fiction—hence her insistence on *Agnes Grey* being a genuine autobiography. As a 'true' fictitious autobiography her novel is formally a straight descendant of *Robinson Crusoe* and *Moll Flanders* (absurd as the comparison with the latter might seem); but in its essential subject—the growth and development of a woman's mind—it is more deeply related to the Romantic tradition of autobiography. Autobiographical form had re-entered the novel via the *Bildungsroman*; in Bulwer Lytton's *Pelham*, for example, it provides some kind of unity and meaning in what would otherwise be merely a set of episodes. But, to my knowledge, no novel of the period is as emphatic as *Agnes Grey* in stressing the 'truth' of its fiction. So anxious is Anne Brontë for her reader to suspend his disbelief that she makes her characters refer to the actual novel form: 'Had I seen it depicted in a novel', says Agnes Grey about some particularly shameful conduct of one of her pupils, 'I should have thought it unnatural.'

It is, I think, this desire for 'true fiction' which has determined the narrative technique and style of *Agnes Grey*. Both are utterly plain and simple—with the strength as well as the weaknesses of those attributes. The narrative structure follows a simple chronological pattern: Agnes Grey, to help the family finances, takes first one position as a governess and then, having been unjustly discharged for incompetence after less than a year, another, which she keeps for a couple of years. While in her second situation, she falls in love with the curate of the parish, Edward Weston. Before she is sure of his feelings, she loses her father, and she and her mother set up a small school in a seaside town called A——. Mr. Weston, who now has his own parish not far from A——, seeks her out, woos and—obviously without any difficulty—wins her. This is told, as by Agnes some years after her marriage, in a consistent first-person narrative, with no recourse to letters or diaries, and—chiefly—in short, simple sentences.

The weakness in this method lies in Anne's occasional failure to perceive how very thin is the borderline between plainness and dullness. In her anxiety to picture life that is drab, she sometimes produces art that is dull. The story drags with repetitiveness as Agnes moves from the miseries of the Bloomfield school-room to those of the Murrays', and the dispassionateness of the style at times verges on boredom. We see, however, that the author herself is aware of the dangers of uncompromising verisimilitude:

> As I cannot, like Dogberry, find it in my heart to bestow *all* my tediousness upon the reader, I will not go on to bore him with a minute detail of all the discoveries and proceedings of this and the following day. (Chapter VII)

The strength of her technique lies above all in its being functional— that is, in the directness of effect. There is nothing to intervene between the reader and the concerns of the novel, no glamorising (this extends to the heroine herself, who is plain and unassuming in appearance), no striving for spectacular effects, no spurious excitement. There is not even a pathetic death-bed, though with the death of Agnes's father the opportunity was there, and few mid-nineteenth-century novelists would have let it pass.[1] There is nothing, in fact, to detract from the reader's growing understanding of how relentlessly drab is a governess's existence.

Practically no use is made of setting and natural scenery. Again, this must have been deliberate, for some of her poems—notably the 'Lines Composed in a Wood on a Windy Day'—show that she was responsive to nature and enjoyed describing its various aspects. But a snowy landscape to a governess is only something which she should try to prevent the children from rolling about in; and parks—however beautiful—are places in which she takes instructive walks with her reluctant pupils. When descriptions of nature do occur in *Agnes Grey*, it is for particular purposes. There is a moving account at the end of the first chapter, of Agnes looking back on her home as she leaves it for the first time:

> We crossed the valley, and began to ascend the opposite hill. As we were toiling up, I looked back again: there was the village spire, and the old grey parsonage beyond it, basking in a slanting beam of sunshine—it was but a sickly ray, but the village and surrounding hills were all in sombre shade, and I hailed the wandering beam as a

propitious omen to my home. With clasped hands, I fervently implored a blessing on its inhabitants, and hastily turned away; for I saw the sunshine was departing; and I carefully avoided another glance, lest I should see it in gloomy shadow like the rest of the landscape.

The landscape here is used only for its obvious symbolical meaning to Agnes. The much more extended descriptions of sea and beach in the final chapters serve a similar function. The reunion with Mr. Weston on the beach at sunrise, and his sunset proposal, mean an end not only to the 'drab-coloured' governess-existence but also to the darkness and despair of a lonely and hopeless-seeming pilgrimage:

I shall never forget that glorious Summer evening, and always remember with delight that steep hill, and the edge of the precipice where we stood together watching the splendid sun-set mirrored in the restless world of waters at our feet—with hearts filled with gratitude to Heaven, and happiness, and love—almost too full for speech.

External nature and internal emotion meet and fuse into one experience for Agnes Grey, much as they do for Wordsworth on the top of Snowdon in *The Prelude*.

The plainness of the style involves a great restraint in the use of metaphorical language. Feelings are generally conveyed directly, by a single adjective—'happy', or 'sad', or 'exasperated'—or not at all. Mostly she just relates the bare facts of an episode and lets the emotions remain implicit. The exceptions to this tend to be somewhat self-conscious, as when she wants to describe Agnes's sense of up-rootedness on arriving in a new family:

I awoke the next morning feeling like one whirled away by enchantment, and suddenly dropped from the clouds into a remote and unknown land . . .; or like a thistle-seed borne on the wind to some strange nook of uncongenial soil, where it must lie long enough before it can take root and germinate, extracting nourishment from what appears so alien to its nature, if, indeed, it ever can.

She finds, in fact, that she has been led into a parable of Agnes's situation rather than an analysis of feeling; and so she breaks off: 'But this gives no proper idea of my feelings at all.'

A similar kind of restraint is exercised when it comes to passing comments on the attitudes, actions or behaviour of people other than Agnes. One of the sources of strength in the novel is the author's ability to bring out, and evaluate, people's character without any button-holing or superfluous comments. Agnes communicates the news of her sister's impending marriage to her pupil, Miss Murray, like this:

'Who is she to be married to?'
'To Mr. Richardson, the Vicar of a neighbouring parish.'
'Is he rich?'
'No—only comfortable.'
'Is he handsome?'
'No—only decent.'
'Young?'
'No—only middling.'
'O Mercy! what a wretch! What sort of a house is it?'
'A quiet little vicarage, with an ivy-clad porch, an old-fashioned garden, and——'
'O stop!—you'll make me sick. How *can* she bear it?'
'I expect she'll not only be able to bear it, but to be very happy. You did not ask me if Mr. Richardson were a good, wise or amiable man; I could have answered yes to all these questions. . . .'
. . .
'And will she go about in a plain shawl, and a large straw bonnet, carrying tracts and bone soup to her husband's poor parishioners?'
'I'm not so clear about that, but I dare say she will do her best to make them comfortable in body and mind, in accordance with our mother's example.'

With great economy of means and a perfect selection of details, she achieves a genuine effect of two people talking and of two diametrically opposed standards of value up against each other. It is the craft of the realistic novelist and the Morality play writer in one.

Descriptions of outward appearance are generally kept down to a thumb-nail sketch. It is conduct that counts, observed in realistic *minutiae*. In our first meeting with Mr. Bloomfield we get both appearance and revealingly selected details of behaviour:

He had a large mouth, pale, dingy complexion, milky blue eyes, and hair the colour of a hempen cord. There was a roast leg of mutton before him: he helped Mrs Bloomfield, the children, and me [we notice the order of precedence!], desiring me to cut up the children's meat; then, after twisting about the mutton in various directions, and eyeing it from different points, he pronounced it not fit to be eaten and called for the cold beef.

The realism is spiced with a sardonic kind of humour here, just as her tongue is in her cheek in the dialogue between Agnes and Miss Murray. One imagines what Dickens would have made out of lunch with the Bloomfields. Anne Brontë's technique, unlike Dickens's, is that of understatement: after Mr. Bloomfield has, volubly, found fault with the beef, too, and with the arrangements made for that evening's dinner, she only allows herself to say that Agnes is

> very glad to get out of the room with my pupils; for I never felt so ashamed and uncomfortable in my life, for anything that was not my own fault.

The same dry realism, and absence of emotional commentary, can be seen in the description of the Bloomfield children's behaviour. Instead of the conventional miniature adults of much early Victorian fiction, we have here children that would not be out of place in a modern Child Guidance Clinic, kicking and spitting and defying authority in all possible ways.

Because of the prevailing reticence, the rare outburst and the rare metaphor get a peculiarly stinging power, as for example in Agnes's disgust at Rosalie Murray's conduct during her engagement. The young lady is having her last fling, desperately flirting with any available man, and making malicious attempts at stealing Mr. Weston. This provokes Agnes to the point of saying:

> I could only conclude that . . . dogs are not the only creatures which, when gorged to the throat, will yet gloat over what they cannot devour, and grudge the smallest morsel to a starving brother;

—an image which suggests that Anne could 'write up' a feeling if she wanted to, but that—in the cause of 'true fiction'—she was deliberately writing down.

Sentimentality, then, is completely absent from *Agnes Grey*. There are fewer tears in this novel than in any other mid-nineteenth-century novel that I have read. Exaggerated sentiment, so the author seems to have reasoned, would only set up a smoke-screen between the reader and the novel; it would falsify the human condition that the novel is about. It is to that human condition that we must now turn our attention.

Agnes Grey is a novel by a governess about a governess. To understand the way that the governess theme is handled here, it is, I think, helpful to compare it with some other novelists' handling of the same theme.[1] Apart from *Jane Eyre* (which will be discussed in Chapter IV), at least four novels in the decade or so before *Agnes Grey* had dealt at some length with the governess problem: Mrs. Sherwood's *Caroline Mordaunt* (1835);[2] Lady Blessington's *The Governess* (1839)—its heroine, somewhat confusingly in this context, named Clara Mordaunt; Harriet Martineau's *Deerbrook* (1839); and Elizabeth Missing Sewell's *Amy Herbert* (1844). With the governesses in all these novels Agnes Grey shares certain basic features. They are all young ladies in straitened circumstances, used to better things, but forced to earn their living among people who are often socially, and nearly always morally and intellectually, inferior to themselves. The course of events which forces Lady Blessington's Clara Mordaunt to become a governess is typical:

> Clara Mordaunt was the only child and orphan of a merchant, whose unsuccessful speculations had led to bankruptcy and— suicide. Brought up in affluence, large sums had been expended in her education, and being gifted with great natural abilities, her proficiency satisfied, not only her doting father, but surprised the professors who instructed her.

The father of Miss Martineau's governess, Maria Young, died and she herself became a semi-invalid in an accident; Miss Sewell's Emily Morton 'lost her father and mother both in one month'; and Mrs. Sherwood's Caroline Mordaunt was deprived of father and mother 'whilst yet in my tender infancy'. Agnes Grey differs from these young ladies in having, at least for the best part of the novel, both her parents alive. But her father is a poor clergyman who has lost his small private fortune in a shipwreck (the only melodramatic touch in the novel), and her mother is the daughter of a country squire who cut her off without a penny when she insisted on marrying Mr. Grey—thus providing Agnes with the requisite background of poverty and gentility combined. This background is not only effective for novel purposes: it also reflects an actual social condition of the period.[1] That condition was acutely, but cruelly, set out by Miss Rigby in reviewing *Jane Eyre* and *Vanity Fair* together with the *Governesses' Benevolent Institution Report for 1847*:

> We need the imprudencies, extravagancies, mistakes, or crimes of a certain number of fathers, to sow that seed from which we reap the harvest of governesses.[2]

The 'there but for the grace of God' attitude which Miss Rigby's comment suggests is perceptible behind all the four governess novels mentioned. One difference in the work of Anne Brontë, writing her novel when finally back at the parsonage after years of homesickness and humiliation, is the feeling that there, despite the grace of God, had she been.

> The real definition of a governess, in the English sense, is a being who is our equal in birth, manners, and education, but our inferior in worldly wealth,

Miss Rigby goes on to say. As an almost inevitable consequence of the social position of the governess, the theme of social humiliation pervades all these novels. Clara Mordaunt is told by one of her pupils that 'Mamma [who is herself hardly a lady] said that governesses were *never ladies*, but merely useful to teach young people how to behave as ladies'.

Emily Morton is first introduced to us in an embarrassing scene where—despite the 'delicate features and sweet expression of the peculiarly lady-like young girl'—she undergoes the indignity of being confused with the lady's maid; and the author seems to take a masochistic pleasure in letting her suffer constant slights, consciously and unconsciously given, in a house of noble young ladies, in comparison with whom the Ingram ladies in *Jane Eyre* are models of tact and consideration. Agnes Grey is very much in this tradition, when on her arrival in a new family she has to wait to see her employer:

> I did not see her till eleven o'clock on the morning after my arrival, when she honoured me with a visit, just as my mother might step

into the kitchen to see a new servant girl—yet not so, either, for my mother would have seen her immediately after her arrival, and not waited till the next day; and, moreover, she would have addressed her in a more kind and friendly manner.

The implications of the comparison with her mother's treatment of a servant need hardly be commented on. Even her pupils never forget that she is 'a hireling and a poor curate's daughter'; no visitor to the family ever condescends to speak to her; no one gives her her due as a lady. Agnes Grey tries hard, despite constant insults and innuendoes, to 'subdue every resentful impulse, suppress every sensitive shrinking, and go on perseveringly doing my best'. Yet, there is more rebellious-ness in her than in the conventional novelist's governess, as appears, for example, when she has to walk back from church with her pupils and their friends:

> It was disagreeable, too, to walk behind, and thus appear to acknow-ledge my own inferiority; for, in truth, I considered myself pretty nearly as good as the best of them, and wished them to know that I did so, and not to imagine that I looked upon myself as a mere domestic.

Here the similarities between *Agnes Grey* and at least three of the other four novels end. For, while the social position and the indignities of these governesses are very similar, the uses made of that position and those indignities for the purposes of the novel are very different. In both *Deerbrook* and *Amy Herbert*, the governesses are slightly out of the focus of the plot. They serve more as catalysts than as active agents. Maria Young, in a novel where the interest is already dispersed between two heroines and two heroes, is passive as far as plot goes, and shows no trace of character development. Referred to in adjectives like 'wise', 'sensible', 'learned', and—most eulogistic of all—'philosophical', she sets up a standard of moral and intellectual womanhood in the novel, facing the miseries of her solitary life with stoical fortitude. *Amy Herbert* is a novel with little structure and less psychological insight. Its interest is sentimental-moral, and Emily Morton, governess in the house of the title-character's aunt and uncle, is only one of two moral examples in the book (the other is Amy Herbert's saintly mother). To her the governess-ship is a blessed trial or martyrdom: it gives her the chance, which she never misses, to exercise Christian patience and humility.

> She had no mother, no friends; her daily life was one of wearying mortification and self-denial; and yet Emily Morton had never been heard to utter a single murmur. She had never been known to compare her lot with others, or to wonder why she was deprived of the comforts enjoyed by them; and her heart was a perpetual well-spring of quiet gratitude, which made the heaviest trials of her life sources of improvement to herself, and of blessing to those around her.

Significantly, neither of these paragons ends up in marriage. Maria Young, at the end of *Deerbrook*, looks forward with masochistic bravery to going to the wedding between her best friend and the man she herself loves (and who courted her before she became lame and poor and an orphan). Emily's haven is reached when she gets a better position where, instead of 'ridicule or contempt', she is treated with 'the truest esteem and regard'.[1] Both these novels, then, insert studies of the ideal governess—not so much *qua* governess as *qua* Christian stoic—into novel structures where they are not essential. Both, while gaining in general and social interest, lose considerably in concentration.

With both Lady Blessington's *Governess* and Mrs. Sherwood's *Caroline Mordaunt* the case is different. In both, as in *Agnes Grey*, the novel centres on its heroine-governess, and its structural pattern, too, simply consists in following the central character from one position to another. But here the three part company. The real interest in Lady Blessington's novel does not lie in the governess *per se*;[2] it lies in the various social milieus that Clara passes through by virtue of being a governess. Clara is a convenient vehicle in a picaresque tour of various strata of English society: the parvenu Williamson family, the cranky poetess Mrs. Vincent Robinson, the high society of the Lord and Lady Axminster establishment, and the gourmand Manwarrings. Much of the treatment of the different social circles is satirical, and most heavily under fire is the vulgarity—'the solecisms in good breeding and still more in grammar'—of the Williamsons. Clara's own high breeding seems to have fitted her not so much for teaching their children as for ridiculing the bourgeois manner of these parvenus, their conversations (they continually misuse and misunderstand French), their taste in clothes (Mrs. Williamson looks like a radish, in pink and green), and so on. The literary circles of would-be poets and poetesses get their share of the satire, too.

Clara does suffer the customary humiliations, but her solution is not to fight it out: it is to be restored, by money and marriage (in that order), to her proper niche in society. Rich heiress becomes poor governess, but the poor governess eventually (thanks to the timely death of a rich uncle) becomes rich heiress again and marries lord. This pattern of success story is common enough in the 'fashionable' novels of Lady Blessington; and the fact that Clara spends her time of ill-fortune as a governess has nothing to do with her ultimate good fortune.

Caroline Mordaunt is, in most ways, an antithesis to Lady Blessington's novel.[1] Caroline's course, through one governess's position after another, is not a picaresque satire but a domesticated Pilgrim's Progress; her various humiliations do not lead to the arms of a lord but to those of The Lord. True, she marries at the end, but the bridegroom is a clergyman (who wants, not romance but 'a housekeeper') of humble means. Mrs. Sherwood's intention is to show how Caroline, who starts as an irreligious and self-opinionated young woman, is brought by degrees to mortification and the Church. Her story, if we are to label it, is as much a Low Church religious novel as a governess tale. It ends by stating its two morals explicitly and emphatically. The first is that the heroine becomes a good Christian by realising 'how my various misadventures had been calculated to humble me, and bring me to a knowledge of myself'; the second is an admonition to mothers to educate their daughters for the task of being 'a respectable wife in a humbler station' rather than governesses of intellectual and social pretensions. Needless to say, this novel has rather less artistic merit than that which treats of the more worldly Miss Mordaunt.

In *Agnes Grey*, as in *The Governess*, there is social contrast between the employing families. The Bloomfields live in 'a manufacturing district, where the people had nothing to do but make money'; they are definitely underbred; and Agnes's mother refers to them as 'those purse-proud tradespeople and arrogant upstarts'. The Murrays belong to the squirearchy and live in a country-house; they even move in the circles (and have the vices) of the society of the 'fashionable' novels.

But social observation of this kind occupies a very subordinate place in the novel.

This, however, does not mean that Anne Brontë is not interested in social issues: on the contrary, *Agnes Grey* is a work much concerned with the nature of human relationships, both in the larger unit of society as a whole and in the smaller unit of the family—husband and wife, parents and children. Underlying the chronological pattern of the autobiography, there is a pattern of what we may call 'social' themes. These themes are developed by simple contrasts, as clear-cut as those in a Morality play. The vicar, Mr. Hatfield, and the curate, Mr. Weston, are as antithetical as the Bad Angel and the Good; and throughout the best part of the novel, episodes are arranged so as to provide testing ground for them. We first meet them in church, where the vicar's exhibitionism is ruthlessly observed:

> He [Mr. Hatfield] would come sailing up the aisle, or rather sweeping along like a whirlwind, with his rich silk gown flying behind him . . ., mount the pulpit like a conqueror ascending his triumphal car; then sinking on the velvet cushion in an attitude of studied grace, remain in silent prostration for a certain time; then, mutter over a Collect, and gabble through the Lord's Prayer, rise, draw off one bright lavender glove to give the congregation the benefit of his sparkling rings, lightly pass his fingers through his well-curled hair, flourish a cambric handkerchief, recite a very short passage, or, perhaps a mere phrase of scripture . . .

Contempt, as usual, brings out Anne Brontë's power of metaphor. Mr. Hatfield's sermons are only concerned with outward observance, 'church discipline, rites and ceremonies, apostolical succession, the duty of reverence and obedience to the clergy'; or else he will take sadistic pleasure in delivering a hell-fire oration, not being ashamed to be seen after the service 'laughing [with the gentry] at his own sermon, and hoping that he had given the rascally people something to think about'. The curate, on the other hand, is characterised by the 'evangelical truth of his doctrine, as well as the earnest simplicity of his manner, and the clearness and force of his style'. What may look at first like a rather specialised ecclesiastical conflict between a Ritualist and an Evangelical churchman, soon proves to be a much more fundamental moral issue. Several chapters take us to the cottages of the poor, whom the vicar despises—one of his favourite topics being 'the necessity of deferential obedience from the poor to the rich'; while the curate sends them coal out of his small stipend, consoles their troubled minds, and goes to any trouble to carry out his pastoral duties. The relationship with the family from the Hall, and with their governess, is another touchstone: the vicar bows and scrapes to the Murrays and ignores Agnes; the curate sees the true worth of people and treats them accordingly. Thus Agnes and Mr. Weston are very clearly lined up against the Murray–Hatfield group; here again the cottagers perform an important thematic function, as the Murrays' condescending, thoughtless and even insulting treatment of them, like the vicar's, is contrasted with Agnes's, and the curate's, true charity. What is at stake in these antithetical attitudes is symbolically expressed in an episode which takes place while Agnes is at the Bloomfields'. A great deal is made of the children's cruelty to animals and the way this is condoned, or encouraged, by their elders. One day Agnes finds the boy with a nest of fledgling birds, gloating at the prospect of slowly tormenting each of them to death. Agnes, in an outburst of revulsion, drops a stone on the intended victims, and is afterwards severely rebuked by Mrs. Bloomfield for interfering with Master Bloomfield's amusements:

> 'You seemed to have forgotten', said she calmly, 'that the creatures were all created for our convenience.'

This, of course, is also the attitude of the family (and of the Murrays and their likes) to their inferiors, be they governesses or cottagers. Mrs. Gaskell tells us how she and Charlotte once discussed this particular passage in *Agnes Grey*, and how it provoked Charlotte to say that

> none but those who had been in the position of a governess could ever realize the dark side of 'respectable' human nature; under no great temptation to crime, but daily giving way to selfishness and ill-temper, till its conduct towards those dependent on it sometimes amounts to a tyranny of which one would rather be the victim than the inflicter.[1]

Agnes Grey is not a social problem novel in the sense that *Mary Barton*, or even *Shirley*, is; but in the comments implied, rather than stated, in its thematic structure, it cries out against *using* your fellow beings.

Relationships within the family unit, and above all on the question of marriage, are also starkly contrasted, in black and white. Here, again, the two clergymen set up an antithesis: the rector's undignified courtship of Miss Murray is developed at length, until it culminates in an ungraciously rejected proposal, in deliberate and pointed contrast to the restrained and slowly-growing affection between Agnes and Mr. Weston. Via the Murray family Agnes gets in touch with the world of high society, where mothers match-make and daughters marry pounds and titles. 'I *must* have Ashby Park, whoever shares it with me', Rosalie Murray proclaims. Anne Brontë is here obviously drawing on the kind of material that the novelists of manners used so profusely; but in comparison with the detachedly amused view of the marriage game in such a novel as Mrs. Gore's *Mothers and Daughters*, Anne's use of the theme is a firmly moralistic one. Thus Rosalie, on a woman's attitude to marriage:

> 'To think that I could be such a fool as to fall in love! It is quite beneath the dignity of a woman to do such a thing.'

But, it is implied, it is not beneath the dignity of a woman to sell herself on the slave-market. This speech is particularly effective, as it is directed to Agnes who has just begun to experience love. The contrasts in attitudes, understandings and moral imagination are all the greater for being implied rather than spoken. But Rosalie is not allowed to get away with it. Just before her reunion with Mr. Weston, Agnes is made to visit her former pupil, now in possession of her coveted Ashby Park, so that we may learn what Rosalie's marriage, after one year, has come to,

> 'I detest that man', whispered Lady Ashby with bitter emphasis, as he [a horseman] slowly trotted by.
> 'Who is it?' I asked, unwilling to suppose that she should so speak of her husband.
> 'Sir Thomas Ashby', she replied with dreary composure.

Rosalie's account of her husband's mode of life is a clear *exemplum horrendum*; it points forward to the more extended use of this kind of material in *The Tenant of Wildfell Hall*.

It is worth noticing how Agnes's own family background is used in this context. Her mother's rejection of the life of an heiress for true love and a worth-while life is another contrast to the Murray way of thinking, and the issue is not just one of the past; it is brought up again when the mother spurns her father's offer of reconciliation at the cost of repentance.

Thus—to return to *The Governess* after this detour—while Lady Blessington is engaged in detached and satirical observation of society through the eyes of her governess, Anne Brontë is deeply 'committed' in the matter of social morality—that is, her novel deals with social situations in so far as they involve moral issues. What a modern reader may find most difficult to take in *Agnes Grey* are the suggestions of self-righteousness which pervade Agnes's attitude to her pupils and their parents, and which are crystallised in occasional comments— as, for example, when the Murray girls are maliciously intervening between Agnes and Mr. Weston and she consoles herself by thinking: 'though he knew it not, I was more worthy of his love than Rosalie Murray'. If we find this quality in the novel intolerable, then we are debarred from enjoying all those works of fiction (of which *Mansfield Park* is as clear an example as *Agnes Grey*) in which the author assumes that he or she shares with the reader an attitude, and the only possible attitude, to moral absolutes. In a novel so sure of what is right and what is wrong, so wholly occupied with mapping its world into black and white areas, as is *Agnes Grey*, being holier than thou becomes a matter of calm *a priori* classification rather than of personal pride. Yet *Agnes Grey* does not, like Mrs. Sherwood's *Caroline Mordaunt*, use the governess theme as a simple moral tract.

The most important distinction between *Agnes Grey* and any earlier governess novel is Anne Brontë's concentration on the task of governess-ship as such and, further, on what happens to the individual mind in situations such as those which Agnes Grey goes through. It is what happens inside Agnes, not around her, that matters. Throughout the first section of the novel—with the Bloomfields—there is transmitted a very clear image of a young girl, full of idealistic educational theories, exhilarated at the thought of making her own way in the world, coming up against the hard reality of spoilt children and unsympathetic employers. Her theories prove of no avail, her own childhood experiences do not apply to this brood, the work wears her out. But still she perseveres: 'They may crush, but they shall not subdue me!' Her pupils in her second position are older, but her efforts at making any kind of impression on them are as unavailing. It is here that we get to the deep hurt at the heart of the book, the insight into a human situation which none of the other governess novels even approaches. The real degradation, to Agnes Grey, is not that of social humiliation, slight and neglect; it is one of absolute human isolation and of emotional and spiritual starvation:

> Never, from month to month, from year to year, except during my brief intervals of rest at home, did I see one creature to whom I could open my heart, or freely speak my thoughts with any hope of sympathy, or even comprehension. . . . Never a new idea or a stirring thought came to me from without; and such as rose within me were, for the most part, miserably crushed at once, or doomed to sicken and fade away, because they could not see the light.

There is a rhetorical force in the language here which suggests that we are approaching the central experience in the novel. Agnes fears that this kind of life is actually contaminating her:

> Already, I seemed to feel my intellect deteriorating, my heart petrifying, my soul contracting, and I trembled lest my very moral perceptions should become deadened, my distinctions of right and wrong confounded, and all my better faculties be sunk at last, beneath the baneful influence of such a mode of life.

Thus it is that the focus widens, from the governess, to any mind deprived of sympathy, isolated from its likes, and exposed to nothing but coarsening influence. The imagery used, and the notion behind it, cannot but recall Wordsworth's *Immortality Ode*: 'The gross vapours of earth were gathering round me, and closing in upon my inward heaven.' The initial enthusiastic Innocence of Agnes Grey is becoming the Experience of moral darkness. On the background of this, her feelings for Mr. Weston are seen as something other than a poor governess's infatuation with an eligible curate:

> Mr. Weston rose, at length, upon me, appearing, like the morning star in my horizon, to save me from the fear of utter darkness.

The pathos of Agnes's need for any ideal outside the moral murkiness and sterility of her position is such as to justify the exalted imagery, with its definite religious undertones. In Anne's portrayal of Agnes's love, there is none of the passion that we find in the novels of her sisters, but there is another kind of intensity: the sense of love as an epiphany, as Grace. The same sense inspired her poem, 'The Power of Love', written after *Agnes Grey* was completed:

> 'Tis not my own strength has saved me;
>   Health, and hope, and fortitude,
> But for love, had long since failed me;
>   Heart and soul had sunk subdued.

In her poems of spiritual struggle, divine intervention is expressed by the same kind of imagery as is first used for Agnes's love for Weston, and as reappears when her love is reciprocated in the last two chapters. The pattern of wavering between 'despair' (or, as in the passage just quoted, 'utter darkness') and hope is, perhaps, most evident in the poem called 'Fluctuations', where the 'cold and gloomy night', the 'gloomy darkness', are contrasted with the brightness of the sun and the 'silvery gleam' of the moon. In itself the imagery is commonplace enough; but in its context it suggests that the pattern of the spiritual and the emotional experience (for they are one and the same thing) in *Agnes Grey* is the same as that in Anne Brontë's most central poems. The denouement of *Agnes Grey*, then, is not just a conventional happy ending, but a victory for Hope against Despair.

To those who know something about the life of Anne Brontë, the ending of *Agnes Grey* may seem like a piece of wish-fulfilment, like the opposite of the poem where she dreams that her 'life of solitude is past', but wakes up to a reality of deprivation:

> But then to wake and find it flown,
>   The dream of happiness destroyed;
> To find myself unloved, alone,
>   What tongue can speak the dreary void!
>
> A heart whence warm affections flow,
>   Creator, Thou hast given to me;
> And am I only thus to know
>   How sweet the joys of love would be?
>   ('Dreams')

69

Maybe it is, and maybe the prototype of Mr. Weston was Willie Weightman, Mr. Brontë's curate, who died in 1842 and whom Anne loved, according to most of her biographers.[1] The cliffs on which Agnes's hope is fulfilled are obviously those of Scarborough which Anne Brontë loved, and where—in one of the most pathetic chapters of the Brontë saga—she was taken to die, within three years of completing *Agnes Grey*. The sunrise epiphany seems to represent a conjunction of images which had long been in her mind: in the Parsonage Museum there is a drawing by Anne of a girl on a cliff facing the rising sun. It is called 'Sunrise over the Sea' and belongs to the Weightman period; its date (November 13, 1839) suggests that she might have had in mind the approaching end to her governess-ship with the Ingrams of Blake Hall. But it is wrong to let the pathos of any autobiographical aspect blind us to the wider meaning of the ending in the 'true' autobiography of *Agnes Grey*. 'All true histories contain instruction.' To have left Agnes with nothing but a 'rayless arch of sombre grey' ('Self-Communion') would have been closer to the actuality of Anne's own life; but it would have been what Professor Pascal in his book on *Design and Truth in Autobiography* calls a 'wrong' truth.[2] By postulating a reciprocated love, fulfilled in marriage, Anne must have felt that she was creating a 'right truth': she made her novel more morally impressive, more generally instructive. This, obviously, does not mean to say that she is 'instructing' by holding out, like a carrot to a donkey, a happy marriage to every persevering governess. It means that *Agnes Grey* is an attempt to hand on to the novel-reading public her own belief, expressed in so many of her poems, that Hope and Joy will eventually come to those who live 'upright and firm, through good and ill' ('*Vanitas Vanitatum*').

(iii)

The most outstanding characteristic of *Agnes Grey* is its simplicity of form and design—the quality which made George Moore call it 'the most perfect prose narrative in English letters'.[3] *The Tenant of Wildfell Hall* is an altogether more ambitious, and therefore more uneven, work. But behind it is the same moral passion. As Anne Brontë puts it in her Preface to the second edition of the novel: 'I wished to tell the truth, for truth always conveys its own moral to those who are able to receive it.'

The structure of *The Tenant of Wildfell Hall* is much more involved than that of *Agnes Grey*. Instead of a straightforward and continuous narrative, we have here three interlocking sections, or, rather, a framework into which is inserted a lengthy flashback. The first section consists of letters from Gilbert Markham to his brother-in-law, relating events which happened between the autumn of 1827 and the summer of 1828. The setting is a village (presumably in Yorkshire) where Markham is a gentleman farmer, and where much consternation arises, when a beautiful and mysterious young (presumed) widow and her small son arrive to occupy the practically derelict Hall. Markham, who has fallen in love with the supposed Mrs. Graham, refuses to listen to the gossip which accumulates around her name. She, on her side, appears to be trying to resist a growing attraction towards Markham; but when he, too, begins to believe in the gossip, she hands him her diary to read. This diary, written by her in instalments between the summer of 1821 and the late summer of 1827, forms the second, and longest, section of the novel. The world of Helen Huntingdon is that of the 'fashionable' novels: the season in London, shooting-parties in the autumn, life at a big country-house. During her first London season Helen becomes infatuated with a young rake, Arthur Huntingdon, and marries him. Her husband turns out to be a heartless and incurable drunkard, gambler and adulterer; and when finally he establishes one of his mistresses in the house as a supposed governess(!) to their son, Helen flees with her child from the profligacies of her husband and becomes the tenant of Wildfell Hall. In the third section, Markham resumes his letters and relates how he and Helen, after the death of Arthur Huntingdon, are eventually united and married.

This technique, in its interplay of past and present, reminds one to some extent of *Wuthering Heights*; but its application is much less imaginative and successful. The machinery creaks sadly at times: there is no intrinsic reason why the framework should be in the form of letters (to a person who has no function in the novel). In fact, as one begins to read, one is not aware of the epistolary form till one reaches the end of the first chapter, where the first letter ends; the rest of the book forms one mammoth epistle, including presumably a copy of the diary. In the third section there are letters within letters, as Helen writes from her husband's death-bed, holding him with one hand and the pen with the other. It is clear that Anne Brontë made herself unnecessarily uncomfortable by using a needlessly elaborate device. On the other hand, she does achieve an interesting effect in playing off the detachment of the framework sections—the letters are written twenty years after the events related—against the immediacy of direct experience in the diary chapters.

Far more than *Agnes Grey*, this novel contains pieces of conventional novel material. There is a suggestion of Gothic romance in the description of Wildfell Hall and the 'ghostly legends and dark traditions our old nurse had told us respecting the haunted hall and its departed occupants', and in the air of mystery surrounding the new tenant in the first section of the book; but this element disappears altogether, as the mystery turns out to be of a domestic and moral nature. There are touches of melodrama, as when Helen repulses an insistent lover with a palette knife; and there are attempts at creating dramatic suspense, as when Gilbert Markham rushes through the country to prevent Helen Huntingdon from re-marrying and arrives at the church just in time to see the blushing bride come out (who, of course, is not Helen but a friend of hers).

More spectacular, but far less conventional in a work by a woman novelist, are some scenes of physical violence and brutality, even verging on sadism, which suggest *Wuthering Heights* more than *Agnes Grey*. Gilbert Markham makes a senseless assault on the man he believes to be the lover of Helen Huntingdon:

> Impelled by some fiend at my elbow, I had seized my whip by the small end, and—swift and sudden as a flash of lightning—brought the other down upon his head. It was not without a feeling of savage satisfaction that I beheld the instant, deadly pallor that overspread his face, and the few red drops that trickled down his forehead, while he reeled a moment in his saddle, and then fell backward to the ground.

The same obsession with gruesome detail is there in the drunken brawl at Helen's house. One guest (Hattersley) pins another to the wall, and Helen, for all her disgust, comes to the rescue:

> I snatched up a candle and brought it to him. He took it and held the flame to Hattersley's hands till, roaring like a wild beast, the latter unclasped them and let him go.

These are the scenes which made the reviewers accuse Anne of a morbid love of the coarse and brutal. Her defence was that they 'have not been more painful for the most fastidious of my critics to read than they were for me to describe'. Her theme, in other words, demanded that depths of human depravity should be depicted; the 'truth' she wanted to tell was not a squeamish one. It is the principle of the *exemplum horrendum* that has determined much of the narrative and descriptive technique in this novel, especially in the diary section.

Superficially, the material of that section is that of the 'fashionable' novel. But what immediately distinguishes *The Tenant of Wildfell Hall* is the intense moral concern in the treatment of any character or episode. The drinking and gambling scenes are played out against a background of remorse and terror, a pervading sense of sin and a fear of 'bottomless pits'. No medieval preacher's use of the *memento mori* could be more effective than the scenes where Lord Lowborough, ever repenting and ever slipping-back, sits in on the orgies of his so-called friends 'like a skeleton at a feast'. With grim irony, the author makes one of the revellers sing in jest what Lowborough (and the reader) is to take seriously:

> Stop, poor sinner, stop and think
> Before you farther go,
> No longer sport upon the brink
> Of everlasting woe.

And when the false gaiety reaches a climax, Lowborough's *dies irae* breaks in on the drunken laughter:

'What *you* see in life I don't know—*I* see only the blackness of darkness and a fearful looking for [forth?] of judgment and fiery indignation!'

The counterpointing here has the fervour of the religious tract, with the artistry of the Morality play. In similar fashion, Anne Brontë is constantly superimposing the ghastly awareness of the wages of sin on the portrayal of those same sins. Needless to say, this is a very different technique from that of the 'fashionable' novelist. Most of Mrs. Gore's rakes do eventually receive some kind of wages, but before then, they (and the reader) have rather enjoyed the committing of their sins.

Thus, Huntingdon and his companions are not primarily a set of

73

rakes but a group of sinners; and their various fates are neatly balanced against each other to form a pattern of repentance or retribution. There is Lord Lowborough, wasted in body and soul, who eventually reforms, through his own will-power. In a bitterly ironic scene we see his joy at having been accepted in marriage by Miss Wilmot, the female villain of the novel. 'I am not a castaway', he says, echoing an image from Cowper and from one of Anne's own poems, 'she will save me, body and soul, from destruction.' Miss Wilmot, in fact, nearly leads him, body and soul, to destruction, as he discovers her adulterous relationship with Huntingdon. Then there is Hattersley, the gayest and most thoughtless of the group, who marries and makes miserable an innocent young girl, but who also eventually reforms, thanks to Helen's warnings, and, above all, to the awful example of Huntingdon's death-bed (thus making the *exemplum* of Huntingdon's career effective within the novel itself). There are others, to whom appropriate rewards or punishment are meted out, according to their deserts. But above all there is Huntingdon, the unrepentant sinner, who pursues his sure course to damnation, through a multitude of vices. There is no Byronic charm about his wickedness: either he is realistically disgusting ('sick and stupid'), or there is a hell-fire atmosphere around him—even, somewhat unrealistically, in the mouth of his four-year old son: 'I am sorry papa's wicked . . . for I don't want him to go to hell.'

Unlike the villagers in the frame section, the people in the diary section do not really form a social group—as, say, Mrs. Gore's people do—where characters meet, make small-talk, dine together, etc. Although the diary entries are carefully dated, there is no feeling of period or place. Not only does Anne Brontë use relatively few characters (while the pages of the 'fashionable' novel are usually crowded with people); but those which she does use are made to interrelate with each other in a uniform and well-defined manner. They make up a sort of moral (or immoral) hierarchy. Over against the set of profligates, who do or do not benefit from the warning example of Huntingdon, there are the young women who, more or less, benefit from Helen's experience. Millicent Hargrave is her best friend; she marries Hattersley, out of the Huntingdon set; she is also the sister of the man who tries to make Helen break her marriage-vows. Esther Hargrave is the young innocent, whose innocence is preserved thanks to Helen. The counterforce here is Mrs. Hargrave who, in the play of moral forces, represents the world. Her one desire in relation to her children is to see them 'all well married, that is, united to rich partners'. Even more than in *Agnes Grey* the traditional match-making mother has been stripped of any redeeming feature: Helen's references to Mrs. Hargrave's conduct in wanting to push her daughter into a loveless marriage ('slavery' Helen calls it) are in such phrases as 'positive wickedness'.

To Anne Brontë's women, marriage is neither a matter of a good match, nor of romance; it is the outstanding test of your moral stamina. How you choose your husband, and how you live with him, are parts of the larger questions of 'What is the real nature of marriage?' and 'What is the power of marriage, for good and for evil?' Thus the conventional marriage-game has become one of the most important moral issues in this novel. This theme also helps to link frame and middle section: all the matrimonial scheming in the village is only the game taken on another social level.

Related to this issue is the question of the double standard of sexual morality. Helen may not tax her husband with unfaithfulness; but he may take her faithfulness for granted. So, at least, Huntingdon argues; but the author implies that the argument is perverse. A climax is reached when Helen, having successfully resisted Hargrave's advances, is accused and abused by her husband, who is living in flagrant adultery and who, at a recent drinking party, has offered his wife to whoever would have her. There is bold defiance of any merely relative moral standard in Helen's reply:

'If your accusations were true, Mr. Huntingdon, how *dare you* blame me?'

The relationship between Helen and Huntingdon gets its peculiar flavour, and much of its interpretation, by being developed against a tightly-woven tissue of religious references. Helen's infatuation with Huntingdon is first brought out in a theological debate between her and her aunt. The aunt, who knows the character of Huntingdon, is warning Helen: 'The wicked shall be turned into hell, and they that *forget* God!' Thus, surely even if her life with Huntingdon here on earth should turn out, against expectation, happy, Helen would not want to face an eternal separation after death? 'You, perhaps, taken into eternal bliss, and he cast into the lake that burneth with unquenchable fire.' The persistence of the girl's love is measured by the fact that she takes it upon her to re-interpret Scripture: she has searched through the Bible and found 'nearly thirty' passages to prove that nobody will suffer eternal punishment. This particular form of controversy is used repeatedly, at key-points, throughout the book. Helen and Huntingdon, newly married, have their first quarrel because Huntingdon resents the idea that she loves God more than him. They quote the Bible at each other, each choosing whatever passage suits his or her argument. Against Huntingdon's version of Solomon, 'There is nothing better for a man than to eat and to drink, and to be merry', Helen sets hers: '. . . but know thou that, for all these things, God will bring thee into judgment'. After this *débat*, Helen has the first glimpse of horrible realisation of whom she has married.

The most prolonged echo of the initial theological discussion is the description of Huntingdon's sick- and death-bed. Helen returns to nurse the man who, if in name only, is her husband; he thinks that this is 'an act of Christian charity, whereby you hope to gain a higher seat in Heaven for yourself, and scoop a deeper pit in hell for me'. This final and eternal contrast between them obsesses him more and more as death creeps nearer: he sees himself 'howling in hell-fire' while Helen stands by as an 'immaculate angel'. Utterly realistic imagery conveys the horror of the man:

> 'Catch you lifting a finger to serve me *then*!—No, you'll look complacently on, and not so much as dip the tip of your finger in water to cool my tongue!'

Against this, Helen has absolutely no doubt of her own salvation; her answer runs thus:

> 'If so, it will be because of the great gulf over which I cannot pass; and if I *could* look complacently on in such a case, it would be only from the assurance that you were being purified from your sins, and fitted to enjoy the happiness I felt.'

Many a reader faces, I think, the same kind of difficulty in this episode as in the interview between Isabella and Claudio in *Measure for Measure*, III.i. Huntingdon's realistically human terror is encountered by what seem like coldly dogmatic statements from Helen. Our moral approval is on one side; our instinctive sympathies go out to the other.

There is a tension here, though of a different kind from that in Shakespeare's play. Nor is it just a question of a sentimental kind of pity around Huntingdon's death-bed, which, as a modern critic puts it, 'must have, in some unregenerate breasts, kindled a flicker of sympathy for the sinner'.[1] The humanity of Huntingdon is used to heighten the agonies of the death-bed, and we are spared none of those agonies, neither the shudder at the thought of physical corruption, nor the terror of impending judgment. Everything is done to build up the horror of a situation without consolation: 'I *can't* repent; I only fear', says Huntingdon. But in this contrast between Huntingdon's fear of damnation and Helen's assurance of salvation, Anne Brontë returns to a problem which concerned her much in her poems. The closest parallel to the situation in *The Tenant of Wildfell Hall* is her anti-Calvinist poem 'A Word to the "Elect"'. It begins with an apostrophe to the elect:

> You may rejoice to think *yourselves* secure;
> You may be grateful for the gift divine—
> That grace unsought, which made your black hearts pure,
> And fits your earth-born souls in Heaven to shine.

But it goes on to question a grace and joy achieved while others suffer:

> But, is it sweet to look around, and view
> Thousands excluded from that happiness . . .?

and to suggest the impossibility, to her, of the two alternatives of damnation and election:

> And, when you, looking on your fellow-men,
> Behold them doomed to endless misery,
> How can you talk of joy and rapture then?—
> May God withhold such cruel joy from me!

The poem is resolved in a kind of coda, which states her own belief in eventual salvation for all:

> And, oh! there lives within my heart
> A hope, long nursed by me;
> (And should its cheering ray depart,
> How dark my soul would be!)

That as in Adam all have died,
    In Christ shall all men live;
And ever round His throne abide,
    Eternal praise to give.

That even the wicked shall at last
    Be fitted for the skies;
And when their dreadful doom is past,
    To life and light arise.

I ask not how remote the day,
    Nor what the sinners' woe,
Before their dross is purged away;
    Enough for me, to know

That when the cup of wrath is drained,
    The metal purified,
They'll cling to what they once disdained,
    And live by Him that died.

I have quoted from this poem at some length in order to show how close this situation in the novel is, in thought and feeling if not in fact, to the stuff of Anne's own experience; and how, therefore, what could easily have been nothing but didactic melodrama is given a further spiritual dimension.

The tone of 'A Word to the "Elect" ' is heard again, as Helen speaks of Huntingdon's death. We are almost prepared to see him, Faustus-like, being torn apart by devils, but

how could I endure to think that the poor trembling soul was hurried away to everlasting torment? it would drive me mad! But thank God I have hope—not only from a vague dependence on the possibility that penitence and pardon might have reached him at the last, but from the blessed confidence that, through whatever purging fires the erring spirit may be doomed to pass—whatever fate awaits it, still, it is not lost, and God, who hateth nothing that he hath made, *will* bless it in the end!

Thus the wheel has come full circle; the argument against eternal damnation which Helen used on her aunt, when she herself was full of love and trust in her own ability to rectify whatever might be wrong with Huntingdon, is now, after all that love and trust have been blasted, used as an epitaph over a life worse than useless.

The story of the love and hatred between Helen and Huntingdon, then, is inextricably knit together with a theological argument. This technique of presenting the meaning of events is used at various other points in the novel. Biblical quotations appear repeatedly, not to adorn situations but to interpret them; they are built into the situations and part of them. Helen by implication sees herself as a Job figure, complaining that

> He hath hedged me about, that I cannot get out; he hath made my chain heavy. He hath filled me with bitterness, he hath made me drunken with wormwood.

She cannot, though she wishes to, add Job's words of consolation and reassurance:

> But though he cause grief, yet he will have compassion according to the multitude of his mercies.

Helen, too, dispatches the man who has tried to seduce her, in Christ's words to Magdalen: 'Go, and sin no more.'

Not all the moral comment, however, is conducted on that level. There is also a great deal of that low-toned technique of understatement which we met with in *Agnes Grey*: the use of implication and irony. One example of this will also show how this technique goes hand in hand with the one discussed above. Helen has repulsed her would-be seducer; they both join the assembled company in the drawing-room, and Hargrave

> went to his mother, who was telling Lord Lowborough how many reasons she had to be proud of her son.

One of the characteristics of the Silver-Fork school is the slickness of dialogue in its novels. The conversation of Mrs. Gore's ladies cuts and dazzles like the repartee in Restoration comedy, and her rakes are experts at conveying a sense of infinite boredom. That Anne's acquaintance with this set is essentially bookish is shown by the awkwardness of some of her dialogue. Thus Huntingdon, talking about a friend:

> He said he had plenty of the needful—or should have, when his old governor chose to quit the stage.

D   79

One need only compare the 'high-life' proposals of marriage (for example Mr. Boreham's and Sir William Wyndham's, respectively) in *The Tenant of Wildfell Hall* and in Mrs. Gore's *Mothers and Daughters*, to see that Anne Brontë was neither acquainted with, nor really interested in trying to imitate, the tone of this kind of society. Yet, in situations of genuine emotional stress, she manages better. In Hattersley's words at Huntingdon's death-bed, she conveys very well the embarrassment of a reformed rake trying to strike the right note with an unreformed one who is dying, and who is terrified of death:

> 'I say, Huntingdon, I *would* send for a parson, of some sort—If you didn't like the vicar, you know, you could have his curate, or somebody else.'

But the real strength of the dialogue, here as in *Agnes Grey*, lies in the encounters between two minds who do not speak the same language, as in Helen's bitter altercations with her husband's mistress, or in the mutually inflicted torments of husband and wife:

> 'Don't you know that you are part of myself? And do you think you can injure and degrade yourself, and I not feel it?'
> '*Degrade* myself, Helen?'
> 'Yes, degrade! What have you been doing all this time?'
> 'You'd better not ask,' said he, with a faint smile.
> . . .
> 'Arthur, you *must* repent!' cried I, in a frenzy of desperation, throwing my arms around him and burying my face in his bosom.
> 'You *shall* say you are sorry for what you have done!'
> 'Well, well, I am.'
> 'You are not! you'll do it again.'
> 'I shall never live to do it again, if you treat me so savagely,' replied he, pushing me from him.

Thus, without any interposed comments, we follow the arguments of two alienated human beings, alienating each other still more.

There are many more set-pieces of description in *The Tenant of Wildfell Hall* than in *Agnes Grey*, and we are aware of nature as a backcloth to the action to a larger extent: whether it is the summer beauties of Grassdale Park, where Helen languishes alone, while her husband is leading a dissolute life in town; or the heavy December snows, through which Gilbert Markham rushes to prevent what he thinks is to be the marriage of Helen Huntingdon. There is also another use of nature, when—as in *Agnes Grey*—it becomes an integral part of an emotion and a spiritual state. The outstanding example of this is one of the central passages in the novel. Helen, out in the garden, has been given decisive proof of her husband's unfaithfulness, and what remained of her world has fallen to pieces around her. Internal agony is reflected in external setting:

> 'God help me now!' I murmured, sinking on my knees among the damp weeds and brushwood that surrounded me, and looking up at the moonlit sky, through the scant foliage above. It seemed all dim and quivering now to my darkened sight. My burning, bursting heart strove to pour forth its agony to God, but could not frame its anguish into prayer; until a gust of wind swept over me, which, while it scattered the dead leaves, like blighted hopes, around, cooled my forehead, and seemed a little to revive my sinking frame.

At this point, as in *Agnes Grey*, the break-through of hope and the sense of Grace are pointed by celestial imagery.

> Then, while I lifted up my soul in speechless, earnest application, some heavenly influence seemed to strengthen me within: I breathed more freely; my vision cleared; I saw distinctly the pure moon shining on, and the light clouds skimming the clear, dark sky; and then, I saw the eternal stars twinkling down upon me; I knew their God was mine, and he was strong to save and swift to hear. 'I will never leave thee, nor forsake thee', seemed whispered from above their myriad orbs.

What more than anything enlarges the moral theme in this novel is the psychological insight and moral imagination displayed in the character of Helen Huntingdon. Like Agnes Grey's, hers is a case of passing from innocence to experience; but the experience is so much more bitter, and the loss of innocence is, to a large extent, self-inflicted. This is what gives Helen a dimension that Agnes never achieves. Helen, brought on to the marriage-market in her first London season, turns down the proposals of, respectively, one elderly profligate and one old bore. (In the treatment of 'Bore'em' we have the nearest approach to satire in the book.) She then becomes infatuated with young, gay and handsome Mr. Huntingdon; she lets herself be taken in, almost wilfully, by him; she marries him, even though she has plenty of intimation of the abyss of moral corruption in him. The story of her marriage is one of progressive disillusionment: it begins with the pathos of a woman giving her love to a man who she *knows* is not worthy of receiving it; it turns eventually into disgust and hatred of an almost Strindbergian intensity. The tragedy of life, as seen by Helen Huntingdon, is that 'the generous ideas of youth are too often over-clouded by the sordid views of after-life'. As with Agnes Grey, the worst of Helen's disillusionment is what it is doing to herself: she feels that, instead of raising her husband to her level, she is being drawn down to his, contaminated and debased by the union with him. Her own moral nature is suffering: the real loss of innocence consists in losing 'that instinctive horror and repulsion which were given me by nature'. There are pathetic glances back at her own innocent and hope-ful self—'fool that I was, to dream that I had strength and purity enough to save myself and him!'—and horrified analyses of what is actually happening: 'Instead of being humbled and purified by my afflictions, I feel that they are turning my nature into gall.' Repeatedly she confides to her diary that her inner self is being dried up, withered, petrified; and we hear that 'a hardness such as this, is taught by rough experience and despair alone'. This theme, of what experience does to a human being, occurs several times in Anne's poems, and nowhere more clearly than in 'Self-Communion', a poem which she was work-ing on from November 1847 to April 1848—thus simultaneously with *The Tenant of Wildfell Hall*. It is her longest poem and the fullest review of her life; and at its centre is her interpretation of experience, expressed in much the same terms as those used by Helen Huntingdon:

> I see that time, and toil, and truth
> An inward hardness can impart,—
> Can freeze the generous blood of youth,
> And steel full fast the tender heart.

That Helen learns this 'inward hardness' and becomes cold and unfor-giving is, I think, an important distinction between her and the con-ventional novel heroine, who, in a position like Helen's, almost inevitably acts the patient Griselda. Miss Edgeworth's 'fashionable' tale *Leonora*, to take just one example, has a situation much like that of *The Tenant of Wildfell Hall*: Leonora's husband is having an affair with a guest in the house, under the heroine's eyes; and she herself is at the same time being wooed by a would-be seducer. But Leonora does nothing but 'understand' and forgive and suffer patiently; and she is, of course, eventually rewarded by the return to her of her erring husband. There is a great deal more human insight in Anne Brontë's description of the 'feeling of malevolent gratification' that Helen experiences in seeing her husband's mistress put out. The development within Helen's own mind also increases the amount of moral inter-action: perhaps the greatest of all the sins of Arthur Huntingdon is what he does to Helen. Though not corrupting her morally in the superficial sense of the word, he causes her springs of love and sym-pathy to dry up; and Anne knows that there is no happy-ending possibility of rebuilding such a relationship.

It is a pity, and a weakness in the novel, that the person who makes possible a happy ending, by giving new warmth and sympathy to Helen, should be such a shadowy character as Gilbert Markham. Perhaps in a deliberate attempt at avoiding the conventional novel hero, Markham has been made far from perfect; he has traits of vanity, petty jealousy, even brutality. But instead of making him more human, these (as related in his letters) merely make him trivial. It is impossible to believe that his mind and Helen's have much in common, and that theirs is the satisfactory true marriage, to counterbalance the central disastrous marriage; one characterised by

> the unity of accordant thoughts and feelings, and truly loving, sympathizing hearts and souls.

Nor, therefore, can we give more than theoretical acceptance to the 'violent conflict between reason and passion' in Helen when, before her husband's death, she banishes Markham. Her choice—which is very similar to that made by Jane Eyre after her interrupted wedding—is part of the moral pattern of the novel; but the object of the choice hardly fits into that pattern. Despite a single embrace 'from which no physical or mental force could rend us', it is impossible to see Markham as either inspiring or returning passion.

It is, of course, difficult for Markham to write much about his own good sides; and much of the flaw lies in the technique which Anne Brontë has chosen. In the central section of the novel Helen can reveal her innermost being to the diary; in the framing letters, Markham is bound to be as objective as possible. This throws the novel out of balance; the frame fails to support the powerful middle portion. The Helen that paints pictures to sell, and goes to tea-parties and picnics, has lost the stature of Helen, the wife of Arthur Huntingdon.

What this goes to show, I think, is that Anne Brontë's real strength as a novelist lies not in width but in depth; not in constructing a multitude of characters and events, but in closely following the moral development, the 'soul-making', of one central character. She is at her best, not when she is straining for talents which she has not got, but when the creative talents she has got are at work on her own hard-won experience of life, transmuting this experience into fiction by the fire of moral passion.

The Tenant of Wildfell Hall is not a feminist novel in the obvious sense. Its central concern has nothing to do with Women's Rights; Helen does not complain of her legal position in marriage, although it means that her husband has charge of all her money (and thus virtually can keep her prisoner in her own home until her brother helps her to escape), and that—whatever he does to her—she cannot divorce him.[1] These points seem hardly to have occurred to Anne Brontë. And yet, through the very nature of its central concern, this novel is feminist in the deepest sense of the word. Without any thought of what ought to be the proper sphere of a woman writer, it analyses passion (and Helen even 'tells her love', first to Huntingdon and then to Markham), exhibits profligacy and demonstrates vice, as demanded by its theme. The Preface to the second edition of *The Tenant of Wildfell Hall*, which I have already repeatedly referred to, is, by implication, the bravest statement for the literary equality of the sexes that any of the Brontës ever made. Replying to those who had attacked her for the 'unwomanly' qualities of her material, she answers with an appeal for truth:

O reader! if there were less of this delicate concealment of facts —this whispering 'Peace, peace', when there is no peace, there would be less of sin and misery to the young of both sexes who are left to wring their bitter knowledge from experience.

While apologising to those who have 'derived more pain than pleasure' from the novel, she will not retract one word:

... be it understood, I shall not limit my ambition to this, [giving pleasure]—or even to producing a 'perfect work of art': time and talents so spent, I should consider wasted and misapplied. Such humble talents as God has given me I will endeavour to put to their greatest use; if I am able to amuse I will try to benefit, too; and when I feel it my duty to speak an unpalatable truth, with the help of God, I *will* speak it, though it be to the prejudice of my name and to the detriment of my reader's immediate pleasure as well as my own.

'I *will* speak it.' This is not the mimosa plant of Miss Stodart, shrinking away from danger and using her talents in writing moral poems for children. To Anne Brontë, the demands of duty outrule those of conventional propriety; she is a moralist first and a woman second; and if the woman gets in the way of the moralist, all the worse for the woman. The truth must be spoken and taught, no matter what sex the author is.

By the standards of her time, both Anne Brontë's novels were unwomanly. By the standards of our time, neither is 'a perfect work of art'. By her own standards, she must have had the satisfaction of knowing that she had put her talents 'to their greatest use'.

III

Emily Brontë: The Woman Writer as Poet

The tigers of wrath are wiser than the horses of instruction.

(Blake, 'Proverbs of Hell')

(i)

THE case of Emily Brontë, and in particular *Wuthering Heights*, is that of an imaginative genius which for over a hundred years now has haunted commentators with something of the same persistence and the same 'pleasure and pain, in exquisite extremes' as those with which the ghost of Cathy haunts Heathcliff. Nor is it any more likely that her baffling genius will be caught and held to a definite interpretation than that we are ever to know the ultimate fate of those two spirits. I do not claim to 'understand' Emily Brontë or even to be able to give an 'interpretation' of *Wuthering Heights*. Nor do I believe that she saw her sex as a central problem in her art. This chapter, then, would seem to need some justification.

Such a justification does not lie in any directly apparent connection with the woman writer's quest for a proper sphere. Ellen Nussey's memory of Emily Brontë doing the housework with a book propped up on the kitchen table;[1] M. Héger's reported impression that the angular English spinster whom he was teaching ought to have been a man—'a great navigator';[2] a modern biographer's somewhat hysterical picture of 'Emily at Haworth, exiled from love, with a man's soul in her female body, hell tormenting her, poetry adding to the torment';[3] C. Day Lewis's insistence that the basic impulse behind her work was 'the limitation of not being a man'[4]—all these would seem, more or less formidably, to indicate a woman deeply caught in the feminist dilemma. But in fact, if we turn to her writings, we have no evidence that Emily Brontë ever, consciously or unconsciously, resented the

limitations of her sex. Her birthday note of 1845, one of the few
personal statements we have from her hand, suggests nothing but
absolute acceptance of her lot in the parsonage where she was 'a very
busy and industrious housekeeper, doing all the ironing for the house
and making all the bread'[1]:

> I am quite contented for myself—not as idle as formerly, altogether
> as hearty and having learnt to make the most of the present and hope
> for the future with less fidgetness [*sic*] that I cannot do all I wish—
> seldom or ever troubled with nothing to [do] and merely desiring that
> every body could be as comfortable as myself and as undesponding
> and then we should have a very tolerable world of it.[2]

It was, perhaps, the essential paradox of her nature that this resolute
contentment with her place in life co-existed with rebellion—Charlotte Brontë speaks in her 'Biographical Notice' of how 'under an
unsophisticated culture, inartificial tastes and an unpretending outside,
lay a secret power and fire that might have informed the brain and
kindled the veins of a hero;'—but it was a rebellion against the whole
human condition. Never, except in the exile poems inspired by her
period as a governess, does her poetry speak of, or imply, frustrations
in her actual social-domestic position; and even in those poems it is not
her sex or her status she laments, but the separation from the parsonage
and the moors. The frustrations in her poetry are the profound and
incurable ones of the human condition: her demand in the poems for
liberty and integrity—

> Through life and death, a chainless soul
> With courage to endure—

is too absolute to be motivated by, or directed towards the alleviation
of, any one particular ill; her most piercing cry—'Oh, dreadful is
the check—intense the agony'—laments the return from a mystical
moment of spiritual liberation, the pain of re-discovering the limitations of humanity,

> When the ear begins to hear and the eye begins to see;
> When the pulse begins to throb, the brain to think again,
> The soul to feel the flesh and the flesh to feel the chain!

87

When, as often happens in her later poems, she turns the world created by her imagination into a vehicle of moral satire, this is aimed at no particular abuse but recalls Johnson's *Vanity of Human Wishes* in the condemnation of a whole world:

> I'll think there's not one world above,
> Far as these straining eyes can see,
> Where Wisdom ever laughed at Love,
> Or Virtue crouched to Infamy;
>
> Where, writhing 'neath the strokes of Fate,
> The mangled wretch was forced to smile;
> To match his patience 'gainst her hate,
> His heart rebellious all the while;
>
> Where Pleasure still will lead to wrong,
> And helpless Reason warn in vain;
> And Truth is weak and Treachery strong,
> And Joy the shortest path to Pain;
>
> And Peace, the lethargy of grief;
> And Hope, a phantom of the soul;
> And Life, a labour void and brief;
> And Death, the despot of the whole!
> ('How Clear She Shines!')

The vital opposites in her poems, then, are not man and woman, but enslavement and freedom (the image of the fettered or caged spirit being one of the most frequently recurring ones), reality and imagination, vice and virtue. The same is true of *Wuthering Heights*, where not only is there no concern with one sex being superior or inferior to the other, but where traditionally masculine and feminine qualities and attitudes are entirely subordinated to the complex of opposites formed by the Earnshaws (and Heathcliff) against the Lintons, the Heights against the Grange. 'Nothing', says Charlotte Brontë, in her Preface to *Wuthering Heights*, commenting on the alleged femininity of Edgar Linton, 'moved her more than any insinuation that the faithfulness and clemency, the long-suffering and loving-kindness which are esteemed virtues in the daughters of Eve, become foibles in the sons of Adam.' Cathy and Heathcliff are woman and man but, more impor-

tantly, they are joint rebels against the human condition, with a desire
and a will as absolute as those of the Philosopher in Emily Brontë's
poem of that name:

> No promised Heaven, these wild Desires
> Could all or half fulfil;
> No threatened Hell, with quenchless fires,
> Subdue this quenchless will.

Needless to say, we have no pronouncement from Emily Brontë
on the 'woman question' and no critical defence to match Anne
Brontë's assertion of the female novelist's autonomy in the Preface
to the second edition of *The Tenant of Wildfell Hall*. Her work must
stand, as her life, self-contained and self-explained, even less affected
by the social and literary pressures of her time than that of either of her
sisters. Every new reading of her work confirms that quality of
Blakean independence which Charlotte summed up as: 'Stronger than
a man, simpler than a child, her nature stood alone.'

And yet Emily Brontë is inextricably part of the theme of this
book, for two main reasons. First, while the contemporary reaction to
her novel is one of the best indicators to the climate of opinion in
which the Bells started to publish, her work itself forms a valuable foil
to that of her sisters, illuminating by contrast various features of their
art. Secondly, while *Wuthering Heights*, as has often been pointed out,
stands as much outside the main tradition of nineteenth-century
fiction as Blake stood outside the main tradition of eighteenth-century
verse, I feel that the kind of wisdom—albeit the wisdom of the tiger
rather than that of the horse—which is the ultimate product of her
imaginative vision is more *of* its time than has been generally recognised. The view of Emily Brontë epitomised in Jocelyn Horner's
daemonic bronze figure opposite the Parsonage Museum post-card
kiosk—the view usually articulated in terms like 'passion', 'power',
'wildness'—has tended to obscure what I feel a close reading of the
novel must bring out: namely that when she followed her sisters in
abandoning poetry for a 'prose tale', and so mapped out her own sphere
in fiction, this came to involve her in an affirmation of values which she
herself might have called 'healthful'[1] and which we think of as Victorian. To the pursuit of these two points, which are inevitably interrelated, this chapter is dedicated.

(ii)

'Books, coarse even for men, coarse in language and coarse in conception, the coarseness apparently of violent and uncultivated men.' Thus—in a vein remarkable only for the monotony of its vocabulary, but otherwise typical of much early criticism of the Brontës—the reviewer in *The Leader* greeted the new edition of *Wuthering Heights* and *Agnes Grey* (1850) and the 'Biographical Notice' by Charlotte Brontë which first set before the public the true story behind the Bell pseudonyms.[1] Three years earlier, in December 1847, there had appeared from the publishing house of T. C. Newby, joined together to fill the traditional three volumes, two novels by 'Ellis and Acton Bell'. Neither *Wuthering Heights* nor *Agnes Grey* made on their appearance anything like the stir created by *Jane Eyre* two months previously; but the name Bell was in itself enough to attract attention, and many reviewers at first believed that they had before them two early works of Currer Bell—a belief that Newby, with an eye to the rising sales-figures of *Jane Eyre*, was only too anxious to encourage. Many also realised that the new volumes contained two works which were very different from each other, and *The New Monthly Magazine* went so far as to suggest that they were exercises of Currer Bell's:

> Ellis Bell and Acton Bell appear in the light of two names borrowed to represent two totally different styles of composition and two utterly opposed modes of treatment of the novel, rather than to indicate two real personages.[2]

When it came to a comparison of these two 'modes of treatment of the novel', *Agnes Grey* was a convenient stick to beat *Wuthering Heights* with: Acton Bell's novel had at least the obvious merit of didacticism and could be safely ranged into a familiar category of domestic fiction. *Wuthering Heights* was a freak, defying every attempt at classification and offending most contemporary canons of taste:

> Canons of art, sound and imperative, true tastes and natural instincts . . . unite in pronouncing it unquestionably and irremediably monstrous.[3]

Thus while the reviewers found in both novels the coarseness of what a later age was to call naturalism, and accordingly rebuked the Bells because

> they do not turn away from dwelling upon those physical acts of cruelty which we know to have their warrant in the real annals of crime and suffering,—but the contemplation of which true taste rejects,[1]

in *Wuthering Heights* there was no apparent moral aim to justify such a violation of true taste. If you could find no other moral in the novel than that it showed 'what Satan could do with the law of entail', then the verdict was bound to be: 'powerful writing . . . thrown away'.[2] Even Sydney Dobell, who wrote in *The Palladium* the first seriously praising review, and who anticipated much modern criticism of *Wuthering Heights* by insisting on its poetical qualities, regretted that the author used 'her wonderful pencil on a picture so destitute of moral beauty and human worth'.[3] The next step was to see the novel itself as positively immoral; to the *Spectator* critic its incidents had 'a moral taint about them';[4] and in her infamous review of *Jane Eyre* Miss Rigby found room to safeguard both the taste and the morality of the Establishment by a scathing attack on Heathcliff and Cathy as being 'too odiously and abominably pagan to be palatable even to the most vitiated class of English readers'.[5]

When, after the appearance of the 'Biographical Notice', it was clear that *Wuthering Heights* was the work of a woman, the moral position became more embarrassing still. *The Athenaeum*, out of consideration, one feels, for the surviving sister, spoke in a tellingly guarded fashion of 'a more than usually interesting contribution to the history of female authorship in England';[6] and when writing to mark the Queen's Jubilee, on 'The Literature of the Last Fifty Years', Mrs. Oliphant still could not forgive Emily Brontë for contributing to the history of female authorship 'the extraordinary and feverish romance "Wuthering Heights", which in very painfulness and horror made an impression upon the mind of the public, greater perhaps than its intrinsic merits justify'.[7]

Under this barrage, and with Emily in the grave even before the *Palladium* review had appeared, it is no wonder that Charlotte Brontë spoke bitterly of critics who 'remind us of the mob of Astrologers,

Chaldeans, and Soothsayers gathered before the "writing on the wall", and unable to read the characters or make known the interpretation'.[1] Yet even she flinched before the moral implications of some of that writing. Thinking it scarcely 'right or advisable to create beings like Heathcliff', she put the blame on her sister's imagination:

> This I know: the writer who possesses the creative gift owns something of which he is not always master—something that, at times, strangely wills and works for itself.[2]

Imaginative and instinctive: Charlotte Brontë here set the tone for much subsequent writing on the novel. Perhaps what is most remarkable about *Wuthering Heights* is the impression it makes of being all of one piece, created, as it were, at white heat, a single, sustained feat of the imagination. It is this quality which has led so many critics to speak of the novel as a spontaneous overflow of powerful feelings, as a work in which the author is unaware of what forces she has set in motion and what means she has used—even 'a kind of prose *Kubla Khan*'.[3] And it is this quality which has often blinded the same critics to the careful and painstaking art of *Wuthering Heights*. Though it may be a truism, it needs to be said that not only the intensity of the author's imaginative vision, but also the workmanship with which she projects and controls it, has created *Wuthering Heights*. I want to stress in this chapter that the poet in Emily Brontë is a Maker as well as a Seer; and that what she makes reveals that she saw ultimately in moral terms.

Charlotte's defence could also be paraphrased as 'imagination at the expense of morality'; and thus, too, it would, willy-nilly, outline the direction of later *Wuthering Heights* criticism. As Art became a more important criterion than Morality, so the spokesmen for the passionate and poetical qualities of the novel became more eloquent. Where Mrs. Oliphant was shocked by the 'extraordinary and feverish' in the novel, Pater praised it as 'the really characteristic fruit' of the spirit of Romanticism.[4] Swinburne was still worried by those parts which he thought like 'a police report or even a novel by a French "naturalist" of the latest and brutallest order', but to him all its 'faults' were compensated for by its poetry, and he saw the novel as a whole as a dramatic poem, to be compared with *Lear* and *The Duchess of Malfi*.[5] Serious modern criticism—by which I rule out the rhapsodic type of account which *Wuthering Heights*, above all the other Brontë novels, seems to invite—has varied less than might have been expected from this pattern. It is true that the twentieth-century interest in the art of the novel generally has been reflected in excellent and sympathetic studies of features of Emily Brontë's art (though popular editions of *Wuthering Heights* still carry Prefaces apologising for its 'faults of construction' and 'defects in realism'). But the view of this novel as a great achievement of the Romantic imagination, its contents a-moral or 'pre-moral' (Lord David Cecil) in nature, has prevailed. G. D. Klingopulos, writing on *Wuthering Heights* in a series of *Scrutiny* articles on 'The Novel as Dramatic Poem' concludes that 'in the world of *Wuthering Heights* good and bad are not applicable terms',[1] and in much the same way Lord David Cecil feels about Emily Brontë that 'the conflict between right and wrong which is the distinguishing feature in the Victorian view of life does not come into her view'.[2] With few exceptions—Miriam Allott's interesting essay on 'The Rejection of Heathcliff' being the most notable[3]—the art of *Wuthering Heights* has been seen as one which does not involve moral awareness.

That its contemporary critics should have failed to find any moral commitment in *Wuthering Heights* does not seem so strange when we consider the degree of moral explicitness expected from a novelist even in the mid- and late 1840s. Charlotte Brontë has a not very subtle dig at the sugared-pill expectancy of her readers when she writes in the last paragraph of *Shirley*:

> The story is told. I think I now see the judicious reader putting on his spectacles to look for the moral. It would be an insult to his sagacity to offer directions. I only say, God speed him in the quest!

But many novelists were not so chary of offering 'directions'. Many thought it safest, having seen their characters home, to point the moral of their tale; thus Mrs. Marsh ends her *Emilia Wyndham* (1846):

> Now, was it not better, dear reader, think you, that all these pairs, once united, should have remained united, done their duties by and learned to love one another. . . ? And, moreover, is it not just possible, think you, that *some* of the discomforts of married life . . . might be ameliorated if husbands now and then . . . learned to correct themselves as well as wives?

This as a conclusion to *Wuthering Heights* would no doubt have gone some way towards appeasing its morally outraged critics! But *Wuthering Heights* ends as a quiet elegy in Gimmerton churchyard, and the narrative method Emily Brontë has chosen does not allow of any intrusive comment to establish a direct moral rapport between her and her readers—not even as general a one as Thackeray's return to his puppet-box image at the end of *Vanity Fair*, or his reference to the 'Ordainer of the lottery' in the conclusion to *Pendennis*. Nor does it allow for the running commentary by which an omniscient author could give his reader the moral bearings of situations and remind him of the exemplary function of characters and incidents—as, again, Mrs. Marsh is for ever commenting on her characters' behaviour in such phrases as: 'Now, if So-and-So had done so-and-so instead of what he did, then all would have been well.' The objective directness and dramatic intensity with which characters and actions in *Wuthering Heights* are presented would, especially in contrast to novels that were virtually case histories illustrating social and moral maxims, have suggested that Emily Brontë was indeed condoning extra-marital love and acts of brutality which ought to have been made explicitly cautionary. Granted Nelly Dean as a narrator, she did not even use the opportunity of making her novel into the cautionary autobiography of a housekeeper. One of the reasons for the popularity of the fictitious autobiography in this period was doubtless its inherent effectiveness as an exemplary tale: 'look at my Experience of Life [the title, in fact, of Elizabeth Sewell's 'autobiography' of a Christian spinster, published in 1853] and learn from it'! George Eliot had not yet appeared, to show how the moral lesson of a novel can reside in its sensitive observation of the interrelationships of people (and even George Eliot had to comment as well as demonstrate). So far only Jane Austen had more subtly used the whole structure and style of her novels to embody her moral vision; but Jane Austen, when read, was mainly admired for her realism. In any case, her best-liked novel in this period was *Mansfield Park* whose heroine is as self-consciously, not to say self-righteously, a moral norm (agreed on by author and reader) in her world as is Agnes Grey in hers.

If we can find a historical explanation for contemporary critics' dismissal of *Wuthering Heights* as immoral, it seems the more odd that modern critics should have confused the dramatic objectivity used by Emily Brontë to present her material with a lack of moral valuation of characters and actions in the novel. To see how this has happened, the case of Anne Brontë may, paradoxically, be a help. Anne Brontë differs from the common run of domestic fiction writers mainly by the intensity with which she moralises all her material. Her method is allegorical. The clear-cutness of Agnes's juxtaposition with the two families she serves, of the contrast between Mr. Weston and Mr. Hatfield; the drinking-bouts with Lowborough as a skeleton at the feast; even Agnes's apocalyptic sun-rise meeting with Mr. Weston and Helen Huntingdon's Christmas rose—all these are reducible to a simple formula; they directly 'stand for' something else, easily definable and paraphrasable. Anne Brontë knows the truth and uses her fictitious material to illustrate it. But what does Lockwood's dream stand for? Or that horrible dream that Cathy never tells Nelly about, or the one she does tell, about being miserable in Heaven without Heathcliff? Did Emily Brontë know? Do we know? If the answer to this is firmly yes, then, I think, we are in danger of not noticing that *Wuthering Heights* uses its material for exploration and discovery; that it does not illustrate an assumed set of relationships or a 'philosophy': that its mode of operation is symbolical. The distinction between symbolism and allegory is a vexed one, but I think it is safe to say that while allegory assumes a relatively simple and complete equivalent for everything in a work of art, a static relationship between the elements of a work of art and a set of concepts (moral or not) assumed outside it, symbolism is dynamic and complex. In *Wuthering Heights*, characters, events and images are presented to us objectively, but so that in the course of the novel they gradually accumulate significances which the reader's mind holds in suspension. Meanings are suggested rather than defined; they hover around, modifying each other and the work as a whole, but they are never totally paraphrasable.

Much modern criticism assumes for *Wuthering Heights* what is applicable to *Agnes Grey*: that everything 'stands for' something else. As it is impossible to make Heathcliff or the Lintons or either Catherine stand for moral categories, and as the forces of nature play such a large part in the novel, the next step is to assume that its people stand for natural, non-moral forces. Hence Emily Brontë becomes morally perplexed or innocent. Even Lord David Cecil's admirable and in many ways epoch-making essay on *Wuthering Heights* tends to make it into a metaphysical allegory, so that, for all that he was the first to bring out many important qualities in the novel, he also helped to squeeze it into a pattern which both oversimplifies and overcomplicates. He reads the novel as a paradigm of what he takes to be Emily Brontë's philosophy: according to him she thinks 'that the whole created cosmos, animate and inanimate, mental and physical alike, is the expression of certain living spiritual principles'. These are the principles of, respectively, storm and calm. Ultimately they are not in conflict but compose parts of a harmony; nor is either inherently destructive: they become so 'only because in the cramped condition of their earthly incarnation these principles are diverted from following the course that their nature dictates'. But, 'when they are free from fleshly bonds they flow unimpeded and unconflicting; and even in this world their discords are transitory'. Hence Emily Brontë does away with 'the ordinary antithesis between good and evil' and also with the antithesis between life and death.[1] Not surprisingly, since most of this philosophy has been derived from the novel, the novel itself then reduces itself neatly into an illustration of these ideas. It shows 'the destruction and re-establishment' of 'cosmic harmony' by playing the children of storm (the Earnshaws and Heathcliff) off against the children of calm (the Lintons): 'unnatural' marriages between Catherine and Edgar and between Heathcliff and Isabella provoke disorder; order is re-established as Heathcliff and the first Catherine are united at last, after death, and Wuthering Heights is left to them as rightful possessors, while Hareton and the second Catherine establish themselves at the Grange.

While the very assurance of such a reading is tempting, it does, I feel, ultimately misrepresent the novel. I feel that the characters in *Wuthering Heights* are, in various ways, presented as moral beings; and, secondly, that they are not used, allegorically, to illustrate a philosophy —one which, in any case, can hardly be substantiated from the poems, the novel, or anything we know about Emily Brontë—but symbolically, to explore the human condition. Support for this belief can be found both in the novel and in the poems of Emily Brontë. To show this, it is natural to turn first to Heathcliff. No one would deny that he is the most compelling and puzzling character in the novel. He is also structurally the protagonist, the only one whose lifetime spans the whole novel. According to Cecil, Heathcliff is *not* a wicked man voluntarily yielding to his wicked impulses. Like all Emily Brontë's characters, he is a manifestation of natural forces acting involuntarily under the pressure of his own nature.

He becomes destructive only because his nature was 'frustrated of its true fulfilment—union with its affinity, Catherine Earnshaw'. But he is no more morally responsible for his destructiveness than 'a mountain torrent directed from its channel, which flows out on the surrounding country, laying waste whatever may happen to lie in its way'. Now, Catherine's betrayal, which sends Heathcliff away on the words, 'It would degrade me to marry Heathcliff now', is clearly the decisive moment in Heathcliff's life, but it is hardly a question of his being changed here from a merely 'alien' to an outright 'destructive' force. Before this moment, we have had the gruesome episode of Heathcliff and Hindley fighting over the colts in Chapter IV; we have heard how Heathcliff's idea of bliss is 'painting the house-front with Hindley's blood'; and we have had the impressive passage in Chapter VII— structurally emphasised as Nelly breaks her narrative there for the first time—where Heathcliff is brooding over how to pay Hindley back and Nelly is advising him to leave revenge to the Lord:

> 'No, God won't have the satisfaction that I shall,' he returned. 'I only wish I knew the best way! Let me alone, and I'll plan it out: while I'm thinking of that, I don't feel pain.'

These are hardly the terms of 'a mountain torrent directed from its channel': clearly we are meant to see the destructiveness in Heathcliff here—nearly three years before Catherine chooses Edgar—as a psychological and moral consequence of his own mind, hardened under the conflict with Hindley. Nor, as he later pursues his double revenge, against the Lintons (by marrying Isabella and marrying off Linton to the second Catherine, thus 'legally' appropriating the Linton estates) and against Hindley (driving him on to death and acquiring Wuthering Heights), is there anything 'inevitable' or 'involuntary' about what Emily Brontë surely wants us to call his 'wickedness'. His acts of aggression and revenge are laid out clearly and often in painstaking detail, down to his trick of bribing the lawyer away from Edgar Linton's death-bed; they are wilful deeds bound up with moral consequences. That we are to see his course of action as immoral is most obvious in the second half of the novel, where we are more concerned with the consequences, rather than the causes, of his acts; and where Edgar Linton's weakness is less emphasised and his kindness and goodness become the channels through which we perceive him. The scene in Chapter XXVII where Heathcliff keeps the second Catherine from her father's death-bed is a very clear (though implicit) placing of Heathcliff against the very standards he is defying: 'Careful and kind,' he sneers, '—that's paternal.' After his return from the three and a half years' absence we only see him (until his death) in scenes where he does harm—mental or physical or both—to other people. The book is full of physical and mental violence, of hurts and pain and people mistreating each other, and we are not asked to suspend our moral judgment in the face of all that violence. 'Terror,' says Lockwood, describing how he treated the waif ghost in his nightmare, 'made me cruel.' As Lockwood is affected, so the reader is surely expected to be affected, to see the spread of cruelty as evil. Physical violence becomes one measure of evil in the book, as it spreads from Heathcliff outwards. It is he, the 'cuckoo', who brings out the brutality in Hindley; this was initially old Earnshaw's fault for preferring the foundling to his own son, but it culminates in the ghastly fights after Heathcliff's return and in Hindley's death—whether he had 'fair play' or not is left open. It is he who turns Isabella from a silly but innocent creature, via apathy, into something like a bloodthirsty monster, so that she can abet, and even half enjoy, his fight with Hindley. He provokes Edgar Linton's one act of violence in the book, turns Hareton from Nelly Dean's innocent nursling into a swearing little savage and later a coarse lout; he beats up the second Catherine and temporarily kills the human emotions of kindness and pity in her. Significantly, it is Heathcliff's own offspring, Linton, that brings out the cruellest streak in him; and the encounters between them, hinted at in their effects on Linton, rather than described, are the most quietly gruesome passages in the book. The zest of Heathcliff's pleasure in destruction underlines, rather than obscures, its perverseness and immorality:

> 'I have no pity! I have no pity! The more the worms writhe, the more I yearn to crush out their entrails! It is a moral teething; and I grind with greater energy, in proportion to the increase of pain.'

Linton's own form of sadism, both inherited and learnt from Heathcliff, but lacking the vitality of Heathcliff's, is particularly nasty—as

Heathcliff himself knows ('He'll undertake to torture any number of cats, if their teeth be drawn and their claws pared'), and as his young bride finds out when Linton draws 'a pleasant picture to Zillah of what he would do if he were as strong as I [Heathcliff]'.

The imagery connected with Heathcliff—whether used by himself or (mainly) by others in reference to him—is uniformly suggestive of savagery and evil. It refers to unyielding, harsh and sterile aspects of nature—'rough as a saw-edge and hard as whinstone;' 'an arid wilderness of furze and whinstone'—or to wild and predatory beasts—he is 'a vicious cur', a 'tiger or venomous serpent', 'a fierce, pitiless, wolfish man', 'a mad dog', has 'basilisk eyes'—or to infernal powers, picturing him as a devil incarnate. This last is much the most frequent type of reference to him. From the moment Old Earnshaw brings to Wuthering Heights the child 'as dark almost as if it came from the devil', to Joseph's triumphant cry, on finding Heathcliff dead, 'Th'divil's harried off his soul', practically every character in the book speaks of him as diabolical. Sometimes this is elaborated into a whole biblical allegory, as in Nelly's worries about Hindley in Heathcliff's claws at the Heights:

> I felt that God had forsaken the stray sheep there to its own wicked wanderings, and an evil beast prowled between it and the fold, waiting his time to spring and destroy;

but mostly it is in a quick reference, like the otherwise mild Edgar Linton's description of Heathcliff to the second Catherine: 'a most diabolical man, delighting to wrong and ruin those he hates'.

Clearly these diabolical references do not suggest the nobly satanic figure of post-Shelley and Byron literature, or the glamorised wickedness of Charlotte Brontë's Angrian Duke Zamorna. Heathcliff has the mysterious origins and the physical appearance—above all the eyes 'full of black fire'—of a Byronic hero; even the untold horrors of the marriage-bed that produced Linton can be paralleled in descriptions of Byron's marriage with Annabella.[1] But it is a Byron with the glamour gone, with cruelty and torture, physical and mental, seen from the point of view of the tortured ones as well, and hence seen for what they are. Mr. Rochester, whom we only see from Jane Eyre's point of view, is forgiven and his moral failings redeemed, where Heathcliff is treated relentlessly. *Wuthering Heights* could, in that respect, be seen as Emily Brontë's 'healthful' reaction to the late-Romantic mode of flirting with glamorised wickedness, to such Byronic heroes in fiction as Bulwer Lytton's Eugene Aram in the very popular novel of that name (1832). The hero and title character of that novel is an infinitely learned and intelligent man, but he has committed a crime and bears with him a burden of guilt, darkly hinted at in the course of the story. He is Faust and Cain and the Wandering Jew thrust into one—'I felt urged on to wander—Cain's curse descends to Cain's children'—and is given every possible excuse, for his crime (he was the accomplice in a murder, committed, to be sure, on a worthless, wicked and wretched individual) was executed to enable him to make some great (unspecified) scientific discovery which was to benefit all mankind. He falls in love with a lovely and innocent young girl, whose father is no less pure and innocent; and both father and daughter are allowed to die believing Aram innocent. Throughout the novel, Aram is pictured in an extravagantly elevated fashion; and maybe his greatest moment is when (having been seized on his wedding-day, tried and against denial found guilty, which causes his intended bride to go into a suitable decline and die) he hears his death-sentence passed:

Aram received his sentence in profound composure. Before he left the bar he drew himself up to his full height and looked slowly around the court with that thrilling and almost sublime unmoved-ness of aspect which belonged to him alone of all men, and which was rendered yet more impressive by a smile—slight, but eloquent beyond all words—of a soul collected in itself: no forced and convulsive effort vainly masking the terror or the pang; no mockery of self that would mimic contempt for others, but more in majesty than bitterness; rather as daring fate than defying the judgment of others—rather as if he wrapped himself in the independence of a quiet, than the disdain of a despairing, heart. (Book V, Chapter V)

Aram's letter of confession, written in his last hours, is as noble and lofty—or, to look at it the other way, as morally specious—a statement as can be found in nineteenth-century fiction. Lord Lytton, however, wants to have his cake and eat it too: he wants the maximum of admiration and sympathy for his hero, but he also wants his own authorial moral position to be impeccably orthodox. To achieve this, he has no other resort but to print a footnote to Aram's letter:

Aram has hitherto been suffered to tell his own tale without comment or interruption. . . . But here I must pause for one moment to bid the reader remark, that that event which confirmed Aram in the bewildering doctrines of his pernicious fatalism, ought rather to inculcate the divine virtue—the foundation of all virtues, Heathen or Christian—that which Epictetus made clear, and Christ sacred—FORTITUDE . . . I must apologise for this interruption—it seemed to me advisable in this place.[1]

Eugene Aram was read, we know, in the Brontë household,[2] but whether Emily Brontë had read it or not does not matter. What matters is her superiority of control, both moral (in 'placing' Heathcliff) and technical (in not having to resort to footnotes and capital letters to place him) over the author of that novel.

I have tried to show how Emily Brontë implicitly, by his interaction with other characters and by the language around him, places Heathcliff morally. Heathcliff himself does not see his life in moral terms; he gives up his revenge not because he realises and repents of any wrongdoing but because, as his desire for union with the dead Catherine approaches consummation, his will loses strength in all but this one direction. As he says to Nelly: 'I have lost the faculty of enjoying their destruction, and I am too idle to destroy for nothing.' This is presumably why a recent critic states that there is 'no . . . recognition of the hero's moral self anywhere in *Wuthering Heights*'.[3] Heathcliff's case—and the first Catherine's—is indeed that of will and natural instinct operating outside a moral context; but the book as a whole provides that context and so, rather than making Heathcliff into a principle, questions and judges him. This is not to say anything so simple as that Heathcliff is an *exemplum horrendum* and that the love story is merely cautionary. It is not to deny that the most impressive, because imaginatively most realised, parts of the novel are those dealing with the love and agony of Catherine and Heathcliff. In such scenes as the one in Chapter IX where Catherine speaks to Nelly about her love for Heathcliff, or Catherine's delirium in Chapter XII, or Catherine and Heathcliff's last meeting, or Heathcliff's last few speeches, we see them through their own eyes and by their own standards, according to which right and wrong means like and unlike: for in those scenes Emily Brontë has imaginatively entered into two a-moral beings. The realisation is the more complete because the story of Catherine and Heathcliff is the combination and culmination of *motifs* and emotional complexes recurrent in her poems. (I shall return to this point presently.) But this does not mean that Emily Brontë is of Heathcliff's party without knowing it; nor am I altogether happy about seeing a dichotomy between her 'emotional commitment' to Heathcliff and her 'intellectual judgment' of him,[1] for in the total imaginative creation which is *Wuthering Heights*, 'head' and 'heart', emotions and intellect, seem to me co-active. What it means is that through Catherine and Heathcliff Emily Brontë explores a kind of experience which takes us right to limits of the human condition and beyond; but in doing so she does not abandon what Cecil calls the 'naïve erections of the human mind that we call moral standards'. She is, rather, more aware of human possibilities for good and evil (seen as good and evil) than her contemporaries. Part of the affirmation of those 'naïve erections' lies in the counterforce to the first Catherine and Heathcliff provided by the second Catherine and Hareton, and I shall return to them later. But for the moment I want to emphasise the point that her characters are not used as illustrations of systematic philosophical ideas (however personal the system) but as means to explore the human condition.

This mode of writing, exploring rather than illustrating, is also revealed in her poetry. In talking at all about Emily Brontë's poems, one at once runs up against the Gondal question, almost as vexed as the Homeric one; and it is as well for me to declare my standpoint. The question is about the degree of subjectivity, what we might call the personal versus the dramatic, in the poems. For our guidance we have at one extreme Miss Ratchford, who in her labour of loving reconstruction of the Gondal saga, *Gondal's Queen*, claims that all Emily Brontë's verse, did we but know how, falls within the Gondal context.[2] But *Gondal's Queen* may, as Mrs. Visick suggests,[3] have done more harm than good to our conception of Emily Brontë as a poet; inevitably it suggests that her poetry is part of a world as freakish and overheated as that of the 'Atys and Cybele' poem which the adolescent Pierrot is writing in Mauriac's *Les Chemins de la mer*. At the other extreme, Edwin Morgan thinks that 'Gondal and its characters are only masked (and often scarcely masked) projections of a personality trying to materialise its inward wars and loves' and that 'the verse is indeed among the most personal ever written'.[4] An intermediary position is taken up by C. Day Lewis who sees in Gondal a 'scaffolding' which acted as a fuse to her imagination and as an objective correlative.[1] Most commentators seem to have felt that some poems are more Gondal than others but that this division does not necessarily coincide with the division between established Gondal and non-Gondal verse; most would say that in 'Cold in the Earth' and 'Silent is the House', both Gondal poems, Emily Brontë is expressing deep personal feelings. The theory that some are exclusively Gondal poems and some exclusively personal derived support from the discovery that, in February 1844, Emily Brontë started to copy out her finished poems into two separate notebooks, one of which was headed with the inscription 'Gondal Poems'. The other came to contain such poetry as the homesickness poems from the autumn and winter of 1838, the poems on nature and the creative imagination from 1841 and 1844, and meditative poems on hope, despair and the transitoriness of things. Now, what this division seems to me to indicate is Emily Brontë's awareness that Gondal could—as C. Day Lewis suggests—strait-jacket her imagination, that it limited the field of human experience she could explore. It does not necessarily mean that the non-Gondal poems are more 'personal', with the autobiographical implications which that word carries. There are, for example, in the non-Gondal notebook four poems of unhappy love, written in rapid succession in the spring of 1840. The first, 'Far, far away is mirth withdrawn', a lament for a dead lover with a 'blighted name', is both in situation and sentiment very close to many Gondal poems; it seems to assume a background story without knowledge of which the feelings in the poem are extravagant. The second, 'It is too late to call thee now', is tauter and more restrained in its meditation on a lost love; the third, 'I'll not weep that thou art going to leave me' is freer of Gondal echoes but still somewhat over-weighted with sentiment. But in the fourth, she has arrived at a self-contained love lyric where the mood establishes itself within the poem, and where the haunting effect of simple words looks forward to poems like 'Cold in the earth' as well as to the speeches of Catherine and Heathcliff:

> If grief for grief can touch thee,
> If answering woe for woe,
> If any ruth can melt thee,
> Come to me now!

I cannot be more lonely,
More drear I cannot be!
My worn heart throbs so wildly
'Twill break for thee.

What is interesting about these poems, seen together, is the way they show us Emily Brontë working on an experience and a mood, whether personal (this, as biographers would point out, was the happy Willie Weightman year at Haworth) or not, and whittling their expression down to its most perfect form. What matters is not whether the poet herself felt, or not, what is felt in the poems; what matters are the poems as explorations of moods and discriminations of emotions. As with Shakespeare's sonnets, which suffer under a similar autobiographical problem, Emily Brontë's poems matter, not as experience but as something *made out of* human experience. If we can agree on this, then we do not need to go from her poems to her novel via a reconstruction (at best hypothetical) of the persons and events of the Gondal saga (interestingly as it has been done by Mrs. Visick); we can instead concentrate on how the accretions of thought and feeling which the poems are, anticipate thought and feeling, and their expression, in the novel.

To see Emily Brontë's poems in the chronological order which C. W. Hatfield's edition helpfully provides is to become sceptical about assertions concerning her 'philosophy'. Single lines or single stanzas may be taken to illustrate one theory or another, but the poems, seen together as wholes, show her exploring different views of life, trying out different attitudes. Also, more commonly it is a mood rather than a philosophical position—i.e. the emotions round a given attitude rather than the attitude itself—that she explores. Thus, for example, in two consecutive Gondal poems from the spring of 1845 she first gives the emotional situation of a fated young man, one of 'the unblessed of Heaven', then, antithetically, she turns to the 'Child of Delight' who is going to save him. This is followed by a non-Gondal poem on the happiness of a stoical-Christian attitude to life; and the next but one again is the famous Gondal poem which contains the mystical vision. We can see in these poems various emotional complexes that are going to recur in *Wuthering Heights*, but we cannot say that any one of them exposes Emily Brontë's philosophy, or that they add up to some kind of coherent pattern.

At times her mind seems to work dialectically, often through implied or explicit dialogue within a poem. She is fond of letting different voices express their opinion and making the structure of the poem as a whole reject or favour either voice. Here we have, I think, the germ of the narrative technique in *Wuthering Heights*. It is the apparent objectivity of Blake's 'The Clod and the Pebble' rather than the subjective resolution of Tennyson's 'Two Voices' which characterises poems as separated in time as 'Strong I stand, though I have borne' (November 1837) and the dialogue between father and child in 'The winter wind is loud and wild' (November 1844). In her later poems, especially the non-Gondal ones, we can see how, through a whole group of poems, she grapples with related questions and comes up with different answers. In an interesting series of poems from the spring and summer of 1841 she begins, in a straightforward 'I' poem, 'Riches I hold in light esteem', with an exploration of the meaning of liberty; this is the poem which contains the famous prayer for 'a chainless soul'. The next poem, 'Shall Earth no more inspire thee', is a dramatised appeal from nature to the poet, leading up to an affirmation of the power of nature as inspiration; and the following, 'Aye, there it is! It wakes to-night', where the poet becomes a 'thou' by looking at herself from the outside, is a kind of synthesis of the previous two. Here the desire for liberty and the stimulus of nature unite into:

> A universal influence
> From Thine own influence free;
> A principle of life, intense,
> Lost to mortality.

The synthesis has about it that quality of raptness which in her poems always seems to accompany the vision of a liberation from the human condition. The ultimate liberation is seen as death and a rejection of earth:

> Thus truly when that breast is cold
> Thy prisoned soul shall rise,
> The dungeon mingle with the mould—
> The captive with the skies.

But the next poem, dated only eleven days later, is about the love of earth:

We would not leave our native home
For *any* world beyond the Tomb.
No—rather on thy kindly breast
Let us be laid in lasting rest;
Or waken but to share with thee
A mutual immortality.

It is a re-working, in a lower key, of a more poignant stanza in 'Shall Earth no more inspire thee'—

Few hearts to mortals given
On earth so wildly pine;
Yet none would ask a Heaven
More like this Earth than thine—

and a comparison of the two suggests why that poem is the greater one: in it her vision, for all its intensity, is more detached, and so it can accommodate the paradoxical opposites of an attachment to, even an identification with, earth and a yearning away from it. The tension of such a paradox prepares us for the emotional life of the first Catherine, her longings to return to 'the heather on those hills' from the prison of the Grange and her longings to leave 'this shattered prison' for 'that glorious world'. But more importantly still, the tendency in the poems to let the thought develop dynamically and to vary the emotional value of images, so that they do not add up to a set symbolism, is characteristic of the novel as a whole.

Furthermore, the poems are not 'pre-moral'. There is identification of man and nature, there are moments when man becomes 'a principle of life, intense, lost to mortality', but increasingly we are referred back to man as a moral being. Even the Philosopher's desires to break through the human situation by a loss of identity are ultimately placed by himself, as in the last stanza he sees his life in terms of 'vanquished Good, victorious Ill'. The voice of a very orthodox and simple piety gets stronger in her later poems, measuring life in terms of good and bad, and seeing death in the Christian terms of salvation and damnation. I cannot see anything unorthodox in the Protestant individualism of the well-known poem 'No coward soul is mine'. In a poem from the summer of 1839 a Giaour-like figure of a damned man, whose eyes like Heathcliff's have a 'basilisk charm', is introduced for the possibilities he offers of creating an atmosphere of mysterious horror ('And now the house-dog stretched once more'). In a poem from the spring of 1844 a damned man is treated entirely in terms of the life he has wasted and the youthful virtues—'Courage and Truth, a generous breast Where Love and Gladness lay'—which he has wilfully perverted in the cause of Pleasure. A development towards a stronger moral conscious-ness is particularly clear if we look at the poems which at various times she wrote to or about imagination. In 1841 there are the two I have already mentioned—'Shall Earth no more inspire thee' and 'Aye, there it is'—which both see imagination as freedom, raptness and ecstatic liberation: 'how wildly fancy plays' is a criterion of (a-moral) goodness. But in the two poems from the autumn of 1844 in which she directs herself to the imagination, seeing it as something apart from herself, it is looked at squarely as escapism. 'I trust not to thy phantom bliss' she says in the first ('When weary with the long day's care'). In the second she realises that she can make the influence of the imagination 'good or ill' but that its function is that of an anodyne, 'deadening me to real cares'. From the poems it would seem that by the time she came to write her prose tale, she was very conscious of the opposition between the a-morality of her creative imagination and the moral rules by which life must be led. To write a novel, then, would have meant a new departure where life in moral terms could be worked out more fully —where, in fact, her creative imagination could embrace morality.

Emily Brontë's poetry as a whole suggests particular emotional intensity around certain imagined experiences. These (which com-pletely overlap the division between the Gondal and non-Gondal poems) are of two main kinds. One is to do with intense longing for one who was beloved and is dead. It leans, as it were, backward. The other is to do, too, with intense longing, but here it is self-centred and forward- or outward-leaning, a desire to be liberated—by death, by nature or by the imagination—from the bonds that enslave the spirit. There is nothing in the poems like Cathy's assurance of identity with Heathcliff—'I *am* Heathcliff'—though there is passionate love and love-hatred; and there is nothing like Heathcliff's assurance that he is to be reunited with the spirit of Cathy. But the Cathy–Heathcliff relationship seems to have sprung from a new combination of these two 'emotional complexes'. The poems can help here, too, in illumin-ating the ambivalence of that relationship. Perhaps the best guide to this is to be found in the word 'wild'. It occurs in at least one-third of all the poems, or fragments of poems, Emily Brontë ever wrote—and in some of these poems more than once; it occurs practically every time as an emotional centre in those two contexts of passionate grief and of ecstatic reaching out for freedom which I have mentioned. In many poems, particularly the early ones, wildness is a feature of the landscape—the sea or the moors or, above all, the wind. It also refers very often to human emotion, and these two uses are intimately linked: the wild winds, or the clouds which 'rush dark and wild' are associated with the 'wild anguish of despair', or the 'passions wild', or the 'hearts wildly pining' of the figures in the landscape. In one poem the 'wind's wild voice' makes the 'glad heart bound wilder still'. At times she avoids cliché (for 'wild' is, of course, a favourite Gothic adjective) and achieves a peculiarly haunting effect by making 'wild' modify another adjective: the purple heather is 'too wildly, sadly dear', and the red-breast's music is 'wildly tender'—just as Cathy later on is 'wildly wretched' when in her delirium she discovers that she is exiled from childhood and from Heathcliff. The fusion of the human and the natural is best seen in the famous poem of mourning and longing, 'Cold in the earth, and the deep snow piled above thee'—

> Cold in the earth, and fifteen wild Decembers
> From those brown hills have melted into Spring—

where 'wild' derives its effect from its ambiguity: the Decembers are wild and snowy, but they have also meant wild repining to the mourner. Similarly in the freedom-poems, nature and human experience meet: the 'wild sky-lark' in 'Loud without the wind was roaring' suggests the spirit's imagined flight back to the moors from 'exile afar'; and in a very early poem (December, 1836) the landscape—

> High waving heather, 'neath stormy blasts bending
> Midnight and moonlight and bright shining stars
> . . .
>
> All down the mountain sides, wild forests lending
> One mighty voice to the life-giving wind—

provides the impulse for the experience of

> Man's spirit away from its drear dungeon sending,
> Bursting the fetters and breaking the bars.

It is the earliest appearance in her preserved writings both of the fully realised 'wild' landscape and of the idea of the spirit escaping from imprisonment. For all its excited turbulence, its sing-song rhythm and facile alliteration, this poem yet anticipates by nine years the well-known lines of mystical ecstasy:

> Then dawns the Invisible, the Unseen its truth reveals;
> My outward sense is gone, my inward essence feels—
> Its wings are almost free, its home, its harbour found,
> Measuring the gulf it stoops and dares the final bound.

These two poems taken together—the experience in the first proved on the pulses, but only half understood, in the second acutely realised, to a point beyond understanding—describe a curve of development similar to that contained within the scope of Wordsworth's 'Tintern Abbey': the growth from those 'wild ecstasies' which the poet did once know and now catches a glimpse of in the 'wild eyes' of his sister, to

> . . . that serene and blessed mood,
> In which the affections gently lead us on,—
> Until, the breath of this corporeal frame
> And even the motion of our human blood
> Almost suspended, we are laid asleep
> In body, and become a living soul:
> While with an eye made quiet by the power
> Of harmony, and the deep power of joy,
> We see into the life of things.

So far we have seen the attraction of wildness: it represents the pitch of emotional experience, it vitalises you to the point where it liberates you from the imprisonment in physical bondage ('this shattered prison', as Catherine calls it). In such Romantic wildness, nature and man meet. All this is, of course, the attraction of the story of Catherine and Heathcliff.

But this very attraction has in it the seeds of repulsion. Semantically the word 'wild' has a kind of ambivalence: it has the emotionally positive associations of the free, beautiful and romantic; but it also has the negative ones of dangerous, ravenous, mad—or, indeed, as Catherine describes Heathcliff to Isabella, 'fierce, pitiless, wolfish'. Very early Emily Brontë had placed 'wildness' morally in a poem-prayer, where she defines it by contrast:

> O may I never lose the peace
> That lulls me gently now,
> Though time should change my youthful face,
> And years should shade my brow!
>
> True to myself, and true to all,
> May I be healthful still,
> And turn away from passion's call,
> And curb my own wild will.
>
> ('All day I've toiled', Spring 1837)

The same awareness of the opposition between the 'healthful' and the 'wild' goes through *Wuthering Heights*. Heathcliff and Cathy in their childhood have a Wordsworthian kind of kinship with the wild moors; 'half savage and hardy, and free' is how Cathy, in her illness, sees that time. When they first look in through the windows of Thrushcross Grange and see the Linton children quarrelling about a puppy, it is rather like two noble savages looking at an effete and unwholesome civilisation. But as they are brought into relationship with other people, into that interaction of wills that a social context implies, childhood wildness does not grow into a Wordsworthian moral attitude. Instead their wildness becomes will operating outside a moral context. Heathcliff's return after his long absence makes Catherine 'breathless and wild'—a pointed contrast to the 'wondrously peaceful' scene on which he breaks in, like Satan into Paradise. The final conflict between her, Heathcliff and Edgar leads to Catherine's Lear-like exclamation: 'I shall get wild'; and in her ensuing delirium, wildness takes the form of yearning, through space and time, for Wuthering Heights and childhood, both identified with Heathcliff. Their last embrace is like that of wild animals. As she is buried, and as Heathcliff tries to recover her, we hear of 'the wild snow blowing outside', and as Heathcliff throws open the window to call the ghost that has appeared in Lockwood's nightmare, 'the snow and wind whirled wildly through'. After Catherine's death, the wildness of yearning passes to

Heathcliff; and it dominates his life, together with those 'wild endeavours to hold my right', as he calls his acts of revenge. As his death approaches, the adjective occurs repeatedly: his look is described as 'wild'; to the second Catherine he appears '*very much* excited and wild and glad'; and he is overheard calling 'the name of Catherine, coupled with some wild term of endearment, or suffering'. 'Wild' in the novel, then, has the force of an iterative image, and it does not carry a static connotation or value. The imaginative engagement with the vital possibilities of wildness is accompanied by the moral judgment on wildness. Catherine and Heathcliff are seen in full awareness of the ambivalence of wildness. They are also, structurally, held in a framework where healthfulness is seen as good. By dramatisation, Emily Brontë allows the impact of wildness; by the narrative framework she places it. It is the complete awareness of the ambivalence which makes *Wuthering Heights* and its wisdom unique. The ambiguity about the ultimate fates of Catherine and Heathcliff is made possible by the narrative technique: how can the more healthful people know? To some they are ghosts, people have seen them, a shepherd boy has been frightened; even Nelly Dean does not know. And so Lockwood's conclusion—for all that, with its note of 'calm of mind, all passion spent', it provides an emotional catharsis—carries a very definite ambiguity of tone:

> I sought, and soon discovered, the three head-stones on the slope next the moor—the middle one, grey, and half buried in heath—Edgar Linton's only harmonized by the turf and moss, creeping up its foot—Heathcliff's still bare.
>
> I lingered round them, under that benign sky; watched the moths fluttering among the heath, and hare-bells; listened to the soft wind breathing through the grass; and wondered how anyone could ever imagine unquiet slumbers, for the sleepers in that quiet earth.

On the background of what has gone before, and through the mouth of Lockwood, how can we take this at its face value? It is very different from the apparently similar churchyard scene, of peace after ravages, at the end of *The Mill on the Floss* which the author uses as an unequivocal summing-up of the action and its meaning. It is very different, too, from the superficially even more similar last paragraph of Goethe's *Wahlverwandtschaften*—a novel which has enough parallels to *Wuthering*

Heights in theme and details of action to suggest that Emily Brontë may have known it and, consciously or unconsciously, drawn on it:

> So ruhen die Liebenden nebeneinander. Friede schwebt über ihrer Stätte, heitere, verwandte Engelsbilder schauen vom Gewölbe auf sie herab, und welch ein freundlicher Augenblick wird es sein, wenn sie dereinst wieder zusammen erwachen.[1]

There is no irony in Goethe's conclusion; the attitude to the lovers is the same awe and idolisation with which the omniscient observer-author has treated them throughout the novel. In the final paragraph of *Wuthering Heights* we are made to ask such questions as: how does this agree with what has gone before? and, how reliable a spokesman is Lockwood? Its irony operates within the frame of the novel as a whole; the dynamism of the novel is such that each part illuminates and modifies the others, right to the last word. The passage suggests that her narrative technique is one of the most important ways in which Emily Brontë controls our vision of her material. We must therefore proceed to a closer look at that technique.

(iii)

It has often been said that the strength of the Brontës, but also their weakness, lay in their isolation: in the narrowness of their experience of life, which drove them into themselves and gave a unique kind of intensity to their writings. For no one is this more true than for Emily; yet her imagination has a quality not to be found in either of her sisters. It is revealed in what, paraphrasing T. S. Eliot, we may call the separation between the woman who feels and the mind which creates. The artistic detachment with which her imagination is combined can be seen, right from the earliest of her poems, in a keen sense of poetic form and structure; but nowhere can it be seen more clearly than in the narrative technique she created for herself.

In the two great novels of Charlotte Brontë, *Jane Eyre* and *Villette*, the narrative method is simple: a woman, looking back over her life, gives a straightforwardly autobiographical account. In *The Professor* the method is much the same: by a simple inversion of the sexes we have, as it were, the autobiography of a male governess. *Shirley* is a more ambitious attempt, perhaps inspired by *Wuthering Heights*, at breaking away from the first-person formula; much of its weakness is due to this. *Agnes Grey* uses the same technique as *Jane Eyre* and is successful within its limits. We have already seen the comparative failure of the more complicated structural devices of *The Tenant of Wildfell Hall*, and how that novel only really comes into its own in the autobiographical sections of Helen Huntingdon's diary. Emotionally, Anne is the one who most directly draws on her own untransmuted experience. Charlotte presents a more complex picture, but it is roughly true to say that she moves from the more detached in *Jane Eyre* to the more directly autobiographical in *Villette*, with *The Professor* as an early and *Shirley* as a more mature, attempt at imposing objectivity on a highly subjective content. Yet, for all the inventiveness of the plot and story of *Jane Eyre*, the emotional content is very directly lived; by the time she gets to *Villette* the experience is almost painfully personal, while here also the plot is, as in *Agnes Grey*, a mixture of direct experience and wish-fulfilment. It is significant, then, that with much the same background of experience and reading as her sisters, Emily Brontë should have been the only one to achieve a successfully sustained distancing effect, in a form as objective as that of a ballad and with a structure as complex as that of a formal epic. Both Charlotte and Anne are in their novels much closer to the personal lyric; if we are to relate them to the epic, it must be to *The Prelude* (which only Charlotte lived to read), i.e. to the Romantic epic which narrows and intensifies rather than expands and generalises. In a measure approached by neither of her sisters, Emily Brontë had the power which Coleridge describes as 'esemplastic', which dissolves, diffuses and dissipates experience in order to re-create. In writing *Wuthering Heights* she had material which was so difficult to handle, so emotionally and morally ambiguous, that only a form which could contain and control such ambiguity would do. Her creative gift guided her to just that form.

The use of two narrators, not themselves central to the action, gives an over-all sense of detachment to *Wuthering Heights*. At the same time, Emily Brontë manipulates her narrators, and her structure, to make us more, and differently, involved in some situations than in others. Incidents are so organised that we are thrown right into the world of the Heights; we wonder, with Lockwood, what it is all about; we see Lockwood's nightmare vision of the ghost of Catherine and hear Heathcliff's frantic appeals to it, before we know who Catherine is. The last few chapters take place less than a year later, as Heathcliff's revenge has nullified itself; and the use of 'flash-back' to narrate the story in between gives a sense of coherence and of intertwining which a simple, chronologically arranged, narrative would not have produced. Breaks in the narrative give structural prominence to some events over others. For example, the emphasis thrown on the birth of Hareton, Nelly Dean's 'first bonny little nursling, and the last of the ancient Earnshaw stock', by the fact that with it Nelly resumes her story after her first interruption, prepares us in some measure for the importance of Hareton in the last few chapters. Similarly, Nelly's first long break comes just after the wedding of Edgar Linton and Catherine Earnshaw, pointing this up as the inauguration of a new era; and another interruption before the last meeting of Catherine and Heathcliff adds to the dramatic impact of that scene. Also, certain episodes are structurally emphasised because they re-appear, seen from different angles, at various times. The fated excursion of Heathcliff and the first Catherine to Thrushcross Grange first appears as a 'scamper on the moors' in the childish diary which Lockwood reads in Chapter III (and which suggests the contents for his nightmare); it is then related in its proper place in the sequence of events, by Heathcliff through Nelly, in Chapter VI. It comes back again in Chapter XII when Catherine's delirious dream of being back in childhood, and the awakening therefrom, seem to bring home to her the real significance of that first meeting between Heights and Grange:

> 'Supposing at twelve years old, I had been wrenched from the Heights, and every early association, and my all in all, as Heathcliff was at that time, and been converted, at a stroke into Mrs. Linton, the lady of Thrushcross Grange, and the wife of a stranger; an exile, and outcast, thenceforth, from what had been my world.'

Here an event accumulates meaning as we see it acting on different minds at different perspectives of time. The story of the evening after Catherine's funeral gradually grows richer in meaning as different characters, almost in a jig-saw puzzle fashion, add their particular experience of that evening. To Nelly, in Chapter XVII, it merely meant a change in the weather, from spring back to winter; to Isabella, later in the same chapter, it meant the wild fight at the Heights as Hindley tried to prevent Heathcliff from entering the house. Finally, in Chapter XXIX, more than seventeen years later, Heathcliff tells

Nelly how that evening in the churchyard he had tried to disinter Cathy, until suddenly 'I felt that Cathy was there, not under me, but on the earth', and how he came rushing to the Heights because he felt sure he would see Cathy there. The fight, to him, was only a small obstacle in the race to catch up with Cathy. In this way, events became *motifs* which weave in and out, interrelating structure and meaning, and making both dynamic.

The two narrators, Nelly Dean and Lockwood, are effectively contrasted and complement each other: Lockwood never becomes a character as such, but enough of his background of silly love-affairs at seaside resorts and autumns spent 'devastating the moors' is filled in for the reader to sense where he is perceptive and where he has been dulled by social habit. He is given exactly the right tone so that we approach Wuthering Heights from the most effective distance, through the perception of a man who can think the Heights 'a perfect misanthropist's Heaven' and call Heathcliff 'a capital fellow'. His tired clichés—such as the one about rural retirement,

> 'many could not imagine the existence of happiness in a life of such complete exile from the world as you spend, Mr. Heathcliff'—

contrast in their loquacious ineptness with the mysterious taciturnity of the inhabitants of the Heights. For this same Lockwood to find a ghostly waif wailing outside his window in the snowstorm, and to pull its wrist on to the broken window-pane and rub it, 'till the blood ran down and soaked the bed-clothes', means an initiation into a world of nightmare and the supernatural, of horror and cruelty, which we apprehend as the more effective for the size of the gap between it and Lockwood's own version of normality. Though in some ways his function is that of Coleridge's Wedding-Guest, he does not easily become a sadder and a wiser man. His outsiderness remains with him when in the middle of January 1802, after having heard Nelly Dean's account of events up to that time, he can still think of the second Catherine in such blatantly complacent terms as:

> Living among clowns and misanthropists, she probably cannot appreciate a better class of people, when she meets them.

In this chapter, as in the early ones, he comes in rather heavily for that irony which critics have denied Emily Brontë:

What a realisation of something more romantic than a fairy tale it would have been for Mrs Linton Heathcliff, had she and I struck up an attachment . . . and migrated together, into the stirring atmosphere of the town.

The absurdity of even the second Catherine being attached to Lockwood and transplanted into 'the stirring atmosphere of the town' should convince us, if we have not already been convinced, that Emily Brontë is using Lockwood very deliberately as a foil to the Wuthering Heights world. He has to listen to the account of Heathcliff's death and witness with his own eyes the growth of love between Hareton and Catherine before he becomes truly sadder and wiser; but even then it is worth remembering that it is he, the limitations of whose understanding of the goings on in this world have been repeatedly before us, who wonders 'how anyone could ever imagine unquiet slumbers, for the sleepers in that quiet earth'. Looking at Lockwood makes it very clear to us that this novel is dramatised, so that not any one statement or angle of vision, but the total interwoven pattern of the whole, is the vision of its creator.

Because we see Lockwood's perception as so often blatantly faulty, we are the more prepared to trust Nelly Dean where she is perceptive. The plot effortlessly puts her in the centre of comprehension. She has no character of her own, for that would dissipate attention away from the main characters, but she stands in some kind of naturally affectionate relationship with all of them: she has played with Hindley, comforted Heathcliff, counselled the first Catherine, nursed both Hareton and the second Catherine, and been for years the sole adult companion of Edgar Linton. It is also remarkable how, without any straining of credibility, Nelly Dean is actually a participant, however passive at times, in all the crucial scenes in the book. She thus has a narrative focus quite different from that of Lockwood, who, except for his nightmare, is never more than an observer where Nelly is never less than a catalyst. For the greater part of the book, although he is technically the narrator, Lockwood is only a transparent window-pane rather than a modifying lens. As he tells us, he uses Nelly's own words; and the whole pattern of the narrative—the vivid individual scenes with only the most economical linkage in between—is justified as a reflection of Nelly's mind. Near the end of Chapter VII Nelly rebukes herself for being too detailed and intends to skip some of her story, using what sounds very much like a conventional novelist's trick: 'You must allow me to leap over some three years; during that space, Mrs. Earnshaw . . .' But there Lockwood interrupts her, relating Nelly's own technique of narration to the very nature of life and people in these regions: 'They *do* live more in earnest, more in themselves, and less in surface change, and frivolous external things.' Thus, in an aside, Emily Brontë points us to the identity of her material and her technique, laying, as it were, a realistic-regional foundation for the extraordinary self-containedness of the *Wuthering Heights* world. Lockwood's articulation here of his brief experience of these people—

> I could fancy a love for life here almost possible; and I was a fixed unbeliever in any love of a year's standing—

points explicitly what the story of Catherine and Heathcliff (which he has not yet been told) is going to point implicitly.

It would be wrong, however, to suggest that Nelly dominates the individual scenes. For most of the time she is only a tape-recorder, giving back what others have told her: as when we have the first glimpse of the Linton family by Heathcliff telling Nelly what he and Cathy saw through the window, or when Isabella tells her, first by letter and then by word of mouth, of the struggles at the Heights between her and Heathcliff or Hindley and Heathcliff. Thus, in the latter case, the scenes of violence in Isabella's account of life at the Heights come to us, not as gratuitous coarseness, but implicitly as a measure of the 'moral teething' she, the delicate young lady, has gone through at the hands of Heathcliff. The implicit callousness in one who has more than condoned the fight, and relates its details with such relish, is sufficient judgment on Heathcliff's educative effect. At other times, Nelly is just a clear window-pane through which we see the action unimpeded. Therefore the full contrast between the Heathcliff–Cathy world and that of Linton is allowed to hit us directly, as when Heathcliff's agonised words of love and reproach to Catherine on his return are interrupted by Linton's worries about the tea getting cold; or when Heathcliff contrasts his own feelings for Catherine with Edgar's—

> 'Catherine has a heart as deep as I have; the sea could be as readily contained in that horse-trough, as her whole affection be monopolized

by him—Tush! He is scarcely a degree dearer to her than her dog, or her horse—It is not in him to be loved like me, how can she love in him what he has not?'—

and Isabella replies: 'Catherine and Edgar are as fond of each other as any two people can be.' Nelly's transparency here gives us the chance to see each speech as true on its own level and, dramatically, to sense the world of difference between these two perceptions. Even after she has run away from the Heights, Isabella can speak of that love in the shocked phraseology of the drawing-room:

'Catherine had an awfully perverted taste to esteem him so dearly, knowing him so well.'

Yet, significantly, when she talks about what Heathcliff has done to herself, her language changes:

'I gave him my heart, and he took and pinched it to death; and flung it back to me;'

and, as her metaphors become of the Heathcliff kind, the contrast between this and her previous mode of speech enacts the merging of the two different worlds:

'Pulling out the nerves with red hot pincers, requires more coolness than knocking on the head.'

She, who had previously known no passion stronger than a romantic heart-flutter, has been made to learn about hate, but not about love.

Though Nelly Dean is contrasted with Lockwood as the insider against the outsider, she is herself placed on a sliding scale of involvement with the world of the novel, and this scale is used to measure experiences. At one extreme we see Nelly as unsympathetically void of understanding. In her delirium, Catherine is given a speech in which the movements of a wandering mind are powerfully enacted:

'That's a turkey's,' she murmured to herself; 'and this is a wild duck's; and this is a pigeon's. Ah, they put pigeons' feathers in the pillows—no wonder I couldn't die! Let me take care to throw it on the floor when I lie down. And here's a moor-cock's; and this—I should know it among a thousand—it's a lapwing's. Bonny bird; wheeling over our heads in the middle of the moor. It wanted to get to its nest, for the clouds touched the swells, and it felt rain coming. This feather was picked up from the heath, the bird was not shot—we saw its nest in the winter, full of little skeletons. Heathcliff set a trap over it, and the old ones dare not come. I made him promise he'd never shoot a lapwing, after that, and he didn't. Yes, here are more! Did he shoot my lapwings, Nelly? Are they red, any of them? Let me look.'

This is followed by Nelly's, 'Give over with that baby-work!' To have let Nelly's deficient perception here colour Catherine's speech would have been like having a Third Gentleman narrate Ophelia's mad-scenes. Nelly's incomprehension is part of the exile under which Catherine is suffering, at the same time as it measures the uniqueness of Catherine's experience.

At the other extreme, Nelly is, at least half, drawn into the experience of her interlocutor. The use of her varying quality of involvement is particularly interesting in Chapters XXXIII and XXXIV, when Heathcliff is rapidly being killed by nervous exhaustion, lack of food and sleep—or killing himself by sheer desire to join Catherine. At the outset of these days Nelly is still very much the outsider; the inadequacy of her comment on Heathcliff's tremendous speech about seeing Cathy everywhere—'in every cloud, in every tree—filling the air at night, and caught by glimpses in every object, by day'—is reminiscent of Lockwood's clichés:

He might have had a monomania on the subject of his departed idol; but on every other point his wits were as sound as mine.

Just a page later, her position as commentator has shifted to the theological one, usually occupied by Joseph: 'I was inclined to believe, as he said Joseph did, that conscience had turned his heart to an earthly hell.' But under pressure Nelly's descriptions match the speech of Heathcliff. Her view of him—

'his frame shivering, not as one shivers with chill or weakness, but as a tight-stretched cord vibrates—a strong thrilling, rather than trembling'—

is a deepening of, rather than a foil to, his self-analysis:

'I'm too happy, and yet I'm not happy enough. My soul's bliss kills my body, but does not satisfy itself.'

Yet it is typical of the technique of these chapters that the paragraph which leads up to that description of Heathcliff begins: 'I set his plate, to keep warm, on the fender.' For through Nelly the other-worldly movement of Heathcliff is set in an utterly concrete everyday world of meals, daily chores and mild, smoky, northern spring. The clash between these two worlds, and Heathcliff's ability to move between them, before one engulfs him, is seen in the episode where Nelly bustles in with a candle and supper, to be taken aback by what appears to her 'not Mr Heathcliff, but a goblin. . . . Those deep black eyes! That smile, and ghastly paleness!' Horrified, she lets the candle out, only to be scolded by Heathcliff, 'in his familiar voice' and in familiar, practical terms. Nelly is partly drawn into the Heathcliff world by that shock and by her subsequent semi-nightmare, in which there is a fine blending of the Gothic kind of terror (she wonders if he might be a 'ghoul or a vampire'), the real mystery that lies around Heathcliff's descent, and the homely awkwardness of social embarrassment in having to dictate an inscription for the gravestone of a man with no surname and no birthdate. She is drawn in, it should be noticed, as was Lockwood at the beginning of the novel: through a nightmare. But, being Nelly Dean, she finds that 'dawn restored me to common sense'.

These chapters show particularly clearly how, by rendering the story through the mind and mouth of Nelly Dean (avoiding by dramatisation the drag of a crippling convention), Emily Brontë has found a way of making the incredible credible—or, rather, of creating a unique kind of union between the incredible and the credible, which is neither sentimental nor Gothic. Though Heathcliff's death does not even have the pathological motivation of Catherine's, it does not occur to the reader to question it in its context. This is because of the way in which a basically non-realistic event has been made part of a realistic world where the daily business goes on as usual, where we see meals set on the table and hear Heathcliff on one of the last mornings of his life instructing Joseph about some farming business, giving 'clear, minute directions concerning the matter discussed'.

As Nelly's perception modifies the texture of the novel in those last chapters, so, at other points in the novel, it is through her that the unbearable is made bearable. For example, Hindley's drunken violence, which must have been one of the pieces of 'coarseness' objected to by contemporary reviewers, is given an almost surrealistic effect by Nelly's telling of it.

> He entered, vociferating oaths dreadful to hear; and caught me in the act of stowing his son away in the kitchen cupboard. . . .
>   'There, I've found it out at last!' cried Hindley, pulling me back by the skin of my neck, like a dog. . . . 'But, with the help of Satan, I shall make you swallow the carving-knife, Nelly! . . .'
>   'But I don't like the carving-knife, Mr. Hindley,' I answered, 'it has been cutting red herrings—I'd rather be shot if you please.'

And so, when he forces the point of the knife between her teeth, she spits it out, affirming that 'it tasted detestably'. There is something Jacobean in the grotesqueness of the horror here, very different from the brawl scenes in *The Tenant of Wildfell Hall*, which are exclusively terrifying and disgusting. The same undertone of grim human comedy saves from melodrama the conclusion of this scene, where his drunken father drops baby Hareton down the stair-well and Heathcliff appears at the right moment to save him, instinctively and, on afterthought, much against his own will and interest; it is clinched by Nelly's image:

> A miser who has parted with a lucky lottery ticket for five shillings, and finds the next day he has lost in the bargain five thousand pounds, could not show a blanker countenance than he did on beholding the figure of Mr. Earnshaw above.

Built into Emily Brontë's narrative technique, then, is a particularly keen awareness that, in Joseph Conrad's words, 'there is a quality in events which is apprehended differently by different minds or even by the same mind at different times'.[1] Perhaps the most important aspect of this awareness is that throughout the progress of the story it enables her to hold in suspension opposite moral attitudes. Lockwood has not got much of a moral existence, but Nelly Dean has a kind of homely and orthodox piety, so that nearly always in her dealings with the first Catherine and Heathcliff, we find one version of the moral bearings of a situation juxtaposed with another. A clear example is the scene where Cathy is trying to explain to Nelly why, though she has promised to marry Edgar Linton, she feels in her soul and in her heart that she is wrong. She wants to tell Nelly of a dream she has had, one of those which she says have 'gone through and through me, like wine through water, and altered the colour of my mind'. But Nelly is 'superstitious about dreams' and refuses to listen, so, 'apparently taking up another subject', Catherine proceeds to say that, if she were in heaven, she would be 'extremely miserable'. To this, Nelly has a categorical enough answer:

> 'Because you are not fit to go there. . . . All sinners would be miserable in heaven.'

To Catherine's mind this explanation is meaningless; and as she goes on to explain in her own terms, we see that she has not, in fact, taken up another subject. The dream of being in heaven which she now relates is not that fearful one which never does get told, but it serves equally well to 'give you a feeling of how I feel':

> '. . . heaven did not seem to be my home; and I broke my heart with weeping to come back to earth; and the angels were so angry that they flung me out, into the middle of the heath on the top of Wuthering Heights; where I woke sobbing for joy. . . . I've no more business to marry Edgar Linton than I have to be in heaven.'

Imaginatively it is, of course, Catherine's side that is more fully realised: the side where Heaven and Hell have reality only in terms of togetherness and separation, and where sin lies only in a betrayal of that togetherness—as Heathcliff says in the scene which is thematically the follow-up of Nelly's and Catherine's conversation:

> 'Yes, you may kiss me, and cry; and wring out my kisses and tears. They'll blight you—they'll damn you. You loved me—then what *right* had you to leave me? What right—answer me—for the poor fancy you felt for Linton? Because misery, and degradation, and death, and nothing that God or satan could inflict would have parted us, *you*, of your own will, did it. I have not broken your heart— *you* have broken it. . . . Do I want to live? What kind of living will it be when you—oh, God! would *you* like to live with your soul in the grave?'

This is the kind of a-moral valuation which many would make Emily Brontë's; and therefore it is worth noticing how even in this most harrowing of all the scenes, this attitude is set against the orthodoxy of Nelly and made to interact with it. At the end of Chapter X, just before we enter on the stage of fatal conflict, Nelly makes one of her rare generalising comments:

> My heart invariably cleaved to the master's, in preference to Catherine's side; with reason, I imagined, for he was kind, and trustful, and honourable: and she—she could not be called the *opposite*, yet, she seemed to allow herself such wide latitude, that I had little faith in her principles, and still less sympathy for her feelings;

and at the beginning of the scene between Catherine and Heathcliff in Chapter XV, those are still the terms in which she sees them:

> Well might Catherine deem that heaven would be a land of exile to her, unless, with her mortal body, she cast away her mortal character also.

But the passionate action before her is made to go through Nelly and modify the colour of *her* mind: in what she has to say there is a powerful mingling of her world and theirs, of her comment and their action:

> He flung himself into the nearest seat, and on my approaching hurriedly to ascertain if she had fainted, he gnashed at me, and foamed like a mad dog, and gathered her to him with greedy jealousy. I did not feel as if I were in the company of a creature of my own species.

Catherine's words now seem to go through Nelly 'like wine through water'; Catherine's emotional certainty that she is about to leave her 'shattered prison' only to 'escape into that glorious world' has enlarged Nelly's moral imagination, and so, as she looks at Catherine's dead body she echoes, 'instinctively', Catherine's words:

> 'Incomparably beyond, and above us all! Whether still on earth or now in heaven, her spirit is at home with God!'

Chapter XVI is, in a sense, a moral inquest on Catherine Earnshaw, with various angles of perception allowed interplay. First there is Nelly Dean's spontaneous, but fully conscious, suspension of her usual orthodox morality:

I see a repose that neither earth nor hell can break; and I feel an assurance of the endless and shadowless hereafter—the Eternity they have entered—where life is boundless in its duration, and love in its sympathy, and joy in its fulness. I noticed on that occasion how much selfishness there is even in a love like Mr. Linton's, when he so regretted Catherine's blessed release!

To be sure one might have doubted, after the wayward and impatient existence she had led, whether she merited a haven of peace at last. One might doubt in seasons of cold reflection, but not then, in the presence of her corpse. It asserted its own tranquillity, which seemed a pledge of equal quiet to its former inhabitant.

Cecil quotes this speech as an example of Emily Brontë's, and her characters', view of death as a fulfilment of one's own nature; but the point of it, in the context where it belongs, is surely that it shows Nelly Dean so affected by Catherine's death as to be prepared to grant even this wayward creature a Christian Heaven. Lockwood, getting the experience, as it were, at second hand, remains unaffected. When Nelly asks him: 'Do you believe such people *are* happy in the other world, sir?', his refusal to answer the question, because it strikes him as 'something heterodox', is bound to seem narrowly priggish. But Nelly Dean has the last word in this conversation, and in her words conventional morality and the imaginative impact of the actual experience meet, interact, and culminate in an ultimate suspension of judgment, the ambivalence of which reminds us of the final paragraph in the novel:

Retracing the course of Catherine Linton, I fear we have no right to think she is: but we'll leave her with her Maker.

Upon this moment of doubtful equipoise follows Nelly's interview with Heathcliff, who has been going through his own agony in the garden; and between the two attitudes here contrasted, there is no possible reconciliation. Nelly rather primly tells Heathcliff that Catherine is

'Gone to heaven, I hope, where we may, every one, join her, if we take due warning, and leave our evil ways to follow good!'

Heathcliff's answer starts as a searing attempt at sarcasm and works gradually up to such personal agony as to leave us with a feeling of Nelly's inadequacy here:

> 'Did *she* take due warning then? . . . Did she die like a saint? . . . May she wake in torment! . . . Catherine Earnshaw, may you not rest, as long as I am living! You said I killed you—haunt me then! . . . Be with me always—take any form—drive me mad! only *do* not leave me in this abyss, where I cannot find you! Oh, God! it is unutterable! I *cannot* live without my life! I *cannot* live without my soul!'

In the total pattern of judgments within the novel, this must be seen with the two opposed versions of Catherine's fate: Edgar Linton, who in his love and goodness has no doubt that she has gone 'to a better world', and Joseph, 'the wearisomest self-righteous Pharisee that ever ransacked a Bible to rake the promises to himself and fling the curses to his neighbours', who is the first person in the novel to mention the first Catherine when he snarls at the second that she will 'goa raight tuh t'divil, like yer mother afore ye!' And, finally, the ghost of Lockwood's nightmare gives strange substance to Heathcliff's assurance that his prayer—to be haunted—has been answered.

A similar interaction of judgments, though narrowed into a shorter space, as he dies so near the end of the book, takes place around Heathcliff's death. To Joseph there is of course no doubt that 'th'divil's harried off his soul'. Nelly, who has seen 'that frightful, life-like gaze of exultation' in his eyes, is in two minds: she mourns him on an ordinary human level, sees to his burial and hopes piously that Heathcliff 'sleeps as soundly' as Catherine and Edgar. Yet, she tells in the same breath of rumours of 'those who speak to having met him near the church, and on the moor, and even within this house', and of how she herself is afraid of being out in the dark now. Hareton who weeps filial tears over Heathcliff's corpse and kisses that 'sarcastic savage face', remains the strongest defender, but this reflects on his 'generous heart', rather than on Heathcliff, and Lockwood implicitly contrasts him and the second Catherine with the limbo of that other pair, by saying:

> '*They* are afraid of nothing. . . . Together they would brave satan and all his legions.'

I have spoken at length about the interplay of judgments on the central action, for it cannot, I think, be said too strongly that conclusive evaluation of character and action must be looked for not in any one speech or passage, however impressive, nor through the mind of any one character, however compelling; it must be provided by the novel as a whole. As within a small compass in many of Emily Brontë's poems, so within the novel we have opposite attitudes and judgments played off against each other; and only the structure of the work as a whole gives anything like a conclusive evaluation.

We are left at the end with the fearful uncertainty of the fates of Catherine and Heathcliff, and with a sense of the costs to themselves and to others and, possibly, to their immortal souls, of a love like theirs. Set against this is the certainty of the love which has sprung up between the second Catherine and Hareton and of the good it has already brought them. The last few chapters have a dual movement: as Heathcliff approaches death (and Catherine?), Hareton and the second Catherine approach each other. The two movements are not at any point fused, but remain counterpointed; the young people do not really exist to Heathcliff, except as two pairs of eyes which he cannot bear to meet because they are so like the first Catherine's. The texture of the writing suggests a different kind of imaginative realisation of Heathcliff's death from that brought to bear on the idyllic and domestic love of Catherine and Hareton. There is an unusually abstract style in the description of how Catherine rouses Hareton from savagery:

> His honest, warm, and intelligent nature shook off rapidly the clouds of ignorance, and degradation in which it had been bred; and Catherine's sincere commendations acted as a spur to his industry. His brightening mind brightened his features, and added spirit and nobility to their aspect.

Not only in style but also in thought this passage could come from practically any of the many Victorian novels in which education is a theme. Indeed, at this stage *Wuthering Heights* becomes a novel about education. Catherine teaches Hareton and thus brings out the suppressed good in him; their wooing, as that of most of the protagonists in Charlotte Brontë's novels, is done in terms of the school-room:

'Con-*trary*!' said a voice, as sweet as a silver bell—'That for the third time, you dunce! I'm not going to tell you, again—Recollect, or I'll pull your hair!'

'Contrary, then,' answered another, in deep but softened tones. 'And now, kiss me, for minding so well.'

Lockwood, who overhears this dialogue, also sees the symbolical sight of 'her light shining ringlets blending, at intervals, with his brown locks, as she bent to superintend his studies'. It is easy to wince at the sweetness of this, or of Catherine sticking primroses in Hareton's plate of porridge, when one contrasts it with the passions of the first Catherine—symbolised by that other mingling of light and dark hair: in the locket that goes into the grave with her—and with Heathcliff's words: 'My soul's bliss kills my body, but does not satisfy itself.' In the first pair, love was seen as a superhuman passion, as an affinity existing outside every social or moral category; in the second, the direction of the lovers' feelings is defined in the human and socially weighted word 'esteem' (a key-word in Charlotte Brontë's vocabulary of love):

> . . . both their minds tending to the same point—one loving and desiring to esteem; and the other loving and desiring to be esteemed —they contrived in the end, to reach it.

If we went by the imaginative quality of the writing only, and by our emotional response to it, we would see the love of the first Catherine and Heathcliff as the great positive statement of the novel, with the second generation as a feeble gesture towards a happy ending and, as many critics have complained, not an answer to the first. But in terms of the structure and the pattern of the whole, the love of the second Catherine and Hareton *is* an answer, as much as the hopeful and pious words of the 'sweet, trustful child' is an answer to his father's dark and troubled dreams of 'moor, and misty hill' in Emily Brontë's poem 'The winter wind is loud and wild' (November 1844). Natural imagery emphasises the positive, life-affirming quality of the answer, for while Heathcliff, always connected with winter and sterile aspects of nature, is dying, the young people are busy planting flowers at the Heights. Ultimately, then, the novel affirms the domesticated virtues of man as a kind and social creature; it develops towards the Brontë version of the good life (which we have seen in the case of Anne Brontë and shall see much more of in the case of Charlotte) which envisages an alleviation of suffering and loneliness through love that is kindness, affection, stronger teaching weaker, in a domesticated context. Emily Brontë is here very close to most of her contemporaries' vision of the good life. What distinguishes her and makes her novel unique is her powerful vision of the other life as well.

(iv)

If the moral consciousness which is part of her total vision makes Emily Brontë more *of* her period than we might at first think, the structural and stylistic means whereby she develops that vision set her apart. If we speak of the novelist in Emily Brontë being a poet, we are also speaking of the way in which, in her novel, all the parts are subordinated to the whole. In what follows I want to examine more closely this aspect of *Wuthering Heights*. The typical Victorian novel is large and leisurely, incorporating a great deal of material for its own intrinsic interest: descriptions of nature, historical events, social life, and so on. In Anne Brontë's first novel, the simplicity of the story and theme gives the novel a *conte*-like unity of form, but when she tries to cover a larger canvas in *The Tenant of Wildfell Hall*, her structure becomes dangerously unbalanced. Charlotte Brontë tries in *Shirley* to give the kind of social panorama which *Jane Eyre*, in its concentration on its heroine, does not have, but her curates and her Luddite elements do not become very integral parts of a whole. Even *Villette* has passages of slack writing, where one feels that she is just trying to bring the story forward. What is outstanding about *Wuthering Heights* is the sense of form displayed by Emily Brontë—a sense which, before her, had been shown only by Jane Austen. Like Jane Austen, she achieves a structure which, in every part, is the visible embodiment of the theme, by the exclusion from the novel of anything not necessary, anything that would dissipate concentration. No more than in Jane Austen do we, in *Wuthering Heights*, have any references to the historical period of the novel, to the goings on at the time in the world at large. But here the similarity stops, for what Jane Austen includes— 'parties, picnics, and country dances' (Virginia Woolf)—is just what Emily Brontë excludes.

The concentration on the world limited geographically by Wuthering Heights to the north and Thrushcross Grange to the south-west,

128

with the chapel, churchyard and Gimmerton brook between them, is complete. We never follow anybody outside it. Hindley just reappears on his father's death, with a wife whom he has found somehow, somewhere. For three and a half years Heathcliff is just gone, and nobody is told where he has been or what he has done. There is not one word about where Isabella and Heathcliff go on their ghastly honeymoon; we pick up their story again with a characteristic sentence: 'The sun set behind the Grange, as we turned on to the moors', and all we hear of it from Isabella is that her heart 'returned to Thrushcross Grange in twenty-four hours after I left it'. Isabella herself vanishes, except for the barest account of facts, as soon as she leaves the Grange carrying the unborn Linton. The events in the novel stem from the moment that old Mr. Earnshaw brings Heathcliff into that world, carried under his coat from the streets of Liverpool; the central conflict from the moment that the first Catherine and Heathcliff peep in through the parlour window at the Grange. The novel is resolved with the second Catherine and Hareton going to live at Thrushcross Grange, leaving the Heights to 'the use of such ghosts as choose to inhabit it'. There is no sense of a geographical or social world outside this—it never occurs, for example, to Edgar Linton that his daughter might find a husband other than Linton Heathcliff.

For all its exclusiveness, this world is also inclusive. It has everything that matters: birth, death, love, hatred, nature, the seasons. And so it gets a larger than naturalistic significance, becomes a microcosm of the human condition. Despite the Yorkshire dialect and the moorland setting, it is not really a regional novel—or, rather, its regionalism is a means, not an end. This is not to say that the world of the novel exists only on a symbolical level, for its every incident has a perfectly realistic plot validity as well as a symbolical validity. Thus, for example, the narrowing down of the social world is one for which the people themselves are responsible. In the early chapters there are hints at the existence of neighbours (they gossip when Hindley brings home a wife) and some social intercourse (there is a visit of the Gimmerton band who 'go the rounds of all the respectable houses ... every Christmas'). Hindley's behaviour after his wife's death makes the Earnshaws socially unrespectable; all the servants, except Nelly and Joseph, vanish; also 'the curate dropped calling, and nobody decent came near us, at last'. After Catherine's marriage, Heathcliff's return sets the seal on the social seclusion of the Heights. A similar development takes place at the Grange. The Lintons, to start with, have a place in society: old Mr. Linton is a magistrate, and on his death Edgar takes over his duties; but after the death of Catherine, Edgar, too, becomes a recluse, resigns his office, and the second Catherine, until she goes to the Heights, has never entered another building than her own home and Gimmerton chapel. Yet, there is none of the trivia of social visiting, business, etc., that was the stock-in-trade of the conventional novelist. (This is where film and stage-versions of *Wuthering Heights* tend to commit one of their greatest outrages, showing us a ball at the Grange or letting Edgar and Catherine talk of their recent visit to the seaside.) Everything not bearing on the main action is as ruthlessly pruned as in a Racinian tragedy, and the result are characters who do not have professions but feelings, who do not *do*, but *are*.

Related to this is the exclusion of all the trivia of plot machinery. We are not told *why* Old Earnshaw has to go to Liverpool: the only important function of that marathon walk is to bring Heathcliff to Wuthering Heights. Cathy 'by some means' gets messages to Edgar where a conventional novelist would have expatiated on the means used (Charlotte Smith in *The Old Manor House* spends the best part of the novel working out ways for her young lovers to have chaste midnight meetings). The correspondence here is inessential, it is getting Edgar to the Heights that matters. On the other hand, the clandestine correspondence between the second Catherine and Linton, via the boy who carries the milk, is carefully described, for here it is an important mesh in the net that Heathcliff is weaving to catch Catherine and revenge himself on the Lintons.

Together with the exclusion of irrelevant details, there is an extraordinarily meticulous attention to such details and facts as matter. It is here that the deliberate nature of Emily Brontë's workmanship is most clearly revealed. In his interesting and useful pamphlet, *The Structure of Wuthering Heights*, C. P. Sanger has shown the accuracy of every detail of timing, pedigree and legal procedure and arrived at the conclusion that the structure is truly remarkable for the degree to which it seems to have been artificially constructed, with minute attention paid to details of apparent irrelevance.[1] Such a detail, to take only one example from outside the important aspects covered by Sanger, is the embalming effect of the soil in Gimmerton churchyard.

We first hear about it, very unobtrusively, in Lockwood's account of his dream about the interminable sermon in the chapel; later on it is a material fact in the preservation of Catherine's dead body for eighteen years: Heathcliff finds that her face is 'hers yet'.

Careful workmanship is shown, too, in the way apparently irrelevant details are woven together with images and incidents to form a developing symbolical pattern. The first hint that an elopement has taken place is Nelly's discovery of 'Miss Isabella's springer, Fanny, suspended to a handkerchief, and nearly at its last gasp'. In Chapter XIV Heathcliff tells Nelly how the first thing he did when eloping with Isabella was

'to hang up her little dog; and when she pleaded for it, the first words I uttered, were a wish that I had the hanging of every being belonging to her'.

As often in the novel, an incident is shown us through the eyes of first one person, then another, its significance gradually expanding. This particular episode marks the sudden disillusioning of Isabella, who, the moment she abandons herself to Heathcliff, loses her romantic infatuation and discovers what his real feelings for her are. Thematically, it echoes back to the image used by Catherine in trying to talk Isabella out of her growing infatuation: 'I'd as soon put that little canary into the park on a winter's day, as recommend you to bestow your heart on him.' Isabella's world is the cosy and artificial world of the cage-bird, or the lap-dog; Heathcliff, as Catherine knows, is a 'fierce, pitiless, wolfish man'. Isabella wilfully and disastrously blinds herself to the incompatibility of the wild and the tame. So the irony is the more powerful when the dog-image comes back in Heathcliff's words the first time we see him and Isabella together after their marriage; and now it is applied directly to Isabella:

'Now, was it not the depth of absurdity—of genuine idiocy, for that pitiful, slavish, mean-minded brach to dream that I could love her? . . . I've sometimes relented, from pure lack of invention, in my experiments on what she could endure, and still creep shamefully cringing back!'

Later, the son of this marriage is seen by Nelly as a frightened and fawning dog before his father. And another incident, at first sight a vignette of unnecessary gruesomeness, falls into place here: Isabella's last glimpse of Wuthering Heights, as she finally escapes from Heathcliff, is Hareton 'who was hanging a litter of puppies from a chairback in the doorway'. Presumably these puppies were not as lucky as Isabella's own dog. It would be absurd to say that these details add up to a symbol which clearly stands for something else: that is not how the symbolism in the novel works. On the other hand they do act as structural unifiers—one action reminding us of another—at the same time as they define and universalise oppositions between characters and their behaviour; their effect is both dynamic and complex.

In looking at this particular pattern of happenings and images, we have already touched on one of the main structural devices in the novel: its use of opposites and of repetition. In her poems Emily Brontë often achieves an eighteenth-century kind of balance and control through the use of antithesis. Even such an ecstatic poem as 'Aye, there it is! It wakes to-night' is held within a firm and simple structure, ending on an antithesis:

> Thus truly when that breast is cold
> Thy prisoned soul shall rise,
> The dungeon mingle with the mould—
> The captive with the skies;

and quite early (November, 1838) she controls a Gondal poem of passionate love-hatred ('Light up thy halls!') by the same means:

> Unconquered in my soul the Tyrant rules me still;
> *Life* bows to my control, but *Love* I cannot kill!

The same habit of mind, it would seem, is reflected in what we might call the skeleton of *Wuthering Heights*, in the opposition between the Heights and the Grange. The antithesis is repeated in terms of locality as well as of the people respectively identified with that locality, so that the whole action could be noted down in outline as a series of clashes between opposites. This is probably why it is so tempting to read the novel as a storm-calm allegory; but at this point, on the evidence of the poems as well as the novel, one ought to remember, as Eliot reminds us in his essay on Baudelaire, that a highly organised and restrained external form in a work of art may reflect a *wish* for inner order rather than an *achievement* of such order. The schematic structure of *Wuthering Heights* gives Emily Brontë the means to explore human material about which she has ambivalent feelings, while at the same time holding it in firm control. Again, the sets of opposites do not add up to a simple contrast; they intertwine into a complex pattern. To begin with, as the windy Heights on the moors are contrasted with the Grange, sheltered in the leafy valley, so the Earnshaws are contrasted with the Lintons. Interior decoration is made symbolical here, as the farm house with its stone floor,

> ranks of immense pewter dishes . . . towering row after row, in a vast oak dresser . . . the chairs, high-backed, primitive structures, painted green: one or two heavy black ones lurking in the shade,

is opposed to the description of the Grange, in which poetry is made out of early-Victorian tastes in a way comparable to Mick's dream of 'teal-blue, copper and parchment linoleum squares' in Pinter's *The Caretaker*:

> a splendid place carpeted with crimson, and crimson-covered chairs and tables, and a pure white ceiling bordered by gold, a shower of glass-drops hanging in silver chains from the centre, and shimmering with little soft tapers.

The Earnshaws have dark eyes and complexion, the Lintons are fair and blue-eyed. The Earnshaws ride to church in winter, the Lintons roll up in the 'family carriage, smothered in cloaks and furs'. With Catherine's attraction to that soft and bright world of the Grange, there develops the opposition of Heathcliff and Edgar, repeatedly contrasted in appearance, manners and character. As Heathcliff goes out and Edgar comes in, the contrast, Nelly thinks, resembled

> what you see in exchanging a bleak, hilly, coal country, for a beautiful fertile valley.

And the first crisis in the book is pivoted on Catherine's analysis of the two kinds of love she has for Edgar and Heathcliff, respectively:

> 'My love for Linton is like the foliage in the woods: Time will change it, I'm well aware, as winter changes the trees—my love for Heathcliff resembles the eternal rocks beneath—a source of little visible delight but necessary. Nelly, I *am* Heathcliff!'

The geographical opposition between Heights and Grange has here developed into natural imagery which defines character opposition. Despite her knowledge that

> 'whatever our souls are made of, his and mine are the same, and Linton's is as different as a moonbeam from lightning, or frost from fire,'

Catherine marries Edgar, and the quality of her relationship with the Lintons is defined by the image of 'the honeysuckles embracing the thorn'. Heathcliff comes back, and in revenge woos Isabella; and these two are the next pair of opposites. Isabella thinks Heathcliff is 'a rough diamond' when Catherine knows he is 'an arid wilderness of furze and whinstone'. To Heathcliff Isabella is 'a strange repulsive animal'; to Cathy, offering Isabella to Heathcliff would be like 'offering Satan a lost soul'. In the confrontation between Heathcliff and Edgar which leads to Catherine's fatal illness, Edgar is in Heathcliff's eyes 'a lamb' which 'threatens like a bull'—'the slavering, shivering thing you preferred to me'. When Edgar asks Catherine to choose between him and Heathcliff, Catherine contrasts herself with him: 'Your veins are full of ice-water—but mine are boiling, and the sight of such chilliness makes them dance.' In the delirium that follows this scene, Catherine recalls the Heights–Grange opposition, as she frets for the moors:

> 'And that wind, sounding in the firs by the lattice. Do let me feel it —it comes straight down the moor—do let me have one breath!'

Out of the two sets of opposites are born the second Catherine and Linton Heathcliff; and much of the second half of the novel is balanced on the opposition, yet relentless bringing together (in which Edgar Linton in his goodness and Heathcliff in his wicked scheming are both agents), of these two. Like her mother, the second Catherine is aware of the opposition, and in a famous passage she is made to develop the antithesis in natural imagery:

> 'One time . . . we were near quarrelling. He said the pleasantest manner of spending a hot July day was lying from morning till evening on a bank of heath in the middle of the moors, with the bees humming dreamily about among the bloom, and the larks singing high up over head, and the blue sky, and bright sun shining steadily

and cloudlessly. That was his most perfect idea of heaven's happiness—mine was rocking in a rustling green tree, with a west wind blowing, and bright, white clouds flitting rapidly above; and not only larks, but throstles, and blackbirds, and linnets and cuckoos pouring out music on every side, and the moors seen at a distance, broken into cool dusky dells; but close by great swells of long grass undulating in waves to the breeze; and woods and sounding water, and the whole world awake and wild with joy. He wanted all to lie in an ecstasy of peace; I wanted all to sparkle and dance in a glorious jubilee.

I said his heaven would be only half alive, and he said mine would be drunk. I said I should fall asleep in his, and he said he could not breathe in mine.'

Thus people are, throughout the novel, schematically contrasted—'My love for Linton . . . my love for Heathcliff . . .', 'I said his heaven . . . he said mine . . .'—with verbal antitheses acting out, as it were, the successive disasters of the Edgar–Catherine, Isabella–Heathcliff and Linton–Catherine unions. Over this outline of opposites is laid another, equally schematic, pattern: that of repetitions. Heredity is used both realistically (Emily Brontë here anticipating the later nineteenth-century interest in heredity which was to culminate in *Buddenbrooks*) and as an image which becomes symbolical through iteration. The second Catherine has traits of both her mother and her father:

a real beauty in face—with the Earnshaws' handsome dark eyes, but the Lintons' fair skin, and small features, and yellow curling hair. Her spirit was high, though not rough, and qualified by a heart sensitive and lively to excess in its affections. That capacity for intense attachments reminded me of her mother; still she did not resemble her; for she could be soft and mild as a dove, and she had a gentle voice, and pensive expression: her anger was never furious; her love never fierce; it was deep and tender.

Linton Heathcliff has inherited the softness and the weakness of the Lintons; yet he also has the sadism of Heathcliff, as Joseph points out:

'That's father! We've allas summut o' either side in us.'

Most notable is the use of heredity in the case of Hareton and the complex of emotions which Heathcliff feels for him—'the thousand forms of past associations, and ideas he awakens, or embodies'. Heathcliff must hate Hareton in so far as he is the son of Hindley, and in revenge he deals with Hareton as he himself was dealt with by Hindley. At the same time, just because of this, he must see in Hareton a repetition of himself—good material brutalised and suppressed—and therefore to be sympathised with. But Hareton is also a repetition of Catherine—his eyes, particularly, being the same Earnshaw eyes—to be loved and feared. And in reply to this paradoxical combination of emotions, Hareton gives Heathcliff a kind of filial love which will not tolerate even the second Catherine speaking ill of him.

The case of Hareton shows how behaviour or action is repeated, as well as hereditary features; interrelationships, too, are echoed, with a difference, until ultimately the second Catherine and Hareton are seen as a parallel to the first Catherine and Heathcliff, and yet different because of all the intervening interrelationships which have shaped them, literally and metaphorically.

What produces both these patterns is, of course, the curiously artificial symmetry of the pedigree of the Earnshaws, Lintons and Heathcliffs:

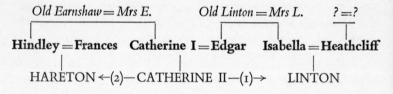

Thus the novel can be inspected like an equation where, all the other terms cancelled out, the second Catherine and Hareton must be united. The effect of this almost mathematical symmetry is like the effect of a metaphor: we get a sense of mastery by seeing the connections, the linkages, the order—emphasised here by the distribution of Christian names—imposed on the flux of time and experience. Fascinated by Catherine and Heathcliff, and yet aware of the dangers of such characters and such a relationship, Emily Brontë has created a pattern which gives her the chance to try out various combinations and permutations of them and their relationship. To see the novel in these terms is once again to throw emphasis on the second Catherine and Hareton as the integral resolution of the novel.

Yet, it is human material Emily Brontë is working on, not figures, and so instead of proceeding along the straight line of an equation or an allegory, *Wuthering Heights* grows cumulatively, like a snowball. Or, to change the metaphor, in this novel, and particularly the second half, one is very conscious of an added dimension which comes through Emily Brontë realising and reminding us of the presence of the past. Often the past rushes in as a visual shock. This is so, for example, at the beginning of Chapter XI, where Nelly, worried by rumours of wild drinking and gambling up at the Heights, sets out to go there and passes on the way the old sign-post round which she and Hindley used to play twenty years earlier. So powerful is the 'gush of child's sensations' which floods Nelly that

> as fresh as reality, it appeared that I beheld my early playmate seated on the withered turf; his dark, square head bent forward, and his little hand scooping out the earth with a piece of slate.
>
> 'Poor Hindley!' I exclaimed involuntarily.
>
> I started—my bodily eye was cheated into a momentary belief that the child lifted its face and stared straight into mine!

In agitation she hurries to the Heights, where

> the apparition had outstripped me; it stood looking through the gate. That was my first idea on observing an elf-locked, brown-eyed boy setting his ruddy countenance against the bars.

Only on further reflection does she realise that this must be Hareton and not his 'devil daddy', as the child has been taught by Heathcliff to call his father. Other such moments of shock are, of course, particularly important in Heathcliff's relation to the second Catherine—in Chapter XXXIII, for example, he is 'ready to tear Catherine in pieces', when 'of a sudden, his fingers relaxed, he shifted his grasp from her head to her arm, and gazed intently in her face'—and to Hareton, through whose Cathy-like eyes the past suddenly impinges on the present.

This device of suddenly 'seeing' the past is, I think, part of a larger feature of construction in the book. At moments, and usually critical moments in the action, Emily Brontë will crystallise a situation into a striking visual image which, as it were, arrests the narrative flow and makes us see a character and its context afresh—the 'film of familiarity' torn off. Usually this is done by way of a few, economically handled, details which etch themselves on to the mind's retina. There is Lockwood looking in through a Heights window to see Catherine bending over Hareton and his book. There is Isabella looking through the window at Heathcliff whom Hindley has locked out of Wuthering Heights:

> His hair and clothes were whitened with snow, and his sharp cannibal teeth, revealed by cold and wrath, gleamed through the dark.

There is Nelly Dean, running to close Heathcliff's window and coming upon him, dead, under it:

> His eyes met mine so keen, and fierce, I started; and then, he seemed to smile. I could not think him dead—but his face and throat were washed with rain; the bedclothes dripped, and he was perfectly still. The lattice, flapping to and fro, had grazed one hand that rested on the sill—no blood trickled from the broken skin, and when I put my fingers to it, I could doubt no more.

Sometimes this visual moment is no more than an aside, as when Isabella runs away from the Heights, pushing aside Hareton who is hanging a litter of puppies over a chairback; or when later Nelly, escaping from imprisonment at the Heights, passes Linton 'on the settle, sole tenant, sucking a stick of sugar-candy'. Sometimes it is more elaborated, defining a character by placing him in the natural setting. Nelly goes into the garden to tell Heathcliff that Catherine has died:

> He was there—at least a few yards further in the park; leant against an old ash tree, his hat off, and his hair soaked with the dew that had gathered on the budded branches, and fell pattering round him. He had been standing a long time in that position, for I saw a pair of ousels passing and repassing, scarcely three feet from him, busy in building their nest, and regarding his proximity no more than that of a piece of timber.

We are dealing here with that poetical quality which gives a kind of visual clarity to even the most abstract of Emily Brontë's poems—as, for example, the vision of Hope in the poem of that title, seen through the bars of the poet's 'grated den'—and which is most obvious in her

nature poems, most of all in those fragments which are imagistic gems.
Thus these lines from 1837:

> Only some spires of bright green grass
> Transparently in sunshine quivering;

or these from 1838:

> Still as she looked the iron clouds
> Would part, and sunlight shone between,
> But drearily strange and pale and cold.

Already in this early poetry there is the sharp visual definition by a
combination of unexpected details and, in the second example, an
approach to an identification of person and landscape. In the novel this
quality is put to use to concentrate experience within a scene, much
as in the over-all pattern of the book action is concentrated into short
dramatic scenes, with the intervening time slid lightly over.

In the handling of descriptive moments in the novel, the principle of
repetition with a difference again comes in. The structure is cemented
and its meanings (often ironies) are pointed by the same image or situation being repeated with a partly different content. There is the first
Catherine lying dead with Edgar asleep beside her, his head on the same
pillow, to be repeated in Heathcliff's dreaming of himself and Catherine side by side in the grave, 'my cheek frozen against hers'. There is
Edgar lying dead with the second Catherine sitting beside him:

> Whether Catherine had spent her tears, or whether the grief were
> too weighty to let them flow, she sat there dry-eyed till the sun
> rose;

and, only a few weeks later, there is Linton lying dead, and the same
Catherine, again emotionally paralysed but now for very different
reasons, 'seated by the bedside, with her hands folded on her knees'.
Sometimes the parallelisms are pointed out to us, as when Heathcliff
comes to claim the second Catherine and to take possession of the
Grange:

> It was the same room into which he had been ushered, as a guest,
> eighteen years before: the same moon shone through the window;
> and the same autumn landscape lay outside.

Because of the schematic organisation of characters and location practically every move between the Heights and the Grange, or reversely, is an echo or an anticipation, or both, of another or others. The first movement from Wuthering Heights to Thrushcross Grange is Catherine's and Heathcliff's escape, on a damp Sunday evening, from the tyranny of Hindley and Joseph; the last—only foreshadowed— will be the removal of the second Catherine and Hareton to the Grange. But in between Edgar Linton has ridden across to the Heights as a suitor and Heathcliff has come to the Grange to see Catherine and woo Isabella; and later Edgar's daughter has ridden across to the Heights again, in the unfortunate wooing of Heathcliff's son. The first Catherine has broken her heart longing to escape back to the Heights and the second Catherine, imprisoned at the Heights, has broken hers to escape back to the Grange. In this way, situations gradually accumulate around them more than naturalistic significances; they become symbolic. The same holds true for objects in the novel, which are naturalistic enough on the surface, but are made symbolic by iteration in important contexts. An instance of this is the inscription over the door to Wuthering Heights. On his first visit, Lockwood notices 'the date "1500", and the name "Hareton Earnshaw"', and at this stage the inscription does little more than whet our curiosity about the Earnshaws. But later on, it is to point the various stages in the relationship between the second Catherine and Hareton: in Chapter XXI Catherine and Linton ridicule Hareton for not being able to read the inscription; in Chapter XXIV Hareton has learnt to read the letters but suffers more ridicule for being unable to interpret the figures. Hareton's troubles are resolved by his becoming literate, which is so closely tied up with the love between him and Catherine; at the same time this love leads to their departure from the Heights, which becomes more momentous as we realise that the departure of *this* Hareton Earnshaw means the end of over three hundred years of Earnshaws at Wuthering Heights.

Most obviously made part of and pointer to a particular complex of feelings is the quaint old closet-bed with its window. We are alerted to its significance in Chapter III by Lockwood's nightmare (anticipated in an early Gondal poem, 'A sudden chasm of ghastly light') and Heathcliff's passionate call through the window. Later, in her delirium, Catherine dreams that she is back in that bed and begs to have the window thrown open:

'Oh, if I were but in my own bed in the old house! . . . And that wind sounding in the firs by the lattice. Do let me feel it—it comes straight down the moor—do let me have one breath!'

Eighteen years later the second Catherine flees through that very same window back to the Grange and Edgar's death-bed, using the same fir tree branch that knocks and disturbs Lockwood's sleep. And finally Heathcliff dies in that bed, under the opened window. (Clearly we must here again beware of the tendency to allegorise: the second Catherine's escape has around it a very different set of feelings from the first Catherine's wild longings to return to that bed and window.) In her delirious dream Cathy is miserable because it takes her back to the first time she was 'laid alone'. At this stage in the novel, the bed and its window has grown into a symbol of the time when Heathcliff was Cathy's 'all in all'. After Heathcliff's death, perhaps neither of them is laid alone? We do not know: the image reminds us how Emily Brontë stops short of the final mystery, but also how she uses her images to explore human situations and emotions right up to it.

In an interesting study of the iterative window-image Dorothy Van Ghent sees it as a metaphor by which the 'break-through and conversion' between two kinds of reality—'a restrictive reality of civilised manners and codes, and the anonymous unregenerate reality of natural energies'—is suggested in the novel.[1] It seems to me that in fact the window-image performs a whole series of functions. At its simplest, it provides occasion for that visual crystallisation of experience which I have been speaking of: Lockwood sees Catherine teaching Hareton to read; Isabella sees Heathcliff's cannibal teeth. But even in these moments there is involved the painful sense of outsiderness or otherness: Catherine and Hareton have together found something that Lockwood could never find; Isabella has suddenly seen Heathcliff as being of another order. This sense of different orders goes through many of the window-images. Heathcliff and Catherine are like two young savages looking in at the splendours of the Grange; compared to the bickering children, they are also noble. At this point, the moral superiority is theirs. But when Heathcliff breaks into the peace of the Grange, years later, with Catherine and Edgar sitting at the window, he comes like Satan. It is not, then, a set series of concepts Emily Brontë is illustrating by this image, but a complex pattern of human emotions.

At its most complex, perhaps, the window-image expands and takes in the whole action of the novel: Lockwood and Nelly are windows through which we, the readers, see the creatures of Emily Brontë's imagination. All the more effective, then, that at the centre of our vision should be the Cathy–Heathcliff window complex; and that the same ambivalence as characterises that complex should prevail when, as often happens, Heathcliff's eyes are compared to windows. When he is found dead, his eyes refuse to be shut over 'that frightful, life-like gaze of exultation', but to Isabella these same eyes are 'the clouded windows of hell'.

No analysis of *Wuthering Heights* can omit the importance of nature in the novel. We have already seen how all the protagonists and their interrelationships are suggested and defined by nature imagery, and how central scenes, like Catherine's delirium, are inextricably tied up with the winds and the life of the moors. But when looking at the novel from the point of view of its structural economy, one notices that there is in the novel not one description of nature and landscape for its own sake. Nature exists as uniquely part of people, places and events: they are defined through nature, as Wuthering Heights itself is defined on the second page of the novel by 'the excessive slant of a few, stunted firs at the end of the house; and by a range of gaunt thorns all stretching their limbs one way, as if craving alms of the sun'; or as the second Catherine is defined by her face being 'just like the land-scape—shadows and sunshine flitting over it in rapid succession' and by her favourite pastime being to sit or swing in the 'breeze-rocked cradle' of one of the trees in the Grange park.

Emily Brontë's poems—which, according to Herbert Read, show 'the most intense rendering of the embodied presence of nature that anywhere exists in English literature'[1]—prepare one for this fusion of man and nature. Her very early poems show that she must have taken pleasure in catching in words a particular visual impression or a particular mood in nature; as in the following fragment from the summer of 1838:

> 'Twas one of those dark, cloudy days
> That sometimes come in summer's blaze,
> When heaven drops not, when earth is still,
> And deeper green is on the hill;

or in the four almost Wordsworthian lines contemporary with those just quoted:

> There are two trees in a lonely field;
> They breathe a spell to me;
> A dreary thought their dark boughs yield,
> All waving solemnly.

At this stage contemplation does not always match description. In a poem from October 1837, she starts with a description of what looks like the Haworth setting—

> The old church tower and garden wall
> Are black with autumn rain—

and then she gets stuck at the point where she feels, in an eighteenth-century manner, that she ought to draw some conclusion, even moralise; and so she gives up:

> And as I gazed on the cheerless sky
> Sad thoughts rose in my mind . . .

Sometimes in the early poems, too, nature is regarded as a kind of Wordsworthian comforter and teacher. In a Gondal poem 'To the Bluebell', the flower breathes 'soothing words'. But this attitude is soon superseded by a deeper sense of nature as inspiration. The thought of the moors will always unlock

> a deep fountain whose springing
> Nor Absence nor Distance can quell;
> ('Loud without the wind was roaring', November 11, 1838)

and we have already seen how in the Romantic landscape of her imagination, whether Gondal or not, wild nature and wild passions fuse. By 1841 inspiration can mean a complete identification with nature:

> And thou art now a spirit pouring
> Thy presence into all—
> The essence of the Tempest's roaring
> And of the Tempest's fall.
> ('Aye, there it is! It wakes to-night')

In two of her earliest extant poems, from the summer of 1836, nature is linked to human fate in an almost emblematic fashion: in the first a new-born child's future is seen as foreshadowed in nature—

> If it darken, if a shadow
> Quench his rays and summon rain,
> Flowers may open, buds may blossom:
> Bud and flower alike are vain;
> Her days shall pass like a mournful story in care and
> tears and pain.
>
> If the wind be fresh and free,
> The wide skies clear and cloudless blue,
> The woods and fields and golden flowers
> Sparkling in sunshine and dew,
> Her days shall pass in Glory's light the world's drear
> desert through;

—in the second a child describes past, present and future in terms of nature. Nine years later, the link between human fate and nature has only become more self-evident, more directly taken for granted. In the ballad-like Gondal poems from May 1845, where the theme appears of two children, the 'Child of Delight! with sunbright hair, and seablue, seadeep eyes' and the 'mournful boy', nature and human mood are assumed identical:

> Heavy hangs the raindrop
> From the burdened spray;
> Heavy broods the damp mist
> On uplands far away;
>
> Heavy looms the dull sky,
> Heavy rolls the sea—
> And heavy beats the young heart
> Beneath the lonely tree.
>
> Never has a blue streak
> Cleft the clouds since morn—
> Never has his grim Fate
> Smiled since he was born.

And in the most haunting of all her poems there is no landscape but an internal one:

> He comes with western winds, with evening's wandering airs,
> With that clear dusk of heaven that brings the thickest stars;
> Winds take a pensive tone, and stars a tender fire,
> And visions rise and change which kill me with desire—
>
> Desire for nothing known in my maturer years
> When joy grew mad with awe at counting future tears;
> When, if my spirit's sky was full of flashes warm,
> I knew not whence they came, from sun or thunderstorm.
>
> ('Silent is the House')

What Emily Brontë's poems, even the late ones, may not have prepared us for, however, and what only the writing of the novel seems to have perfected in her, is a handling of nature in which complete and accurate realism co-exists with symbolism. The Gondal civil war poem which she wrote after completing *Wuthering Heights*, 'Why ask to know the date', is similar to the novel in this respect. Events in the novel are always placed in time and weather: this is equally part of the firm actuality of its action and of its symbolical overtones. There are, of course, differing degrees of symbolical use of nature, from the brief note which makes an event more concrete—'a bright, frosty afternoon; the ground bare, and the road hard and dry'—to the setting which is suffused with potential symbolism, as in the return of Heathcliff:

> On a mellow evening in September, I was coming from the garden with a heavy basket of apples which I had been gathering. It had got dusk, and the moon looked over the high wall of the court, causing undefined shadows to lurk in the corners of the numerous projecting portions of the building.

Through the combination of action and imagery, the figure lurking in those shadows becomes a figure of Satan intruding into the Garden of Eden. (Catherine and Edgar are sitting at a window overlooking the park, the valley and the moors—the whole landscape of the novel, and the characters in it, being at that moment an image of peace, soon to be seen as the calm before the storm.) Sometimes the intention of a description may seem mainly picturesque:

145

On an afternoon in October, or the beginning of November, a fresh watery afternoon, when the turf and paths were rustling with moist, withered leaves, and the cold, blue sky was half hidden by clouds, dark grey streamers, rapidly mounting from the west, and boding abundant rain; . . .

but those threatening rain clouds become both an ominous symbol of Heathcliff's threat to get power over the second Catherine (an important step towards this is taken during the walk introduced by the above description), and a very practical plot reason why Nelly gets her feet soaked and catches a cold which leaves Catherine free disastrously to develop her forbidden intercourse with the Heights. The violent storm over the Heights on the night that Heathcliff runs away is used symbolically to express the shattering of Catherine's childhood world which his disappearance implies. But again it is used realistically, too, to give a physical reason for Catherine's illness (and, later, for the death of the old Lintons, who catch her fever).

In the climactic passages of the novel, mood is controlled very finely by weather. The limpid spring weather around Heathcliff's death is not simply a contrast—Heathcliff not belonging, as do Catherine and Hareton, in the world of apple-blossom and pale primroses—but is part of the very texture of the experience of those days: hazy, yet transparent. On one of his last evenings, Heathcliff leans against a window, his face 'turned to the interior gloom', yet himself part of a scene which is described thus:

The fire had smouldered to ashes; the room was filled with the damp, mild air of the cloudy evening, and so still, that not only the murmur of the beck down Gimmerton was distinguishable, but its ripples and its gurgling over the pebbles, or through the large stones which it could not cover.

I do not think that those who have traced the road to *Wuthering Heights* have pointed out how close this is in mood, vocabulary and sentence construction to a passage in what was probably the most popular biography in the period, namely Lockhart's *Life of Scott*.[1] This is Lockhart describing the death of Sir Walter Scott:

It was a beautiful day—so warm that every window was wide open— and so perfectly still, that the sound of all others most delicious to his ear, the gentle ripple of the Tweed over its pebbles, was distinctly audible as we knelt around the bed, and his eldest son kissed and closed his eyes.

If this is a source, it is probably unconsciously so: Emily Brontë drawing on half-remembered material stored up in her memory. The importance of the parallelism here lies not in the possible source as such, but in the fact that it points Emily's desire to achieve for the dying days of Heathcliff the authenticity of a biography—and her passage particularises, over Lockhart's, the course of the beck—while at the same time fitting them both into the total mood of the novel's last few chapters and into the larger context of the novel. For 'the murmur of the beck down Gimmerton' is the same sound that sets the mood for the last scene between Catherine and Heathcliff in Chapter XV:

> Gimmerton chapel bells were still ringing; and the full, mellow flow of the beck in the valley, came soothingly on the ear. . . . At Wuthering Heights it always sounded on quiet days, following a great thaw, or a season of steady rain—and of Wuthering Heights, Catherine was thinking as she listened.

Catherine's last few days pass in a setting of 'soft thaw winds, and warm sunshine, and nearly melted snow'; the last time we hear Edgar speak to her, he tells her how 'the sky is blue, and the larks are singing, and the becks and brooks are all brim full'. But in the evening of the day of her funeral, the weather breaks (as it breaks into rain on the night of Heathcliff's death), to bring a reversal of the preternaturally early spring, with 'the wild snow blowing outside'. So the mood is modulated, into the wild anguish of Heathcliff—the mood of 'Cold in the earth'—and to link it with the mood of Lockwood's nightmare at the beginning of the novel, when, as Heathcliff opens the window, 'the snow and wind whirled wildly through'. And yet that snow has a 'realistic' explanation, too, in the 'real' snow storm which strands the incautious Lockwood at the Heights for the night and so immerses him in the whole story of the novel.

What we see in looking at nature in the novel, then, is another aspect of the close-knittedness of its structure, of the fine definition of its texture, and of the simultaneousness of its realistic and its symbolical level.

(v)

The outstanding features of the structure of *Wuthering Heights*—economy and precision, which means an exclusion of everything not relevant and an acute exploration of that which is relevant; balance, which means that simplicity of detail is combined with intricacy of overall effect—are also the characteristics of the style of the novel. The economy of the style is perhaps best seen in those passages where Emily Brontë gets across information which is necessary for the progress of the story but thematically not very important. Like Anne she commands a brisk and unsentimental realism. The death of Frances, Hindley's wife, is a good example:

> He told his wife the same story [that she was better], and she seemed to believe him; but one night, while leaning on his shoulder, in the act of saying she thought she should be able to get up to-morrow, a fit of coughing took her—a very slight one—he raised her in his arms; she put her two hands about his neck, her face changed, and she was dead.

For all the lack of death-bed sentimentality here, the stylistic economy becomes an image of Frances' own insignificance, and so a peculiar kind of pathos is achieved. The death of old Mr. Earnshaw is similarly low-toned, and the two old Lintons are dispatched in an almost ruthless manner. After Catherine's first brain-fever, Mrs. Linton takes her to the Grange to convalesce,

> but the poor dame had reason to repent of her kindness; she, and her husband, both took the fever, and died within a few days of each other.

The absence of emotive comment gives a surprisingly modern kind of objectivity to the passages of violence in the book. We have already seen how Isabella's description of Hindley's abortive attack on Heathcliff becomes, implicitly, a measure of her own 'moral teething'; it is also worth noticing how in the wording of it—

> The charge exploded, and the knife, in springing back, closed into its owner's wrist. Heathcliff pulled it away by main force, slitting up the flesh as it passed on, and thrust it dripping into his pocket.

He then took a stone, struck down the division between two windows and sprang in—

no objective detailed is spared us, while at the same time there is no attempt at guiding our reactions by subjective comment.

It is this same quality of language which helps to transmute apparently Gothic material into something unique. *Wuthering Heights* has, of course, often been related to the tradition of the Gothic novel. The ghost of the first Catherine, the figure, and especially the death, of Heathcliff, and the graveyard elements are, superficially, Gothic in their combination of the supernatural and the gruesome. The chief aim of the Gothic novelist was to achieve the maximum of emotional effect, and the way to do so was usually to set out extravagant events in emotionally inflated writing. We can only properly appreciate the different effect Emily Brontë achieves through the objectivity of her style, if we set side by side some passages from *Wuthering Heights* and others from typically Gothic works. One fruitful example is provided by an alleged source of *Wuthering Heights*, an anonymous short story called 'The Bridegroom of Barna', which appeared in *Blackwood's* in November 1840.[1] A criminal called Lawlor is being pursued, in a suitable Gothic setting:

the ruined tower of the Abbey, and the grey walls by which it was surrounded, crowning the summit of a lonely hill directly before them, and glancing white in the broadening moon.

The pursuers advance into the cemetery and encounter a scene 'which, when fully comprehended by the spectator's astonished gaze, made the blood run tingling and freezing through his veins'. Thus teased into excitement, we are given a description of the scene:

By the side of Ellen Nugent's new-made grave sat the murderer Lawlor, enclosing in his arms the form that had once comprised all earth's love and beauty for him, and which, like a miser, with mild [wild?] and maniac affection, he had unburied once more to clasp and contemplate. The shroud had fallen from the upper part of the body, upon which decay had as yet made slight impression. [She has been buried for three days.] The delicate head lay reclined upon that shoulder which had been its home so often, and over which now streamed the long bright hair like a flood of loosened gold, the wan face turned up to his as if it still could thrill to the mad kisses in which he steeped it, while he had twined one of the white arms frantically about his neck.

In this position, Lawlor is shot dead, and he is buried with his beloved: those who dig the grave 'did not venture to separate in death the hapless pair who in life could never be united'. If this story of unfulfilled love and anguished disinterment was one of the seeds of *Wuthering Heights*, it has been translated into an altogether different dimension. Compare to that mixture of sentimentality and necrophilia—with its ladies' magazine cliché of hair like 'a flood of loosened gold' and its bean-stalk bathos of twining what surely must have been a very recalcitrant arm about the lover's neck—to Heathcliff's account of his disinterment of Catherine, with its stress on the factual side of the enterprise:

'I'll tell you what I did yesterday! I got the sexton, who was digging Linton's grave, to remove the earth off her coffin lid, and I opened it. I thought, once, I would have stayed there, when I saw her face again—it is hers yet—he had hard work to stir me; but he said it would change, if the air blew on it, and so I struck one side of the coffin loose—and covered it up—not Linton's side, damn him! I wish he'd been soldered in lead—and I bribed the sexton to pull it away, when I am laid there, and slide mine out too; I'll have it made so, and then, by the time Linton gets to us, he'll not know which is which!'

The experience comes to us here, not ready-made with conventional emotive adjectives describing a cliché situation, but with a forcefulness and suggestiveness due, paradoxically, to the matter-of-factness of the tone and language—the same being sustained even in dealing with decomposition:

'And if she had been dissolved into earth, or worse, what would you have dreamt of then?' [Nelly Dean] said.

'Of dissolving with her, and being more happy still!' he answered. 'Do you suppose I dread any change of that sort? I expected such a transformation on raising the lid, but I'm better pleased that it should not commence till I share it.'

Because of the factuality, there is a frightening interpenetration of the restrained and the passionate, the real and the unreal, culminating in the implications (reminiscent of poems like Donne's 'The Relique' and 'The Funerall') of 'by the time Linton gets to us, he'll not know which is which'.

Thus, by implying emotion rather than flooding her lines with it, and by her own method of following the Coleridgean principle of transferring 'from our inward nature a human interest and a semblance of truth sufficient to procure for [persons and characters supernatural, or at least romantic] that willing suspension of disbelief for the moment, which constitutes poetic faith', Emily Brontë avoids the precarious balance of the traditional Gothic novel between the high-flown and the bathetic.

> Count Rudiger's stature was colossal; the grave in which he stood, scarcely rose above his knees. His eyes blazed; his mouth foamed; his coal-black hair stood erect, in which he twisted his hands, and tearing out whole handsful by the roots, he strewed them on the coffin, which stood beside his feet.

Thus 'Monk' Lewis, in *Mistrust, or Blanche and Osbright*, describing a feudal lord whose son has been murdered.[1] Not only is the situation a cliché, but the writing is obviously synthetical, heaping horror on horror, like Pelion on Ossa, till all topples over into unintentional comedy. Compare this to the organic use of horrifyingly grotesque detail in Catherine and Heathcliff's last embrace on earth:

> Her present countenance had a wild vindictiveness in its white cheek, and a bloodless lip, and scintillating eye; and she retained, in her closed fingers, a portion of the locks she had been grasping.

Truly may Nelly Dean say that she did not feel she was 'in the company of a creature of my own species'. Or, compare the treatment of domestic sadism—a favourite subject in the Gothic novel—in Mary Shelley's short story, *The Heir of Mondolfo*, with that in *Wuthering Heights*. The way Mrs. Shelley's Lodovico is treated by his father, who hates him, is similar to young Heathcliff's humiliations under Hindley Earnshaw, and Lodovico develops into misery and hatred as does Heathcliff; even Lodovico's appearance is similar—and yet different:

> His complexion was dark—hardship had even rendered it sallow; his eyes, once soft, now glowed with fierceness; his lips, formed to

express tenderness, were now habitually curled in contempt; his dark hair, clustering in thick curls round his throat, completed the wild but grand and interesting appearance of his person.[1]

Heathcliff looks 'very black and cross'; he has the expression of 'a vicious cur that appears to know the kicks it gets are its desert, and yet hates all the world as well as the kicker, for what it suffers'; and, at the age of sixteen, 'without having bad features, or being deficient in intellect, he contrived to convey an impression of inward and outward repulsiveness'. Emily Brontë is not afraid to make clear the brutalising effects of continued humiliations—Heathcliff 'acquired a slouching gait, and ignoble look; his naturally reserved disposition was exaggerated into an almost idiotic excess of unsociable moroseness; and he took a grim pleasure, apparently, in exciting the aversion rather than the esteem of his few acquaintances'—but Mary Shelley is anxious to keep a romantic glow around her hero, and so his appearance is summed up —with a bathos worthy of *The Young Visiters*—as 'wild but grand and interesting'.

The modern critic who speaks of 'the almost impossibly inflated style'[2] of *Wuthering Heights* must have had in mind the emotional impression it makes on him, rather than the stylistic means whereby that impression is achieved. For even in the emotional crises of the novel—in the great speeches of Catherine and Heathcliff—the direction is towards deflation and understatement. Emotion is caught and implied in a few simple words, or in a brief image, and it is the rhythm set up within each clause, and by the combination of clauses, rather than any heightening in the diction, that expresses the passion of the speaker. Thus Heathcliff to the dying Cathy:

'You teach me now how cruel you've been—cruel and false. *Why* did you despise me? *Why* did you betray your own heart, Cathy? I have not one word of comfort—you deserve this. You have killed yourself. Yes, you may kiss me, and cry; and wring out my kisses and tears. They'll blight you—they'll damn you. You loved me— then what *right* had you to leave me? What right—answer me—for the poor fancy you felt for Linton? Because misery, and degradation, and death, and nothing that God or satan could inflict would have parted us, *you*, of your own will, did it. I have not broken your heart—*you* have broken it—and in breaking it, you have broken mine. So much the worse for me, that I am strong. Do I want to live? What kind of living will it be when you—oh, God! would *you* like to live with your soul in the grave?'

There is hardly an emotive word in the whole speech: the language has, as it were, become a transparent medium, through which the passion and the anguish of the situation are enacted for us by the rhythm. Most of the staccato sentences are entirely monosyllabic, giving the effect of being wrung out of the direst pain. (One of the few words of any length, 'degradation', echoes back to that sentence on which Heathcliff ran away from Cathy and the Heights: 'It would degrade me to marry Heathcliff, now.') There is hardly a single metaphor; the curve of the feeling is described by the structure of the sentences and of the speech as a whole. Emily Brontë's method of working here is much the same as in her most intense poems; Heathcliff's speech even has the same knotty, throbbing, quality as the lines on the pain

> When the ear begins to hear and the eye begins to see;
> When the pulse begins to throb, the brain to think again,
> The soul to feel the flesh and the flesh to feel the chain.

The weakness of the writing in much nineteenth-century fiction is that it takes the situation for granted and indulges in the emotion; Emily Brontë lets her words explore and define the situation itself. Instead of saying to the reader: 'This is what you must feel about it', she says: 'This is what it feels like'. This quality is very apparent in the first Catherine's delirious speeches, but we can see it, too, in the speeches of Heathcliff as he is being driven to his death:

> 'It is not my fault, that I cannot eat or rest', he replied. '. . . I'll do both, as soon as I possibly can. But you might as well bid a man struggling in the water, rest within an arm's length of the shore! I must reach it first, and then I'll rest. . . . I'm too happy, and yet I'm not happy enough. My soul's bliss kills my body, but does not satisfy itself.'

The plain diction and the firm antitheses give a precision here to the unfathomable, where vagueness would have been fatal; even the metaphor aims at a kind of factual definition of his physical and mental state rather than at provoking emotional reaction to it—just as a little earlier he analysed his condition:

> 'I have to remind myself to breathe—almost to remind my heart to beat! And it is like bending back a stiff spring; it is by compulsion, that I do the slightest act, not prompted by one thought.'

Even in those passages where the imagery is clearly symbolical, radiating out meanings, it is at the same time also used in a strictly analytical fashion, defining states of mind and relationships between people with peculiar precision, as in the first Catherine's speeches about Heathcliff:

> 'He's more myself than I am. Whatever our souls are made of, his and mine are the same, and Linton's is as different as a moonbeam from lightning, or frost from fire;'

or:

> 'My love for Heathcliff resembles the eternal rocks beneath: a source of little visible delight, but necessary. Nelly, I *am* Heathcliff!'

This double movement of metaphors—inward as well as outward, defining as well as suggesting—is typical of the novel; it corresponds to its quality of making everything exist at once on a symbolical and a realistic level. Our ultimate reaction, of course, to the precision and the objectivity of the style, is the greater wonder and the greater emotional involvement. And here, I think, the style has led us back to the central paradox of *Wuthering Heights*, to the combination of involvement and detachment which makes this novel into a poem.

For, when we have taken the novel apart, Emily Brontë remains perhaps the one novelist in the language to live up to Coleridge's definition of a poet:

> The poet, described in *ideal* perfection, brings the whole soul of man into activity, with the subordination of its faculties to each other, according to their relative worth and dignity. He diffuses a tone and spirit of unity, that blends and (as it were) *fuses*, each into each, by that synthetical and magical power, to which we have exclusively appropriated the name of imagination. This power . . . reveals itself in the balance or reconciliation of opposite or discordant qualities:

of sameness, with difference; of the general, with the concrete; the idea, with the image; the individual, with the representative; the sense of novelty and freshness, with old and familiar objects; a more than usual state of emotion, with more than usual order; judgment ever awake and steady self-possession, with enthusiasm and feeling profound or vehement; and while it blends and harmonises the natural and the artificial, still subordinates art to nature; the manner to the matter; and our admiration of the poet to our sympathy with the poetry.[1]

Emily Brontë was a true poet in that her only allegiance was to her own imagination. In *Wuthering Heights* that imagination included morality in its scope, and so produced a unique kind of wisdom. 'She was in the strictest sense a law unto herself, and a heroine in keeping to her law', Ellen Nussey said; but she also said: 'She invited confidence in her moral power'.[2] It is for us to accept that invitation. Swinburne no doubt sensed it when he spoke of 'the double current of imaginative passion and practical compassion which made her a tragic poet and proved her a perfect woman'.[3] Whether she was a perfect woman or not, the art of Emily Brontë makes us see that there is an order of creative genius where the sex of its possessor ceases to matter. The only vital 'woman question' in her case is: why are there no women poets like her?

IV

Charlotte Brontë: The Woman Writer as an Author only

Lonely as I am—how should I be if Providence had never given me courage to adopt a career? . . . I wish every woman in England had also a hope and a motive: Alas there are many old maids who have neither. (Charlotte Brontë to W. S. Williams, July 3, 1849)

Indeed . . . it is a solemn and strange and perilous thing for a woman to become a wife. (Charlotte Brontë to Ellen Nussey, August 9, 1854)

(i)

UNLIKE either of her sisters, Charlotte Brontë regarded her writing as a career. Unlike Anne she saw herself as a novelist rather than a moralist; unlike Emily she had literary ambition and saw her own work in relation to the tradition of the novel. 'It is my wish to do my best in the career on which I have entered', she wrote two months after the appearance of *Jane Eyre*; and the same note—writing as a deliberately chosen and pursued occupation which gives meaning and justification to her life—is sounded throughout her correspondence, until she enters on that all-too-brief second career of marriage, with all the responsibilities of a Victorian clergyman's wife.

Involved in, indeed inseparable from, her emphasis on the importance of a career is her attitude to the 'woman question'. As I have said before, Charlotte, unlike either of her sisters, not only felt strongly about but also pronounced herself on the position of woman in society. Her letters show that she was interested in the many books and articles on the subject which were appearing in the late '40s. They also show that her interest was not of a reformatory kind and that she did not envisage the possibility of a fundamental change. 'Certainly there are evils which our own efforts will best reach', she writes to Mrs. Gaskell,

> but as certainly there are other evils—deep-rooted in the foundations of the social system—which no efforts of ours can touch; of which we cannot complain; of which it is advisable not too often to think.[1]

What she did think about, and what forms the keynote in many of her letters, is the ideal of independence for the unmarried woman. A week before posting off to the publishers the volume that was going to be *Poems, by Currer, Ellis and Acton Bell*, she writes to her old teacher, Miss Wooler (in whose school she had also had a spell as governess), that, to her mind,

> there is no more respectable character on this earth than an un-married woman who makes her own way through life quietly persevering—without support of husband or brother;

and the same theme runs through many of her letters in subsequent years, the success her novels met with and the lionisation she experienced on her few timid visits to London making little or no change in her attitude to herself as someone 'making her own way through life quietly persevering'.

Independence, then, is a keynote in her thinking about her own life and the life of all unmarried women. It is also a central theme in all her novels. In *Shirley*, in other ways her least characteristic novel, there is Shirley Keeldar who has already, by birth and fortune, achieved an independence which she relishes enormously; there is also Caroline Helstone who, however hesitantly, desires independence and often complains that women do not have enough to do and to live for. The other three novels all have an orphan heroine who makes her own way, through nothing but her native wit, moral integrity and strength of will, to what Lucy Snowe calls 'an independent position'. In both *The Professor* and *Villette* that position consists in a realisation of what to the Brontë sisters remained a pathetically abortive plan: the establishment of a boarding-school for young ladies. In *The Professor*, the drive to get on is very much seen in economic terms: the hero and the heroine, who have natures and careers so similar as to make them one character distributed over two sexes, are a respectively male and female

Robinson Crusoe, a version of that *homo economicus* which Ian Watt discusses in *The Rise of the Novel*.¹ William Crimsworth and Frances Evans Henri both make their careers in teaching, and Frances continues to do so after their marriage, only discontented because her husband earns three thousand francs while she gets a mere twelve hundred. Their joint life reaches its fulfilment when, after ten years of Frances running her own school, they have 'realised an independency', and can retire to enjoy the fruits of hard work and sensible investments. In *Jane Eyre*, independence is much more a matter of status in the widest sense: personal identity and self-esteem. Jane measures her governess-ship at Thornfield Hall not by the wages it brings her but by the fact that, as she says to Rochester,

> 'I have not been trampled on. I have not been petrified. I have not been buried with inferior minds, and excluded from every glimpse of communion with what is bright, and energetic, and high. I have talked, face to face, with what I reverence; with what I delight in,— with an original, a vigorous, an expanded mind.'

The case of Lucy Snowe in *Villette* represents an interesting fusion of attitudes in *The Professor* and in *Jane Eyre*. Independence is to her a dire economic necessity (and the end brings material well-being), but there is also a passionate emotional and intellectual involvement with it, so that Lucy's pursuit of it has an almost religious intensity. When in Chapter V Lucy Snowe's mistress has died, leaving her penniless, alone and with nowhere to go, there is a scene of dedication which in the fervour of its expression reminds one of Wordsworth's youthful dedication of his life to poetry, in Book IV of *The Prelude*. To Wordsworth it is a summer sunrise landscape which so fills his heart and mind that

> I made no vows, but vows
> Were then made for me; bond unknown to me
> Was given, that I should be, else sinning greatly,
> A dedicated Spirit.

To Lucy Snowe a clear, frosty winter's night brings her the strength which makes her decision to strike out as a teacher abroad, mundane enough in itself, have the force of a spiritual pilgrimage:

In spite of my solitude, my poverty, and my perplexity, my heart, nourished and nerved with the vigour of a youth that had not yet counted twenty-three summers, beat light and not feebly. Not feebly, I am sure, or I should have trembled in that lonely walk, which lay through still fields, and passed neither village, nor farm-house, nor cottage; I should have quailed in the absence of moon-light, for it was by the leading of stars only I traced the dim path; I should have quailed still more in the unwonted presence of that which tonight shone in the north, a moving mystery—the Aurora Borealis. But this solemn stranger influenced me otherwise than through my fears. Some new power it seemed to bring. I drew in energy with the keen, low breeze that blew on its path. A bold thought was sent to my mind; my mind was made strong to receive it.

The path of her own life is foreshadowed in the natural imagery of this scene: it, too, will be cold and sparsely lit—above all the light of love and friendship will be as fitful and incalculable as the Aurora Borealis—but after every major obstacle on it, Lucy Snowe re-dedicates herself with a similar intensity to her 'advance in life', knowing that giving in would mean sinning greatly.

In the novels of Charlotte Brontë, then, *homo economicus* has turned female, and from one point of view her works are female success stories showing that hard work and good morals bring their reward. (Even Jane Eyre is rewarded with a legacy.) But we have already seen that this is not all. There may be 'no more respectable character on this earth than an unmarried woman who makes her own way through life quietly persevering', but what sort of a life is respectability on its own? 'An old maid's life must doubtless be void and vapid—her heart strained and empty', says Frances Crimsworth out of the fulness of her wifehood, and Caroline Helstone, with outstanding examples of independent and persevering spinsters before her, makes much the same point. Intimately bound up with the drive towards independence in the novels is the awareness that, ultimately, independence is not enough. Plot, characterisation and every other element in the novels go to emphasise the other aspect of Charlotte Brontë's concern—the theme which Mrs. Oliphant, writing retrospectively about her in 1887, called 'the desire of a lonely creature longing for its mate'.[1] The real subject of all Charlotte Brontë's novels is the emotional and intellectual needs (the two inextricably related) of a woman, and her art is the expression of a personal vision of those needs.

For Charlotte Brontë was no propagandist. Reviewing *Shirley* in the *Revue des Deux Mondes*, Eugène Forçade suggested that the novel ought to have had the sub-title of 'la condition des femmes dans la classe moyenne anglaise'.[1] This no doubt amused Charlotte, for even in this novel where she shows the most explicit concern with the condition of women, she yet laughs in her final paragraph at the reader who might be looking for a moral. 'I am no teacher', she wrote to Ellen Nussey soon after *Shirley* was published, and in a letter to her publisher, George Smith, she developed this point in relation to *Villette*:

> You will see that 'Villette' touches on no matter of public interest. I cannot write books handling the topics of the day; it is of no use trying. Nor can I write a book for its moral. Nor can I take up a philanthropic scheme, though I honour philanthropy.[2]

Although she writes deferentially to Mrs. Gaskell about the philanthropic purpose and 'social use' of *Ruth* over *Villette*—the two novels appeared almost simultaneously; Charlotte asked for hers to be held back, so that publication dates would not clash—there is no sense of inferiority or humility about her statements that she cannot write a novel with a purpose. Instead her pronouncements sound rather as if they had come from the mouth of one of her own heroines. 'My own Conscience I satisfy first', she writes to Ellen Nussey in explaining why she is 'no teacher'; to that epitome of didacticism, Harriet Martineau, she boldly points out that self-expression is a higher mode of art than writing for a 'purpose' ('Better the highest part of what is in your own self than all the political and religious controversy in the world'[3]); and her publishers are firmly told:

> Unless I have something of my own to say, and a way of my own to say it in, I have no business to publish.

Here the theme of proud independence crops up again, now as an artistic principle, shaping her novels:

> Unless I can look beyond the greatest Masters, and study Nature herself, I have no right to paint. Unless I can have the courage to use

the language of Truth in preference to the jargon of Conventionality, I ought to be silent.[1]

Independence here means self-expression, in terms both of content and form, rather than art which is didactic and imitative. That she became aware of the difficulty of actually practising such imaginative autonomy within the framework of a novel and under the pressure of a reading public, we gather from the letter to Mrs. Gaskell, written several months after the publication of *Villette*, in which she speaks of the problem, when composing, of being 'quite *your own woman*, uninfluenced, unswayed by the consciousness of how your work may affect other minds; what blame, what sympathy it may call forth', and of how in such a situation a cloud seems to come between the writer and 'the severe Truth as you know it in your own secret and clear-seeing soul'.[2] That the consciousness of how her work might affect other minds could be beneficial to her art we know from her own accounts of how *Jane Eyre* was written in response to publishers' criticisms of *The Professor*. That being true to the 'severe Truth' as she saw it, involved Charlotte Brontë in accusations of impropriety and coarseness, we also know. In this case her artistic principles brought her into conflict with the principles of conventional femininity and so involved her, willy-nilly, in a feminist rebellion.

At this point we ought, I think, to look briefly at Charlotte Brontë's artistic beliefs, for they help us to see why she wrote as she wrote; and what she wrote about and how she wrote it are uniquely parts of the same question. Here again, unlike her sisters, she has left enough evidence—mainly in her letters—for us to be able to build up a picture of her aesthetic creed, apart from the novels. 'Truth', as we have already seen, is the foundation of that creed; and throughout her writing career it stands for the expression of her own, personal, vision of life. Especially in the first few years of that career, it also stands for such qualities as simplicity, homeliness, life-likeness. Her passionate devotion to 'truth' in this sense and at this stage has, no doubt, a great deal to do with her half-guilty avoidance of the Angrian regions in which her imagination had indulged itself so long. In (probably) 1839 she wrote a formal 'Farewell to Angria'—

I long to quit for awhile that burning clime where we have so-journed too long—its skies flame—the glow of sunset is always upon it—the mind would cease from excitement and turn now to a cooler region where the dawn breaks grey and sober, and the coming day for a time at least is subdued by clouds—[1]

which is echoed in the Preface she wrote much later for *The Professor*, her first and much-rejected novel. The move to a deliberate and sustained realism in *The Professor* is mainly a personal effort, but perhaps also partly a reflection of the taste of the period as a whole: away from romanticised fiction and towards more realistic modes. It may be worth noting that when, in this novel, the hero and the heroine read poetry together, she takes easily to Byron, who excites her, and soon comes to love Scott, whereas Wordsworth, with his 'deep, serene, and sober mind', she has to have explained to her and to work at. Charlotte tells G. H. Lewes how in writing *The Professor* she had been governed by the intention to follow 'Nature and Truth' but had stranded on the demands of public and publishers for ' "startling incident" and "thrilling excitement" ';[2] and she clearly has in mind the same dichotomy between the realistic and the romantic-melodramatic when she delivers a brief lecture on the subject 'Truth is better than Art' to her publishers who have criticised *Shirley* for lacking in 'artistic treatment'.[3] The word 'realism' had, of course, not yet entered the general critical vocabulary: the earliest N.E.D. entry for it in the modern sense is 1856. But the implications of the word 'truth' to her are sometimes close to an even photographic realism. When her publishers, having seen part of the MS of *Shirley*, have reservations about the first chapter and its curates, she feels very strongly about it: 'as I formerly said of the Lowood part of "Jane Eyre", *it is true*. The curates and their on-goings are merely photographed from the life'. When it comes to the MS of *Villette*, George Smith seems to have criticised it on structural grounds—'the transfer of interest in the third volume from one set of characters to another'—and Charlotte defends herself by claiming that keeping one single hero would have been 'unlike real life—inconsistent with truth—at variance with probability'.[4] But she agrees that she has failed over the character of Paulina: 'the fault lies in its wanting the germ of the *real*—in its being purely imaginary'. Yet Charlotte Brontë's 'truth' must not be equated too easily with 'realism', for she soon begins to oppose 'true' to 'real'. Much of her correspondence with G. H. Lewes turns on this, involving some of her most significant criticism of other novelists—Jane Austen, Thackeray, Balzac, George Sand. Lewes's strictures on the melodramatic tendencies in *Jane Eyre* and her replies to them form an interesting document in the development of the notion of realism in the English novel,[1] but above all they show the crystallisation of her ideas about her own art. Lewes warns her against straying 'far from the ground of experience' and to this she replies by reference to the limitations of actual experience and to the workings of the imagination, 'a strong, restless faculty which claims to be heard and exercised'. Here, then, she sees art as the 'reality' of actual experience transformed into the 'truth' of imaginative experience. This idea is developed further, into an analysis of the creative imagination, in her third letter to Lewes:

> When authors write best, or, at least, when they write most fluently, an influence seems to waken in them, which becomes their master—which will have its own way—putting out of view all behests but its own, dictating certain words, and insisting on their being used, whether vehement or measured in their nature; new-moulding characters, giving unthought-of turns to incidents, rejecting carefully elaborated old ideas, and suddenly creating and adopting new ones.[2]

As a comment on the experience of writing *Jane Eyre*, this suggests that, though the novel might have been started as an attempt at giving-them-what-they-want, it had turned into an outflow of the imagination, and that Charlotte was aware of this. It also reminds one of the very similar digression on imagination in Chapter IV of *Shirley*, which was probably written about the same time, and of her comment on 'the creative gift' in the Preface to the 1850 edition of *Wuthering Heights*. Charlotte Brontë's argument may have impressed Lewes more than he, in his character of literary adviser, wished to recognise, for in his essay a few years later, on 'The Lady Novelists', although he praises Jane Austen as 'real' because she does not transcend her own experience, he also praises Charlotte because she has given 'imaginative expression to actual experience' (thus practically using her own words). But at this point their ways parted. Lewes became more and more preoccupied with the value of realism. By the time he comes to discuss 'The Novels of Jane Austen', in *Blackwood's*, July 1859, he speaks harshly of Charlotte's inability to appreciate Jane Austen and sees her as a type of those whose 'passionate and insurgent activities demand in art a reflection of their own emotions and struggles'.[1] Charlotte Brontë, on the other hand, was moving away from realism as a criterion of goodness.

'Jane Austen', she says in 1848 to Lewes, who has made her read *Pride and Prejudice*, 'is more *real* than *true*.' What she misses in Jane Austen, she defines as 'poetry'—this being to her what 'elevates that masculine George Sand, and makes out of something coarse something godlike'—and as 'sentiment', by which she seems to mean a Wordsworthian kind of sympathy. Thackeray is 'true' because of such sympathy: he cherishes 'deep feeling for his kind'. George Sand is a greater novelist than Balzac because her heart is warmer than his.[2] Two years later, her feelings about Jane Austen have not been essentially modified, only strengthened and deepened, as she writes to W. S. Williams that well-known passage on Jane Austen's skill in 'delineating the surface of the lives of genteel English people curiously well' and her lack of acquaintance with 'that stormy Sisterhood', the Passions:

> . . . what throbs fast and full, though hidden, what the blood rushes through, what is the unseen seat of Life and the sentient target of death—*this* Miss Austen ignores; she no more, with her mind's eye, beholds the heart of her race than each man, with bodily vision, sees the heart in his heaving breast.[3]

This is written without the restraint she no doubt imposed upon herself when writing to Lewes; more importantly, it is written while she is on the way from *Shirley* to *Villette*. Itself an ardent vindication of passionate and imaginative literature, it is expressed in that passionate, patterned rhetoric which she will soon be using at the moments of high emotional tension in *Villette*. The imagery, too, expresses that devotion to the inner, rather than the outer eye which the passage is about, and which much of *Villette* builds on. It is significant that she should conclude her criticism of Jane Austen (unfair as it is in itself) by the following distinction:

> Jane Austen was a complete and most sensible lady, but a very incomplete, and rather insensible (*not senseless*) woman;

for it suggests that a woman writer's business, if she is to be 'true'—

i.e. allow her creative imagination free play—is bound to be with the passions.

Charlotte Brontë's artistic theory, then, is increasingly concerned with imaginative truth—reality recreated by the imagination; with the freedom of the individual, of whatever sex, to write what his or her imagination prompts; and with the special contribution natural to a woman writer of rendering 'what throbs fast and full, though hidden'. Her ideal novel would, in the end, seem to be one with a plot and structure close to the 'real' and with characters in whom 'truth' has been achieved: this points to *Villette* as the realisation of her own developed aesthetics. And this, in its turn, suggests that her own ideas about the art of the novel may be a vantage point from where we may attempt to define the peculiar qualities of her novels—qualities which are not so easily apparent if we approach them by the absolute standards of the Great Tradition.

(ii)

I intend, then, to examine Charlotte Brontë's novels by trying to see how her principle of artistic 'truth' operates in them: how she achieves truth in her two senses of life-likeness and of personal experience imaginatively transmuted. As far as such a division is possible, I intend to deal first with the more external features of narrative technique, plot, and structure, secondly with language, and thirdly with the emotional and intellectual contents of the novels. But, needless to say, all these elements are inextricably interrelated, so that no strict separation can be made.

All through her four novels, Charlotte Brontë stresses the life-likeness of her material, from the programme-declaration at the beginning of Chapter XIX in *The Professor*: 'Novelists should never allow themselves to weary of the study of real life', to the reminder near the end of *Villette* (Chapter XXXIX): 'Let us be honest, and cut, as heretofore, from the homely web of truth.' She often does this, as these quotations show, by intrusive comments on the art of the novel— but not for its own sake: her claims for life-likeness are an attempt to create a bond of agreement between her and the reader. Thus in *Shirley* she repeatedly steps out of the narrative to lecture the reader on what she is doing, often also implying a criticism of the kind of thing she is *not* doing. In the second paragraph of the novel the reader is warned not to expect anything but realism:

If you think . . . that anything like a romance is preparing for you, reader, you never were more mistaken. Do you anticipate sentiment, and poetry, and reverie? Do you expect passion, and stimulus, and melodrama? Calm your expectations; reduce them to a lowly standard. Something real, cool, and solid, lies before you; something unromantic as Monday morning.

And at the beginning of the last chapter, 'The Winding-Up', satire of the curates develops into some rather heavy-handed satire on public reactions to realism:

> The unvarnished truth does not answer; . . . plain facts will not digest . . . the squeal of the real pig is no more relished now than it was in days of yore.

No doubt she is paying back some of the criticism of *Jane Eyre* when she describes how the truth tends to be received with exclamations of 'impossible!', 'untrue!', 'inartistic!' By similar means she urges her reader to accept her characters—

> You must not think, reader, that in sketching Miss Ainley's char- acter I depict a figment of the imagination—no—we seek the originals of such portraits in real life only—

or a change in narrative view-point, as in Chapter XIII where we first listen to the dialogue between Robert Moore and Shirley via the ears of Caroline, but then, Caroline being too delicate and too overcome with jealous emotion to stay, continue listening without an intermediary, because 'the reader is privileged to remain, and try what he can make of the discourse'; or as in Chapter XXIX where it is necessary that we should learn the progress of the story from what Louis Moore writes in his note-book, and therefore are invited: 'Come near, by all means, reader . . . stoop over his shoulder.'

Devices of this self-conscious kind are not needed in *Jane Eyre*, where an all-over claim to authenticity is made by the fiction of auto- biography; yet the reader is often appealed to, in order that he be drawn into closer involvement with the story. These appeals tend to come at crucial moments in the action: when, in the afternoon of their interrupted wedding, Rochester asks Jane to forgive him ('Reader!— I forgave him'), or when the happy ending approaches ('Reader, I married him'), or, most insistent of all, when Jane runs away from Rochester:

> Gentle reader, may you never feel what I then felt! May your eyes never shed such stormy, scalding, heart-wrung tears as poured from mine. May you never appeal to Heaven in prayers so hopeless and so agonized as in that hour left my lips: for never may you, like me, dread to be the instrument of evil to what you wholly love.

In *Villette* the button-holing of the reader is often simply used at the beginning of a new chapter or a new section, to gather up the threads of the narrative. ('Has the reader forgot Miss Ginevra Fanshaw?', or 'The reader will, perhaps, remember . . .', or 'The reader is advised not to be in any hurry with his kindly conclusions'.) Yet at times we are close to the *Shirley* type of appeal to our taste for realism:

> My reader, I know, is one who would not thank me for an elaborate reproduction of poetic first impressions;

and at least once the appeal to us from out of the autobiographical framework creates an unhappy anti-climax. In the superbly realised moment when Lucy Snowe has been led, almost against her will but desperately needing to talk to *someone*, to go into the confessional, our involvement is suddenly destroyed by an anti-Catholic diatribe:

> Did I, do you suppose, reader, contemplate venturing again within that worthy priest's reach? As soon should I have thought of walking into a Babylonish furnace.

But in the main we are asked to assent to the psychological realism of the novel:

> Reader, if in the course of this work, you find that my opinion of Dr. John undergoes modification, excuse the seeming inconsistency. I give the feeling as at the time I felt it; I describe the view of character as it appeared when discovered—

the appeal here, in keeping with the whole character of the novel, referring us back to the emotions of Lucy Snowe; for it is here that 'truth' in this novel rests.

The fact that the direct appeals to the reader increase rather than decrease in frequency in her later novels, suggests that Charlotte

Brontë used them as a very deliberate device. In *The Professor* they are not frequent, and they are chiefly used to cheer the reader on, to involve him with the story—as at the opening of Chapter VII: 'Reader, perhaps you were never in Belgium? . . . This is Belgium, reader! Look, don't call the picture a flat or a dull one'—or with the hero, explaining his attitudes: 'Know, O incredulous reader! that a master stands in a some-what different relationship towards a pretty, light-headed, probably ignorant girl, to that occupied by a partner at a ball, or a gallant on the promenade'. The reader need not have the life-likeness of individual characters or situations pointed out to him, for the plot and structure of the novel as a whole are entirely shaped so as to be true to life. 'I said to myself', wrote Charlotte Brontë in the Preface she prepared when, after the appearance of *Jane Eyre* and *Shirley*, she again hoped to get her first novel accepted for publication,

> that my hero should work his way through life as I had seen real living men work theirs—that he should never get a shilling he had not earned—that no sudden turns should lift him in a moment to wealth and high station; that whatever small competency he might gain, should be won by the sweat of his brow . . . that he should not even marry a beautiful girl or a lady of rank.

This is a very adequate description of both plot and structure in this uneventful story of a young man, an orphan, who leaves school, has a short spell as a clerk under his unpleasant industrial magnate of a brother, then goes to Brussels and becomes a teacher, sharing his duties between a boys' school and a 'Pensionnat de Demoiselles'. In the latter he gets to know its owner, Mlle. Reuter, whose amorous advances he soon sees through, and also a young girl, Frances Evans Henri, of half-English descent. She is a poor and persecuted teacher of sewing in the school but also comes to his English lessons. Without too many vagaries of fate, he marries Frances, and through their joint industry in teaching, they in ten years accumulate enough money to retire with their one son, at a surprisingly early age, to an idyllic house in the English countryside (from which they intend to send the boy, like his father before him, to Eton!). The novel closes quietly with a family tea on the lawn.

As in *Agnes Grey*, the desire to portray realistically a life that is tough and often dreary has led to art that is drab and dull. But where

Agnes Grey is saved by the utter simplicity of its design, *The Professor* sometimes irritates us by its narrative and structural features. The narrative technique is awkward. The first chapter is a letter from the hero to an old school acquaintance; it takes us up to his arrival at Crimsworth Hall, his brother's residence, and there, for no particular reason, it ends, and we are simply told that 'to this letter I never got an answer'. From then on the absent friend disappears altogether from the novel, and William decides to dedicate the rest of his life story to 'the public at large'. Accordingly, the rest of the novel is a straightforward first person narration—which, of course, it would have been better to stick to in the first place. Inexperience, of the kind that got Anne Brontë involved in a laborious narrative structure in *The Tenant of Wildfell Hall*, is obviously reflected here. It is as though Charlotte Brontë, having determined on a male hero, had found it difficult to come to terms with him; and she herself later thought the beginning of the novel 'very feeble'. Again, unlike the completeness which Anne Brontë achieves in *Agnes Grey* by carefully selecting her details, Charlotte Brontë introduces some situations and characters which the story cannot allow to be developed. The sadistic elder brother (in whom Miss Ratchford justifiably sees a survival of an Angrian motif),[1] occupies a central position in the first few chapters, but is then dropped, except for a brief reference to his bankruptcy and an even more perfunctory reference to his successful railway speculations in the final paragraph. On the other hand, Frances, the heroine, is introduced only well over a third of the way through the book. The structure is organised and held together purely by the character of the hero, and rather than being a *Bildungsroman* where the character is shaped by his contacts and conflicts with society, it becomes a kind of bourgeois pilgrimage, in which the hero's rectitude and will-power remain static and society around him learns to recognise and reward his virtues. William Crimsworth is very clear and explicit about being better than most of the people he meets. Charlotte Brontë tries to avoid priggishness in her hero by having the cynic Hunsden place him, but the total effect is much more of William Crimsworth placing Hunsden. It is significant that Charlotte Brontë later saw the value of *The Professor* as being that it gives 'a new view of a grade, an occupation, and a class of characters', for it is a very socially conscious novel. Through Hunsden, who is an aristocrat and something of a snob, the question of 'caste' is explicitly raised: Crimsworth is an inverted snob in that he glories in introducing his chosen bride to Hunsden as a lace-mender. Thematically the novel establishes a meritocracy consisting of people who are intelligent and work hard (William and Frances), and it thus looks forward to the later Victorian preoccupation with the sanctity of work—to a novel like *Great Expectations*, in which the hero is saved from his corruption and snobbery when he learns to make his own way and earn his own money. The appeal of *The Professor* is economic as much as, or more than, aesthetic: the pleasure of seeing a good man getting on in the world, from a poor and humble start, by his own efforts. It is the appeal of much mid-Victorian fiction, just as it was the appeal of much of the didactic fiction of the early nineteenth century. *The Professor* is a link between the tales of Mrs. Hofland and Mrs. Craik's *John Halifax, Gentleman*, a novel which appeared in 1856, the year before *The Professor* finally got into print. But even in the homely and bourgeois world of John Halifax there are some spectacular events—a flood, an approach to a Luddite riot, an election—and, albeit seen at a disapproving distance, there is high life, including debauchery and a fallen woman. Nothing so colourful lights up the pale world of *The Professor*, the merits of which Charlotte Brontë—re-reading her first work while casting around for a successor to *Jane Eyre*—saw entirely in terms of 'reality':

> The middle and latter portion of the work, all that relates to Brussels, the Belgian school, etc., is as good as I can write: it contains more pith, more substance, more reality, in my judgment, than much of 'Jane Eyre'.[1]

As she was writing this, only she could have been aware of the self-abnegation through which this kind of realism had been achieved. From what we now know of her own stay in Brussels and the letters she wrote after her return, there is no doubt that the most decisive emotional experience in her life was her love for Constantin Héger, her teacher and the husband of Madame Héger to whose *pensionnat* she and Emily went to learn French and German in 1842, and where Charlotte returned alone in 1843 for a further year, after the death of Aunt Branwell had brought them home to Haworth. Enough has been written on this love, so one-sided and so truly begotten by despair upon impossibility; and I do not want to overemphasise the autobiographical elements in her novels. But nor do I think it can be denied that this was the experience most formative for her art: that when she speaks of 'truth' as actual experience transmuted by the imagination, this was the experience which she most intensely worked on; that, in one way or another, each of her novels is a different version of the same 'truth'. Therefore we cannot rightly understand the art of *The Professor* without appreciating the extent to which in it personal experience has been hammered into objectivity.

The declaration of love between William and Frances in *The Professor* is brought about via a technically awkward device: listening outside her door he hears her recite part of a poem (in French, but we are given William's translation) which she has obviously written herself; entering he reads the rest for himself. It is a poem about a pupil who loves her master—her name, Jane, looks forward to Charlotte Brontë's next novel—and it makes the state of Frances's feelings sufficiently clear to William. The poem is in fact one of which the original draft is in an exercise-book used by Charlotte Brontë in Brussels in 1843. It has little value as art, but in terms of the Brussels experience, it is a sad little piece of wishful thinking; in its stilted way it also suggests the tension in one who had come seeking the knowledge necessary to realise her ambition to start a school but had also discovered other needs:

> The strong pulse of Ambition struck
> In every vein I owned;
> At the same instant, bleeding broke
> A secret, inward wound.

Charlotte Brontë's share in the *Poems, by Currer, Ellis and Acton Bell* in 1846 suggests that her gift is not lyrical. She does not have the quiet sense of form that Anne has, nor the structural and verbal power of Emily. Though often in song form, most of her poems are dramatic monologues, and sometimes enough of character and situation is implied to make them into miniature novels. Most frequently the situation is one of love and passion, ill-fated, spurned or ill-rewarded. To describe the creative process behind them, one could use the very words in which William Crimsworth speaks of Frances's poem: it is not exactly, he says, the writer's own experience, but a composition by portions of that experience suggested. Thus while egotism was avoided, the fancy was exercised, and the heart satisfied.

Or, one could use T. S. Eliot's term and speak of the search for an objective correlative. Two of Charlotte Brontë's poems—not, of course, published in her lifetime—speak directly of an unhappy and frustrated love, 'Unloved I love, unwept I weep' (the first stanza of which is worked into the 1846 poem 'Frances') and 'He saw my heart's woe, discovered my soul's anguish'; and, as in the two personal poems on the deaths of her sisters, occasional lines in them have a poignancy of their own:

> In dark remorse I rose; I rose in darker shame;
> Self-condemned I withdrew to an exile from my kind.

But in the main it is not inherent poetical qualities but biographical pathos which forms their appeal:

> Unloved I love, unwept I weep,
> Grief I restrain, hope I repress;
> Vain is this anguish, fixed and deep,
> Vainer desires or dreams of bliss.
>
> My life is cold, love's fire being dead;
> That fire self-kindled, self-consumed;
> What living warmth erewhile it shed,
> Now to how drear extinction doomed!
>
> Devoid of charm how could I dream
> My unasked love would e'er return?
> What fate, what influence lit the flame
> I still feel inly, deeply burn?
>
> Alas! there are those who should not love;
> I to this dreary band belong.

The poems suggest that Charlotte Brontë sorely needed to put some objectifying distance between her and her experience in order to make art of it. *The Professor* shows her to us caught in the dilemma of being too anxious to draw on her own experience and at the same time too anxious to objectify. Her first novel is an example of truth to life gained deliberately at the expense of imaginative truth.

I have spent some time on Charlotte Brontë's least successful novel, because, of all her works, it shows most clearly the artistic problems facing her when she tries to find her proper sphere as a novelist. The novels that follow can be dealt with more briefly because in them—at least in *Jane Eyre* and *Villette*—she has found the form that suits her and that allows for realism as well as imagination. The decisive move from *The Professor* to *Jane Eyre* lies, I think, in her turning to a female narrator. Both *Jane Eyre* and *Villette* are autobiographies, as was *The Professor*, but in both the problem of being a woman stands at the centre and gives life, form and shape to the whole narrative, in a way impossible in *The Professor*.

The plot of *Jane Eyre* is too well known to need repeating. Clearly Charlotte Brontë had decided to take the publishers' advice to supply the reading public with something more exciting than the rejected first novel; clearly, on the other hand, writing with an audience in mind did not lead to a piece of book-making: the attempt at a greater imaginative scope touched off the fuse to a new kind of 'truth'. Thus, as Robert B. Heilman has shown in an interesting article on 'Charlotte Brontë's "New" Gothic',[1] the Gothic plot elements—Rochester's mad wife in the attic, the spectacular burning of Thornfield Hall, the weird, premonitory dreams—are used by Charlotte to achieve psychological realism of a kind previously unknown to the English novel. The events around Jane are there to test her, and to give the author the opportunity to probe into her mind: above all to explore love as it affects a woman's mind in all its aspects. Again, because of the nature of the narrator, as an orphan and a governess with a strong will and mind of her own, refusing to put up with social injustice, all the themes of the novel can be focused on the one character: Jane embodies in herself the woman problem, the governess problem and the class-question. I shall deal more with Charlotte Brontë's handling of these themes, and of love in the novel, later in this chapter; here we need only note the structural unification which is achieved through Jane.

To Charlotte, as we have already seen, realism in *Jane Eyre* lay above all in the Lowood chapters because, built on her experience at Cowan Bridge school, they faithfully reflected life as she had known it. To us the realism of the novel as a whole lies in its acute psychological observation, and the school section is realistic because it shows us, unmistakably, the mind of the child that was going to grow into Jane Eyre, the woman. They belong, structurally, in a novel which otherwise is largely about the Jane–Rochester relationship, because they are part of the logic that governs the book. That logic is one in which events appear only in so far as they affect Jane's mind: there is no sense of narrative material being brought in for its own sake; every incident and every character has a bearing on the growth of Jane into a woman of passion and absolute moral integrity.

Much the same narrative technique and structural pattern recur in *Villette*, Charlotte Brontë's last novel, after she had made a detour (which we shall follow presently) in *Shirley*. *Villette* is again a governess story: orphaned and poor Lucy Snowe goes to Belgium where, in Villette (Brussels) she finds employment, first as a nurse for the children of Madame Beck, the owner of a *pensionnat*, but very soon as a teacher of English in the school itself. In Villette are also living the Brettons, mother and son (Graham, or as he is known in the *pensionnat*, Dr. John), with whom Lucy had spent some time in her early adolescence. Lucy falls in love with Graham who, far from returning this love, first has an infatuation for a flighty English schoolgirl in the *pensionnat*, and thereafter falls seriously in love with Paulina, another Villette inhabitant from Lucy's past. But by this time a second love has come into Lucy's life in the shape of M. Paul Emanuel, a teacher in the school, and the novel ends with Lucy established—by Paul Emanuel—in a school of her own, while he goes off for three years to look after some family properties in the West Indies, and is shipwrecked (or so the end hints) on the way home. So much for the plot, which, as Charlotte Brontë's publishers complained, on the surface lacks concentration, moving longitudinally through two sets of characters, with Lucy as the only link. Charlotte Brontë, as we have seen, defended this structure by a reference to its true-to-lifeness; and in this case, what she defended as realism is also the source of the deeper truth of psychological realism. For the story is Lucy's, and Lucy is the focus, even more so than is Jane Eyre in her novel. The story certainly lacks a neat structural pattern—it does not even fall into those natural divisions which are created in *Jane Eyre* by Jane's movements to and from Thornfield Hall—but its unique power lies in that very lack.

In its stubborn concentration on Lucy, *Villette* becomes a novel about loneliness, lovelessness, about a woman with a sense that 'Fate was my permanent foe, never to be conciliated'. Lucy's emotions, rather than any external events, create the real structure of the novel: a series of crises, in which utter depression threatens Lucy, and, between them, stretches of the empty life of an unloved being. The first major crisis comes in the chapter called 'The Long Vacation' (XV) where Lucy is left alone, apart from a cretinous child, in the school, while all the others are off to visit their friends and relations. Physical illness, fever—matched by the equinoctial gales outside, as Lucy's states of mind always reflect her 'dreary fellowship with the winds and their changes' —and sleepless suffering are powerfully realised; they are gathered up into one nightmare which touches the depths of human depression: a nightmare

> sufficing to wring my whole frame with unknown anguish; to confer a nameless experience that had the hue, the mien, the terror, the very tone of a visitation from eternity. Between twelve and one that night a cup was forced to my lips, black, strong, strange, drawn from no well, but filled up seething from a bottomless and boundless sea.

One evening Lucy goes out, ill but not delirious, and is driven by 'a pressure of affliction on my mind of which it would hardly any longer endure the weight' into the confessional of a Catholic church. Relieved by having spoken to a human being, she leaves the church, struggles against the wind and faints. The intensity with which the situation is rendered is such that we are forced towards a symbolical reading: Lucy is found by Graham and taken back to his mother; and the temporary companionship they offer Lucy gets all the meaning of a re-birth into hope after the death of utter despair. The next movement of the novel is governed by Lucy's agonies of waiting for Graham's letters, the only thing that gives hope to her emotional life; and it ends in the unwitting cruelty of Graham telling Lucy about his love for Paulina. By this time, however, the rising movement of Lucy's relationship with Paul Emanuel is being prepared for; it grows stronger, and eventually culminates in another feverish nocturnal climax: a fête-night in Villette when Lucy wanders around and sees the love and friendship of others (including, as she believes, Paul Emanuel with a girl who is to be his wife), herself an outsider. The *peripeteia* of the novel is Lucy's irrepressible cry of despair when it looks as though she is to be separated from Paul Emanuel for ever:

> Pierced deeper than I could endure, made now to feel what defied suppression, I cried—'My heart will break!'

Lucy's heart does not break; instead it finds a briefly granted solace in Paul Emanuel's love. But it is the probings into the deprivations of that heart and into the neuroses of its owner which make the novel into what must be one of the greatest psychological novels in English in the nineteenth century. If we compare it to *The Professor*, of which it is obviously another, artistically maturer, version, we can see that it is the product of a woman who had now realised that her proper sphere lay in drawing on her own experience for imaginative truth.

Shirley is another matter altogether, and is in many ways the odd one out among Charlotte Brontë's novels. Both *Jane Eyre* and *Villette* take one woman through a long period of time; in *Shirley* she tries to give a cross-section of a piece of Yorkshire society over a shorter period. To do so, she abandons her usual method of first-person narration and becomes, as we have already seen, a somewhat self-conscious omniscient observer, who repeatedly lectures the reader on what she is doing, and why. The effect is, almost inevitably, a lack of focus, and this is strengthened by the fact that, to cover her larger canvas, she introduces several, not always interdependent, themes and several modes of writing. The love-interest is split, as in Miss Martineau's *Deerbrook*, between two couples: Caroline Helstone, orphan niece of the vicar of the parish, and Robert Moore, half-Flemish mill-owner; Shirley Keeldar, orphan heiress and owner of Fieldhead Manor, and Louis Moore, poor tutor brother of Robert. The social interest is divided between Luddite troubles, culminating in an attack on Robert Moore's mill, and the troubles of governesses, as represented by Shirley's companion, Mrs. Pryor (who, in one of the few melodramatic devices of the novel, turns out to be Caroline's mother); but there is also a great deal of social satire, especially of the three unfortunate curates who, as far as the plot of the novel goes, are completely superfluous. And all around the major characters, there is a set of secondary ones—like the radical Yorke family—who, one feels, have each been developed for their own sake, rather than for any central purpose.

Shirley shows that Charlotte Brontë had taken G. H. Lewes's advice to heart and was deliberately working at observational realism, after the flights of (apparent) fantasy in *Jane Eyre*.[1] (It is ironical that Lewes should have criticised *Shirley* so strongly on the grounds that the author had tried to step out of her own experience.) Together with the fragment of a novel left on her death and published in *The Cornhill Magazine* as 'Emma',[2] it is the nearest Charlotte Brontë ever got to the mode of Jane Austen. Social manners are very nicely observed: the vicarage tea-party, the 'Jew-basket', the small domestic concerns of a country parish. Where her wider social satire is often heavy—such as the disquisition on Selfishness and the British Merchant—on this ground she can create social comedy with a sure touch: one remembers the mock-heroic battle when the Church of England Sunday school procession meets, in a narrow lane, the 'Dissenting and Methodist schools, the Baptists, Independents, and Wesleyans, joined in unholy alliance' and puts its opponents to the rout by singing 'Rule, Britannia' to the tune of their brass band.

Perhaps her deliberate effort at realism is best seen from the point of view of *Shirley* as a novel dealing with the problems of industrialism. 'Details, situations which I do not understand and cannot personally inspect, I would not for the world meddle with . . . my observation cannot penetrate where the very deepest political and social truths are to be learnt', she wrote to W. S. Williams;[3] and this attitude informs her treatment of the Luddite situation. We know that, apart from memories of stories she had heard during her school days at Roe Head, she went to some trouble to find out about the conditions in the West Riding heavy woollen district during the time of the Orders in Council;[4] and clearly she tried to make her story as authentic as possible. At the same time she refuses to turn into a social critic:

> Child-torturers, slave masters and drivers, I consign to the hands of jailers; the novelist may be excused from sullying his page with the record of their deeds. (Chapter V)

There is implied in this comment the same distaste at seeing the novel used for illegitimate—because ill-informed—social criticism as we find in her reference to the 'ridiculous mess' of Mrs. Trollope's *Michael Armstrong*.[5] By moving her action back a generation, to Luddite rather than Chartist times, she is excused from handling 'topics of the day'; her handling of the theme of child-labour reminds us of her confessed inability to write for a philanthropic purpose:[6]

The little children came running in, in too great a hurry, let us hope, to feel very much nipped by the inclement air. . . . The signal was given for breakfast; the children, released for half an hour from toil, betook themselves to the little tin cans which held their coffee, and to the small baskets which contained their allowance of bread. Let us hope they have enough to eat; it would be a pity were it otherwise. (Chapter V)

If we compare this with what Disraeli makes of a similar situation in *Sybil* (Book III, Chapter I)—

See, too, these emerge from the bowels of the earth! Infants of four and five years of age, many of them girls, pretty and still soft and timid. . . . They endure that punishment which philosophical philanthropy has invented for the direst criminals. . . . Hour after hour elapses, and all that reminds the infant trappers of the world they have quitted and that which they have joined, is the passage of the coal-wagons for which they open the air-doors of the galleries—

we see the difference between a novel-with-a-purpose and one which uses a situation without sermonising about it. Yet it would be wrong to think that Charlotte Brontë was as unconcerned about social injustice as the above quotation might suggest. She will not preach theoretically, but, when it comes down to the individual character, she can realise poverty and misery in moving terms: we see this in her treatment of William Farren and his family, who have had to sell

't'chest o'drawers, and t'clock, and t'bit of a mahogany stand, and t'wife's bonny tea-tray and set o'cheeney 'at she brought for a portion when we were wed.'

From passages like this, we can understand why Charlotte, on reading *Mary Barton*, should have thought herself 'in some measure anticipated both in subject and incident'. She has certainly achieved social realism here; but in *Shirley* as a whole, this kind of realism has been gained at the expense of the psychological depth of *Jane Eyre* and *Villette*, and one cannot help feeling that in *Shirley* she betrays her own best gifts.

(iii)

The language of Charlotte Brontë's novels, like their form and structure, shows her working towards her two kinds of truth, realism and poetry; and again she achieves her best results when the two fuse: when psychological realism is arrived at by imaginative means.

Compared to its contemporaries, *Agnes Grey* and *Wuthering Heights*, *The Professor* suggests that Charlotte Brontë had not yet arrived at a style of her own, nor one which was in keeping with what she was trying to do in the novel. There is none of the effortlessness of the dialogue in *Agnes Grey*, or of the absolute rightness of both dialogue and narration in *Wuthering Heights*; the dialogue is stiff and awkward (quite apart from the intrusive habit of quoting snatches of speech in French—one which is still retained in *Villette*), and the narrative and descriptive passages have a self-consciously 'literary' ring about them. The style, in other words, is at war with the other elements of the novel. The promise of strength to come lies mainly in the imagery, which occasionally is vigorous and suggestive, as when a life wasted in vice is seen as 'a rag eaten through and through with disease, wrung together with pain, stamped into the churchyard sod by the inexorable heel of despair'. But the image just quoted is part of a general contemplation on life (from which the hero extracts himself rather clumsily by a 'Well—and what suggested all this? and what is the inference to be drawn therefrom?'); rather than being informed by, and illuminating, plot or character, it is a piece of added decoration. Much the same holds true for Charlotte Brontë's handling, at this stage, of one of her favourite stylistic devices, the personified abstract. Mental conflicts in *The Professor* are depicted as a debate between Reason and Passion or Prudence and Conscience, often in such a way as to make them only mock-serious. At one point the hero, though he has to make a living, has given up his teaching post, as keeping it would have meant an involvement with Mlle. Reuter. His action is imprudent, but right. This is how its effects on him are described:

> I walked a quarter of an hour from the wall to the window; and at the window, self-reproach seemed to face me; at the wall, self-disdain: all at once out spoke Conscience:—
> 'Down, stupid tormenters!' cried she; 'the man has done his duty; you shall not bait him thus by thoughts of what might have been; he relinquished a temporary and contingent good to avoid a permanent and certain evil; he did well.'

Instead of helping to realise a mental struggle, the personifications here put a bar of rhetoric between us and it. This tendency is even more apparent when personifications are used, as it were, as a shorthand device for handing over mental states—as if a concept or feeling became more vivid as soon as it is spelled with a capital letter. Thus the Professor on Mlle. Reuter:

> I knew her former feeling was unchanged. Decorum now repressed, and Policy masked it, but Opportunity would be too strong for either of these—Temptation would shiver their restraints.

The effect sometimes touches on the ridiculous, as when the Professor finds Frances after a four weeks' search for her:

> Amazement had hardly opened her eyes and raised them to mine, ere Recognition informed their irids with most speaking brightness;

and sometimes it is one of sentimentality, as when Frances in her room is described thus:

> Twilight only was with her, and tranquil, ruddy Firelight; to these sisters, the Bright and the Dark, she had been speaking, ere I entered.

It is the language of an author steeped in eighteenth-century descriptive poetry (as is the case with many novels of the first half of the nineteenth century); and Hunsden's description of the state of the English country-side—

> 'Just put your head in at English cottage doors; get a glimpse of Famine crouched torpid on black hearth-stones; of Disease lying bare on beds without coverlets, of Infamy wantoning viciously with Ignorance, though indeed Luxury is her favourite paramour, and princely halls are dearer to her than thatched hovels'—

sounds like a not very good prose paraphrase of some of Goldsmith's *The Deserted Village*.

Altogether, then, the language in *The Professor* intervenes between us and the characters: another indication that Charlotte Brontë was deliberately holding them away from her, distancing herself, and therefore us, from them. In *Jane Eyre* the relationship is the reverse: the descriptive passages draw us into the action, the dialogue realises the interplay of minds, and the imagery carries over to us emotion proved on the pulses.

The dialogue between Jane and Rochester—from the stichomythia of their first meeting as strangers on the road and their later interview at Thornfield Hall, via the declarations of love and the banter of affianced lovers, to the agonised battle of their parting—all this is not only 'true' in both Charlotte Brontë's senses, but also new to the English novel. Particularly so are the interchanges between lovers—a form of dialogue which Jane Austen had carefully avoided, cutting short the problem in a way of which the engagement of Edmund and Elinor in *Sense and Sensibility* is typical:

> How soon he had walked himself into the proper resolution, however, how soon an opportunity of exercising it occurred, in what manner he expressed himself, and how he was received, need not be particularly told. This only need be said;—that when they all sat down to table at four o'clock, about three hours after his arrival, he had secured his lady. (Chapter XLIX)

Bulwer Lytton similarly refuses to cope, though, unlike Jane Austen, hinting at oceans of sensibility:

> We will not tax the patience of the reader, who seldom enters with keen interest into the mere dialogue of love, with the blushing Madeline's reply, or with the soft vows and tender confessions which the rich poetry of Aram's mind made yet more delicious to the ear of his dreaming and devoted mistress. (*Eugene Aram*, Chapter X)

The lady novelists of the '40s liked to have a try, but the result is often like Lady Fullerton's, in *Ellen Middleton*, both hysterical and hyperbolical, over-strained and over-patterned, in more than one sense unspeakable. In the following passage, the heroine relates how sometimes in her lover's embrace she would murmur 'in a tone of thrilling and passionate emotion, "Let me die *here*" ', and how, not unnaturally, he would ask why:

> 'Ask not', I would then reply. 'Ask not why some flowers shut their leaves beneath the full blaze of the sun. Ask not why the walls of the Abbey Church tremble, as the full peal of the organ vibrates through the aisles. Ask not why the majesty of a starry night makes me weep, or why the intensity of bliss makes me shudder.'
>
> 'But I love you, my Ellen,' Edward would answer, 'I, too, love

you with all the powers of my soul. My happiness is as intense as yours; and yet, in the very excess of both, there is trust and peace.'

We need only put beside this a piece of the dialogue between Jane and Rochester after their abortive wedding to see what has been gained in directness of expression, and therefore in depths of genuine feeling: Rochester asks Jane,

'If you were mad, do you think I should hate you?'
'I do indeed, sir.'
'Then you are mistaken, and you know nothing about me, and nothing about the sort of love of which I am capable. Every atom of your flesh is as dear to me as my own: in pain and sickness it would still be dear. Your mind is my treasure, and if it were broken, it would be my treasure still. . . .'

But dialogue alone gives little sense of the power with which emotion is realised in *Jane Eyre*—this no doubt is one reason why dramatisations of the novel tend to fall so miserably short of the impact of the original. The core of the book lies in Jane's description of what goes on in her own mind, and it is here that not only the most striking but also the most functional imagery in the novel is to be found. In Chapter XXVI, after the tumult that follows upon the interrupted wedding, Jane is finally left alone, to think and to receive in her consciousness the full impact of the blow. To begin with, she can still see herself from the outside, in the third person, as 'Jane Eyre, who had been an ardent, expectant woman' but is now 'a cold, solitary girl again'; she sees her prospects blasted as by a frost at mid-summer, her hopes, in characteristic Biblical imagery, 'struck with a subtle doom, such as, in one night, fell on all the first-born in the land of Egypt'. And as Macbeth could see pity, 'like a naked new-born babe', so she sees her love, 'like a suffering child in a cold cradle'. Through this progression of images, observer and observed, subject and object, merge; and the mental crisis naturally culminates in the caving-in of consciousness which is the total surrender to despair:

My eyes were covered and closed: eddying darkness seemed to swim round me, and reflection came in as black and confused a flow. Self-abandoned, relaxed, and effortless, I seemed to have laid me down in the dried-up bed of a great river; I heard a flood loosened in remote mountains, and felt the torrent come: to rise I had no will, to flee I had no strength. . . .

It was near . . . it came: in full, heavy swing the torrent poured over me. The whole consciousness of my life lorn, my love lost, my hope quenched, my faith death-struck, swayed full and mighty above me in one sullen mass. That bitter hour cannot be described: in truth, 'the waters came into my soul; I sank in deep mire: I felt no standing; I came into deep waters; the floods overflowed me'.

Character, situation and image are absolutely fused here, into a single rhythm, by a language which has become a superb tool of psychological analysis. One can well see how, after writing passages like this, Charlotte Brontë found that Jane Austen's style suggested unfamiliarity with 'the stormy sisterhood' of the deeper feelings. Her images are not always so fully developed as here; sometimes a brief metaphor will embody a whole situation. 'A hand of fiery iron grasped my vitals', is how Jane expresses the tension between her desire to be Rochester's and her moral knowledge that she must leave him. Nor, of course, is the imagery always so inextricably knit into the context: at one extreme it stops the internal action and grows into self-contained allegory which draws attention to itself rather than to any psychological development. Thus, for example, when Jane returns to Thornfield Hall after hearing Rochester's mysterious call, and finds it gutted by fire, Charlotte Brontë arrests the flow of the narrative with a 'Hear an illustration, reader', and then proceeds to elaborate on an analogous situation—that of a lover who finds his mistress asleep on a mossy bank and, when he bends over to kiss her, discovers that she is dead. This could, I suppose, be defended on functional grounds—there is a valid parallelism—but the effect of the image remains a dilution, rather than a concentration, of the impact on us of Jane's shock. It suggests what other parts of the novel confirm, that Charlotte's language only becomes truly imaginative when she is working on a mind in an agony of passion. In such cases even the half-allegorically developed situation becomes an intimate and revealing part of Jane's mind: we can see this in the two haunting dreams of the little child which Jane tells Rochester on the eve of their wedding and which look forward to the impending disaster, the 'suffering child in a cold cradle'; and we can see it in the descriptions of Jane's paintings in Chapter XIII, which again both define her mind and anticipate her fate.

The fullness and consistency with which she has realised the Jane–Rochester relationship is seen in her use of iterative imagery to accompany it. For example, Rochester keeps likening Jane, thinking both of her physical and her mental qualities, to an eager little bird, and in the early stages of their relationship, Jane sees herself as one of the 'stray and stranger birds' to which Rochester throws his crumbs. When she has run away from Rochester, her heart becomes 'impotent as a bird' which, 'with both wings broken. . . . still quivered its shattered pinions in vain attempts to seek him'; but when she returns, to find a struck and mutilated Rochester, the bird image is transferred to him: her first impression of him is that of a 'fettered wild beast or bird, dangerous to approach in his sullen woe', and their final relationship, in which he is dependent on her, is that of 'a royal eagle, chained to a perch' which is 'forced to entreat a sparrow to become its purveyor'. Events and objects in the novel, too, become iterative images: most notably the horse-chestnut at the bottom of the orchard, which is struck and split into two on the night when Jane and Rochester declare their love for each other, which Jane sees as an ominous allegory on the eve of her wedding, and to which Rochester compares himself when he proposes to Jane a second time, near the end. Whether reading *Wuthering Heights* had taught Charlotte Brontë something about the use of iterative imagery to cement the inner structure of a novel, or whether the intense realisation of her subject produced this spontaneously, we cannot say; but it is certain that none of this quality is foreshadowed in *The Professor*.

As in *The Professor* so in *Jane Eyre* Charlotte Brontë's language tends to turn, in moments of crisis, to personifications; but in the second novel personifications draw strength from their context and so give strength back to it. This is Jane, rousing herself from her stupor of despair, and saying to herself,

'. . . that I must leave him decidedly, instantly, entirely, is intolerable. I cannot do it.'

But, then, a voice within me averred that I could do it; and foretold that I should do it. I wrestled with my own resolution: I wanted to be weak that I might avoid the awful passage of further suffering I saw laid out for me; and conscience, turned tyrant, held passion by the throat, told her tauntingly, she had yet but dipped her dainty foot in the slough, and swore that with that arm of iron, he would thrust her down to unsounded depths of agony.

'Let me be torn away, then!' I cried. 'Let another help me!'

'No; you shall tear yourself away, none shall help you: you shall, yourself, pluck out your right eye: yourself cut off your right hand: your heart shall be the victim; and you, the priest, to transfix it.'

Meaning—individual, emotionally comprehended meaning—is given here by the context of the plot and character to words like 'conscience' and 'passion'; and these concepts then engage in a drama, a morality play whose climax is the cruel irony of morally inevitable self-mutilation. They form, as it were, an inner action which the language superimposes on the outer action, so that we perceive as one Jane's agony and its emotional and spiritual implications. What was merely a set of counters in *The Professor*, distancing us from the characters and suggesting the distance between them and their creator, has here become a vital bond between author, character and reader.

It is interesting to notice how much rarer personified abstracts are in *Shirley*: no character in this novel is trying to analyse his or her feelings or states of mind to the same extent as Jane Eyre. Caroline Helstone is the character who most feels the pangs and tensions of love, but in her there is no struggle because no strength; she just suffers the traditional Victorian heroine's 'decline'. Around her there is sometimes an inane, even bathetic, use of personifications, as when she hopes to pass her evening 'with Happiness and Robert'; or when, on the same page, False Hope whispers to her that Robert might come and see her. In the novel as a whole, personifications cluster around the Louis–Shirley relationship. One of Charlotte Brontë's most elaborate allegories is Louis's heraldic-emblematic vision of his position in regard to Shirley:

Her Gold and her Station are two griffins, that guard her on each side. Love looks and longs, and dares not: Passion hovers round and is kept at bay: Truth and Devotion are scared. There is nothing to lose in winning her—no sacrifice to make—it is all clear gain and therefore unimaginably difficult.

The imagery does not define or suggest anything; the abstracts remain abstract; the whole relationship remains as theoretical as, one feels, it must have been to Charlotte Brontë's mind. Louis Moore is as much of a male governess heroine as was William Crimsworth, and one feels that he must have been the most difficult character in the novel for Charlotte Brontë to realise. He was needed for the plot and the thematic pattern, but he never seems to spring alive from those abstractions with which he is surrounded whenever he appears, musing at great length on Solitude or soliloquising on his previous contacts with Shirley, 'when Confusion and Submission seemed about to crush me with their soft tyranny'. Louis, though an extreme case, is an indication of some of the overall quality of the style in *Shirley*. Instead of abstracts being turned into emotional realities by the heroine-narrator in *Jane Eyre*, we have here the generalisations of an omniscient (and, inevitably, less emotionally involved) narrator, such as the discourse on Youth, Death, Reality, Hope, Love and Experience at the beginning of Chapter VII. They suggest how anxious Charlotte Brontë was in this novel to place the love-stories in an objectified context, and how, accordingly, her style becomes in some respects a throw-back to *The Professor*.

Where *Shirley* presents us with a new kind of writing, and where in particular the personifications are subsumed in a new kind of stylistic 'truth', is in those sections of the novel that deal with social and economic problems. Having got the introduction of her curates safely out of the way, Charlotte Brontë in the second chapter of the novel turns to map out the political and social situation of the country:

A bad harvest supervened. Distress reached its climax. Endurance, over-goaded, stretched the hand of fraternity to sedition. The throes of a sort of moral earthquake were felt heaving under the hills of the northern counties. But, as is usual in such cases, nobody took much notice.

Before this, her typical sentence had been a period one, often with interlinked clauses forming a cumulative pattern. Here her subject needs authority and lucidity, and she achieves both, through short sentences so arranged that the pause after each implies the causal connection between it and the next. Too vivid personifications would distract—and indeed the third of the quoted sentences is the least successful one, threatening to destroy the tone she is establishing—whereas the brief metaphor of the 'moral earthquake' is an economic way of making the situation both concrete and ominous; it also forms an effective contrast to the flat comment in the last sentence, and helps to make this into a pointed anticlimax. The same qualities inform the paragraph where she puts the Luddite situation into a nutshell and at the same time relates it to her own material:

> Misery generates hate: these sufferers hated the machines which they believed took their bread from them: they hated the buildings which contained those machines; they hated the manufacturers who owned those buildings. In the parish of Briarfield, with which we have at present to do, Hollow's-mill was the place held most abominable; Gérard Moore, in his double character of semi-foreigner and thorough-going progressist, the man most abominated.

Here, too, her fondness for a rhetorical pattern built on the repetition of a crucial word is put to a functional use. The first clause gives the premise (and Professor Asa Briggs has shown how its social truth has made it into a catch-phrase[1]), the others follow with inevitability, so that objectivity of attitude and economy of style are equally achieved. Unfortunately, she does not maintain this tone consistently; in the excitement of the attack by Luddite rioters on Hollow's-mill she resorts to personified abstracts which weaken the effect where they were meant to strengthen it:

> Wrath wakens to the cry of Hate: the Lion shakes his main, and rises to the howl of the Hyena: Caste stands up, ireful, against Caste; and the indignant, wronged spirit of the Middle Rank bears down in zeal and scorn on the famished and furious mass of the Operative Class.

Such a passage seems over-written, especially when compared with the way she handles differences of 'caste' in the dialogue, as in William Farren's conversation with Shirley and Caroline in the chapter 'Which The Genteel Reader Is Recommended To Skip, Low Persons Being Here Introduced'. The dialogue in *Shirley* is often excellent—whether it serves the comedy-of-manners by letting us listen in to a vicarage tea-party, or shows up Shirley's spirit as she gives the wrong answers to her snobbish uncle's catechism, or brings alive the children of the Yorke family, whose slightly mannered and infinitely knowing way of speech makes them sound as if they had come out of an Ivy Compton-Burnett novel. But there is also often a wrench from natural dialogue to stiff generalising comment, which suggests that Charlotte Brontë is not altogether happy with her role as omniscient narrator, and that the novel lacks a narrative focus.

In *Villette* we are back with the single focus, the autobiographical narrator, and with the style which is at its best when it probes the mind of that narrator. At the end of Chapter XXIII in *The Professor* there is a passage in which 'hypochondria' is personified: William Crimsworth's mind is invaded by 'a horror of great darkness' and this makes him remember how in his boyhood he was visited by this demon, 'taking me entirely to her death-cold bosom, and holding me with arms of bone'. Powerful in itself, this passage has no justification in plot or character; there is nothing either before or after to suggest such nervous sensibilities in the very sensible hero. His breakdown here is introduced, it would seem, only to give an excuse for what is a welling-up from the suppressed ego of the author. We know that in Brussels and after her final return from there Charlotte Brontë had experienced such hypochondria; and in that sense there is truth to life here, but this truth clashes with the truth of the novel as a whole. In *Villette*, on the other hand, Charlotte Brontë has, in Lucy Snowe, found an adequate objective correlative; and personal truth is transmuted into the true agonies of Lucy's mind. To analyse that mind Charlotte Brontë again uses highly metaphorical language. Lucy, having set out on her pilgrimage to Villette, feels

> the secret but ceaseless consciousness of anxiety lying in wait on enjoyment, like a tiger crouched in a jungle. The breathing of that beast of prey was in my ear always; his fierce heart panted close against mine; he never stirred in his lair but I felt him: I knew he waited only for sun-down to bound ravenous from his ambush.

This piece is typical of much of the writing in *Villette*: to convey the tensions and neuroses of Lucy's mind a brief image is not enough; it has to be fully developed, as a tool of exploration. As in *Jane Eyre*, Charlotte Brontë often draws on Biblical analogies, and here they tend to grow into miniature dramas or *tableaux*, as at the beginning of Chapter XVII, when Lucy sees her own emotional needs like the physical needs of the cripples lying around the pool and waiting for a miracle. The key to Lucy's character lies in what she says about herself in Chapter VIII: 'I seemed to hold two lives—the life of thought and that of reality'; and Charlotte Brontë manages to give us the sense of a character with a cold and composed exterior (it is worth remembering that Charlotte changed her heroine's name from Snowe to Frost and back to Snowe again and insisted that Lucy *should* be a repellent character) and a passionate and troubled inner life. It is because of the persistence with which the inner life, 'the life of thought', of Lucy Snowe is explored that a basically uneventful story, with a central character superficially just as plain and narrow as is William Crimsworth, gets scope and depth.

Time and time again, as Lucy's inner needs are thwarted by her outer circumstances, her state of mind is rendered to us in terms of a *psychomachia*, a dialogue in her soul between Reason and Imagination (or Hope, or Feeling, the three being almost synonymous for Lucy). There is a particularly full example of this in the chapter called 'Reaction' (XXI), where Lucy returns from her stay with the Brettons to her usual loveless existence in the *pensionnat*, with only the doubtful promise of letters from Graham to live on. As soon as she is alone, Reason, here as always surrounded by images of cold and pain, appears, like an old hag, 'laying on my shoulder a withered hand, and frostily touching my ear with the chill blue lips of eld'; and the bitter struggle which ensues makes Lucy remember all her other struggles:

> Often has Reason turned me out by night, in midwinter, on cold snow, flinging for sustenance the gnawed bone dogs had forsaken: sternly has she vowed her stores held nothing more for me—harshly denied my right to ask better things . . . Then, looking up, have I seen in the sky a head amidst circling stars, of which the midmost and the brightest lent a ray sympathetic and attent. A spirit, softer and better than Human Reason, has descended with quiet flight to the waste—bringing all round her a sphere of air borrowed of eternal summer.

As in this example, the personifications produced by Lucy's emotional crises tend to lengthen out into whole allegories; these do not arrest the action of *Villette*, for in a sense they *are* the action: even more than in *Jane Eyre* the imagery in *Villette* tends to act out an inner drama which superimposes itself on, or even substitutes for external action. It is therefore unfortunate that Charlotte Brontë sometimes, with a kind of Byronic irony, undercuts her own technique, as when after a vivid elaboration of the moods of a night spent longing for 'something to fetch me out of my present existence, and lead me upwards and on-wards', she interrupts herself:

> By which words I mean that the cool peace and dewy sweetness of the night filled me with a mood of hope;

or when the personifications are so handled as to mock the self they usually express:

> Must I, ere I close, render some account of that Freedom and Renovation which I won on the fête-night? Must I tell how I and the two stalwart companions I brought home from the illumin-ated park bore the test of intimate acquaintance? . . . Freedom excused himself, as for the present, impoverished and disabled to assist; and Renovation never spoke; he had died in the night suddenly.

Maybe these are meant to be seen as examples of Lucy's Reason at work; but in effect they point to an uncertainty of tone in the author.

But in the great emotional crises of the novel, there is no such uncertainty; there is a unique and sustained tone. In that nightmarish, hallucinatory night of the fête Lucy Snowe sees Paul Emanuel with his ward and believes (quite unjustifiably) that he is going to marry her. The way Lucy's reaction is presented makes it something quite other than the frequent misunderstandings and pangs of jealousy which conventionally prevent the course of true love from running smooth in the Victorian novel. Lucy rushes at what she thinks is the truth and works herself up to a kind of orgasm of self-abnegation:

> I gathered it [the truth] to me with a sort of rage of haste, and folded it round me, as the soldier struck on the field folds his colours about his breast. I invoked Conviction to nail upon me the certainty ab-horred while embraced, to fix it with the strongest spikes her strongest strokes could drive; and when the iron had entered well my soul, I stood up, as I thought, renovated.
>
> In my infatuation, I said, 'Truth, you are a good mistress to your faithful servants! . . . and here I stand—free!'

The narrative technique here makes possible both the immediacy of Lucy's emotions and the placing of them by the later Lucy, the one who tells the story in retrospect ('as I thought', 'in my infatuation') and therefore knows how illusory that achievement of 'freedom' is. Only in creating St. John Rivers had Charlotte Brontë previously got anywhere near this image of masochism, but St. John is cold almost right through, where Lucy's coldness is self-enforced. In this passage the frenzy of rhythm and imagery—as the simile of the mortally wounded soldier develops into a metaphor virtually of crucifixion—contradicts the direction which Lucy *wants* her feelings to take; and the total effect is one of a mind shattered and utterly disordered. Here, as in all the greatest passages of *Villette*, Charlotte Brontë has by poetic means reached the truth of psychological realism.

(iv)

I said at the beginning of this chapter that the real subject of all Charlotte Brontë's novels is the emotional and intellectual needs of a woman, and that the content of her art is, ultimately, a personal vision of those needs. It remains now for us to see what that vision is, and the best way to do so is, it seems to me, by looking at how, through the progression of her novels, she handles the man–woman relationship.

As we can see from her Angrian writings, the imaginative world of her adolescence and early womanhood—she was in her twenty-fourth year when she wrote her 'Farewell to Angria'—was one of stormy passions and often highly spiced erotic adventures. 'Caroline Vernon', which Miss Ratchford takes to be Charlotte's last long manuscript in the Angrian cycle,[1] indicates that its author had a thorough imaginative insight into sexual passion—not just of the wild romantic kind, but involving the power-game, the sudden and paradoxical changes and re-groupings within the relationship between a man and a woman. One passage in this 'novel' springs to mind. The Duke of Zamorna has just returned home, burning with a newly-aroused desire for his young ward, his wife's sister Caroline; he finds his wife waiting and begins to make excuses for withdrawing from her, when suddenly his mood changes:

His Grace smiled without turning his head. That smile confessed that his headache was a sham. The Duchess caught its meaning quickly. She also caught an expression in his face which indicated that he had changed his mood since he came in and that he was not so anxious to get away from her as he had been.

She had been standing before him and she now took his hand. . . .

He forgot her superiority often, and preferred charms which were dim to hers. Still she retained the power of awakening him at intervals to a new consideration of her price, and his Grace would every now and then discover with surprise that he had a treasure always in his arms that he loved better, a great deal better, than the far-sought gems he dived among rocks so often to bring up. . . .

Dismissing Caroline Vernon with this thought, he allowed himself to be pleased by her elder and fairer sister Mary. . . .

That night she certainly recalled a wanderer. How long it will be before the wish to stray returns again is another thing.[1]

Even where the situation has less of the domestic and more of the post-Byronic trappings, we can still sense a genuine interest in the way one mind, and body, gains control over another. The following scene is, in some ways, an anticipation of Jane Eyre's great temptation:

'Did you never guess before that I took a pleasure in watching you, in holding your little hand, and in playing with your simplicity which has sported many a time, Caroline, on the brink of an abyss you never thought of?'

Miss Vernon was speechless. She darkly saw, or rather felt, the end to which all this tended, but all was fever and delirium round her.

The Duke spoke again in a single blunt and almost coarse sentence, compressing what remained to be said, 'If I were a bearded Turk, Caroline, I would take you to my harem.' His deep voice as he uttered this, his high featured face, and dark, large eye burning bright with a spark from the depths of Gehenna, struck Caroline Vernon with a thrill of nameless dread. Here he was, the man Montmorency had described to her. All at once she knew him. Her guardian was gone, something terrible sat in his place.

The fire in the grate was sunk down without a blaze. The silent, lonely library, so far away from the inhabited part of the house, was gathering a deeper shade in all its gothic recesses. She grew faint with dread. She dared not stir from a vague fear of being arrested by the powerful arm flung over the back of her chair. At last through the long and profound silence a low whisper stole from her lips, 'May I go away?'

No answer. She attempted to rise. This movement produced

the effect she had feared; the arm closed round her. Miss Vernon could not resist its strength. A piteous upward look was her only appeal. He, Satan's eldest son, smiled at the mute prayer.

Through the Byronic satanism around the hero, and through the over-heated language (in *Jane Eyre* Jane and Rochester share a joke about the Turk's harem), there comes across an insight into Caroline's mind:

> . . . infatuation was stealing over her. The thought of separation and a return to Eden was dreadful. The man beside her was her guardian again, but he was also Montmorency's Duke of Zamorna. She feared, she loved. Passion tempted, conscience warned her. But in a mind like Miss Vernon's, conscience was feeble. Opposed to passion its whispers grew faint and were at last silenced, and when Zamorna kissed her and said in a voice of fatal sweetness which has instilled venom into many a heart, 'Will you go with me tomorrow, Caroline?' she looked up in his face with a kind of wild devoted enthusiasm and answered, 'Yes'.[1]

If we compare this to Jane's temptation in Chapter XXVII of *Jane Eyre*, which also could be summed up as 'Passion tempted, conscience warned her', we see at once that the difference does not just lie in the fact that Miss Eyre says 'no' where Miss Vernon said 'yes'. In the seven or eight years separating the two scenes, Charlotte Brontë has achieved a greater command of language, a deeper psychological insight, and a deeper insight into moral problems. But more than, though including, all this, there is a widening of the issues involved. Jane is not only a girl with powers to attract a male; she is an *individual* whose key-line is: '*I* care for myself.' And so the later temptation scene becomes a microcosm of all human relationships, a vision of life.

But this is not to say that it reads, or is to be read, as an abstract allegory. I doubt if one could find in nineteenth-century literature a more concrete picture of desire reaching the point of no control than in Jane's description of Rochester as he threatens her with violence:

> His voice was hoarse; his look that of a man who is just about to burst an insufferable bond and plunge headlong into wild licence. I saw that in another moment, and with one impetus of frenzy more, I should be able to do nothing with him.

Or again later:

... he crossed the floor and seized my arm, and grasped my waist. He seemed to devour me with his flaming glance: physically, I felt, at the moment, powerless as stubble exposed to the draught and glow of a furnace.

But this sentence continues: 'mentally, I still possessed my soul, and with it the certainty of ultimate safety'. She is safe, because her mind is impregnable, and because she knows her own value:

'*I* care for myself. The more solitary, the more friendless, the more unsustained I am, the more I will respect myself. I will keep the law given by God; sanctioned by man. I will hold to the principles received by me when I was sane, and not mad—as I am now. ... They have a worth—so I have always believed; and if I cannot believe it now, it is because I am insane—quite insane: with my veins running fire, and my heart beating faster than I can count its throbs.'

And Rochester, too, recognises that without her soul and spirit she is not worth having. In the magnificent speech which begins 'Never ... never was anything at once so frail and so indomitable', he sees that spirit as a 'resolute, wild, free thing' looking out of her eyes; and then the bird-image, which we have noticed before, returns: her spirit becomes the bird and her body the cage,

'And it is you, spirit—with will and energy, and virtue and purity— that I want: not alone your brittle frame.'

We are not just back to the morality situation of Comus and the Lady, nor to the assailed virtue in Richardson and his followers; Rochester has come to love Jane *because of* her 'virtue and purity' and these are inextricably tied up with her 'will and energy'. Furthermore, it is because he recognises and allows that will and energy in her that Jane has come to love him; and because he recognises her as an individual who, though his social inferior, is spiritually not only equal but superior to him. It is significant that even at the crisis of their struggle, Jane is able to enjoy her own sense of power:

I felt an inward power, a sense of influence, which supported me. This crisis was perilous; but not without its charm: such as the Indian, perhaps, feels when he slips over the rapid in his canoe.

We can see, then, that in the thematic structure of the novel, the St. John Rivers relationship is introduced as the antithesis to Jane's relations with Rochester. Physically, the two men are deliberately contrasted:

> My master's colourless, olive face, square, massive brow, broad and jetty eyebrows, deep eyes, strong features, firm grim mouth—all energy, decision, will—were not beautiful according to rule;

and, where Rochester is ugly and dynamic, St. John is static and beautiful—Jane indeed describes him like a statue:

> He was young . . . tall, slender; his face . . . was like a Greek face, very pure in outline; quite a straight, classic nose; quite an Athenian mouth and chin. It is seldom, indeed, an English face comes so near the antique models as did his. . . . His eyes were large and blue, with brown lashes; his high forehead, colourless as ivory, was partially streaked over by careless locks of fair hair.

The physical contrast is a direct reflection of the spiritual one. When St. John asks Jane to marry him, she sees him thus:

> To me, he was in reality become no longer flesh, but marble; his eye was a cold, bright, blue gem; his tongue, a speaking instrument —nothing more.

His inhuman will is channelled into the one direction of self-sacrifice —anticipated in Charlotte's poem 'The Missionary'—and as he tries to force Jane's will in the same direction, their relationship develops into a step-by-step contrast with the Jane–Rochester story. Where Rochester recognised Jane's independent will, St. John, 'by degrees . . . acquired a certain influence over me that took away my liberty of mind'; and Jane speaks of her 'servitude' to him. Where Rochester stood for life and warmth and energy, St. John exercises over her a 'freezing spell' and becomes a sort of death-image: 'My iron shroud contracted round me,' says Jane, as his influence steals over her. His cold purity is the antithesis of life—

> if I were his wife, this good man, pure as the deep sunless source, could soon kill me: without drawing from my veins a single drop of blood, or receiving on his own crystal conscience the faintest stain of crime—

and his very proposal of a loveless marriage is death: 'If I were to marry you', says Jane to him, 'you would kill me. You are killing me now.' Partly because this situation is so far removed from the traditional romantic one, a modern reader may find it more uniquely perceptive than the Jane–Rochester relationship. Slowly St. John brain-washes Jane, using, in the final stages, his predestinarian religion to force her to believe that obeying him will mean election, while rejecting him would make her a 'castaway'. For the reading before family prayers on the evening in which their relationship reaches its climax, he chooses Chapter XXI in Revelation, the chapter about the new Jerusalem, 'prepared as a bride adorned for her husband'; and it is not the bride imagery but the antithesis between the blessed and the damned which is meant to work on Jane. And it does work, as does his prayer after-wards: Jane describes her reaction as a movement from 'wonder', to being 'touched', to being 'awed', culminating in a 'veneration so strong that its impetus thrust me at once to the point I had so long shunned'. Already Jane had sensed the physically paralysing effect of his mental power over her: 'I shuddered as he spoke,' she says on a previous occasion, 'I felt his influence in my marrow—his hold on my limbs.' Now her will and spirit are about to surrender—

> I was tempted to cease struggling with him—to rush down the torrent of his will into the gulf of his existence, and there lose my own—

the imagery here recalling the imagery of floods and torrents in the earlier, Rochester, crisis in Chapters XXVI and XXVII, and also recalling—though without suggesting direct influence—George Eliot's later use of the river-image to express the suspension and abandonment of will in Maggie at the moment of crisis in *The Mill on the Floss*. Jane is deliberately made to draw our attention to the parallelism between this temptation and the earlier one, between, as it were, an attempted physical rape and a more grievous attempted spiritual rape, when she says: 'I was almost as hard beset by him as I had been once before, in a different way, by another.' It is the mysterious call through the night that saves her and prevents what would have been a total loss of her own self; and significantly the *peripeteia* is seen in terms of the return to her of 'energy to command well enough'—that is, to resist, and therefore subdue, St. John. As she breaks away from St. John, Jane sees her position as one of regained will-power, and thus regained identity:

> It was *my* time to assume ascendancy. *My* powers were in play, and in force.

And so, as a free individual as well as a passionate woman, she returns to Rochester.

In *Jane Eyre*, as we have already seen, the love story, the woman question and the governess (social) problem coalesce. Jane initially wins the love of Rochester through her own fearless sense of equality (what must have annoyed the *Quarterly's* Miss Rigby are things like Jane's statement of her superiority to her supposed rival, the moneyed and aristocratic—and beautiful—Miss Ingram). Her spirited assertion of equality is an essential step in the great love-scene in Chapter XXIII —'You glowed in the cool moonlight last night, when you mutinied against fate, and claimed your rank as my equal', Rochester says— and without it she would not have returned to ask Rochester to marry 'her who loves you best'. The nearest we get to this kind of fusion of themes in *Shirley* is in the crucial moment of the declaration between Louis Moore and Shirley:

> What change I underwent, I cannot explain; but out of her emotion passed into me a new spirit. I neither was crushed nor elated by her lands and gold; I thought not of them, cared not for them: they were nothing: dross that could not dismay me. I saw only herself; her young beautiful form; the grace, the majesty, the modesty, of her girlhood.

Thus Louis; and the triumphant resolution of this scene is Shirley's (rhetorical) question: 'And are we equal then, sir? Are we equal at last?', which echoes Jane Eyre's climactic thrust in her wooing scene:

> 'I am not talking to you now through the medium of custom, conventionalities, nor even of mortal flesh:—it is my spirit that addresses your spirit; just as if we both had passed through the grave, and we stood at God's feet, equal,—as we are!'

In a sense, Louis Moore is the Jane Eyre of *Shirley*—in his position as a tutor he suffers all the humiliations of a governess. Socially, he is presumably an even greater revolutionary than Jane, for it must have been even more uncommon for an heiress to marry her cousin's tutor than for a country squire to marry his ward's governess. But Louis is a man and cannot thus be used to link up all the thematic strands, as can Jane. In fact, no one in this novel is so used—as we have seen, the discussions of women's position and of governesses' position are set-pieces in the novel, not truly integrated with its plot and characters. Only Shirley's passionate assertion of her freedom of will can be seen as such an integration; but in the end it is the 'lioness tamed' we see, the wild animal caged and glorying in its subjugation—a sort of inversion of the Jane–Rochester relationship, where Jane has become Louis and Rochester, Shirley. And Caroline is only too pleased to have her concern for girls' education stifled in marriage. It is made very clear, by digressions and by the use of the two spinsters, Miss Ainley and Miss Mann, that the life of an old maid is unfulfilled; that lovelessness is the greatest form of human misery and poverty; and that the self can only be realised in mutual love.

But *Shirley* also returns to a theme which *The Professor* had first introduced: that superior intelligence, as exhibited and put to use in the relationship between master and pupil, is a powerful aphrodisiac. As early as 1839, Charlotte Brontë wrote to Ellen Nussey, having just refused a somewhat dreary proposal of marriage from Ellen's brother:

> If ever I marry, it must be in that light of adoration [i.e. 'that intense attachment which would make me willing to die for him'] that I will regard my husband ... And if he were a clever man, and loved me, the whole world weighed in the balance against his smallest wish should be light as air.[1]

Her feelings for M. Héger must have confirmed this attitude and lie behind the fact that in her novels the man–woman relationship is nearly always that of teacher-taught. It is seen at its simplest in *The Professor*: William and Frances have never once met outside the class-room situation before he knows he loves her (and rather expects her to return his feelings); when first they are together outside the school, they are only really comfortable as she reads *Paradise Lost* and he corrects her intonation; at the meeting after this, he proposes and is accepted. The love plot becomes slightly absurd, for feelings are not being realised in the language and brought to life in the reader's imagination, so that the relationship remains theoretical. Frances is on the surface timid; we are told of passion 'latent' in her—it is spoken of alternately as a 'fire . . . high and vivid' and a 'wild vigour', but unlike Jane Eyre she is given little chance to act out her vigour in the novel: it flashes forth once, eight years after her marriage, and it is seen more sustainedly once, in her sparring with Hunsden in Chapter XXIV, during which she dares convention not only by pitting her intellect against a man's (and a man of superior social rank at that) but by allowing herself to use the word 'hell'. It is her mental qualities that first attract the Professor; later he finds her physically attractive; but to her he always remains the intellectual master that she first fell in love with.

Charlotte Brontë is not just making plot use of the truth that many intelligent girls fall in love with their teachers (or, in modern terms, that many dons marry their students). The teaching-situation is Charlotte Brontë's favourite version of the love-and-power-game. In *Jane Eyre* the more imaginative plot and structure make possible the exploration of a wider range of relationships, but the situation is there as an underlying metaphor, as Jane and Rochester teach each other (and Jane likes to call Rochester 'master,' while he also tells her: 'you please me, and you master me'), and as St. John brain-washes Jane. In *Shirley* the thematically vital relationship is that between Shirley and Louis—Caroline's and Robert's being much more the conventional romantic one, though even they appear as pupil and master in their joint French and English poetry readings; and Robert is given a revealing passage where he speaks to Mr. Yorke about his ideal of a wife:

> 'Supposing, Yorke, she had been educated . . . supposing she had possessed a thoughtful, original mind, a love of knowledge, a wish for information, which she took an artless delight in receiving from your lips, and having measured out to her by your hand.'

This is very close to Louis's speech about how he wants to find 'some young, penniless, friendless orphan girl', to whom he can be 'first tutor and then husband'. And it is as her tutor that he feels he can claim Shirley. In his notebook he analyses his feelings in the days when he was actually teaching her:

> It was unutterably sweet to feel myself at once near her and above her: to be conscious of a natural right and power to sustain her, as a husband should sustain his wife.

> I worship her perfections; but it is her faults, or at least her foibles, that bring her near to me . . . these faults are the steps by which I mount to ascendancy over her.

The teaching-situation, then, not only obliterates conventional social superiority; it is also in itself an image of the ideal man-woman relationship. An interesting document here is the French composition on 'La Première Femme Savante' which Shirley had written while a pupil of Louis's a couple of years back, and which in the novel Louis, impossibly, recites verbatim from memory (the author translating it, 'on pain of being unintelligible to some readers'). A strange schoolroom exercise it is, on the 'bridal-hour of Genius and Humanity'—a kind of Blakean allegory. It deals with a primitive maiden, an Eve-figure, who receives a divine visitation. 'The Evening flushed full of hope: the Air panted; the Moon—rising before—ascended large'; and out of this love-charged atmosphere comes a voice:

> 'I take from thy vision, darkness: I loosen from thy faculties, fetters! I level in thy path, obstacles: I, with my presence, fill vacancy: I claim as mine the lost atom of life: I take to myself the spark of soul —burning, heretofore, forgotten!'

This whole story is like a mythifying of the Louis–Shirley relation (it serves a similar function here to that of Frances's poem in *The Professor*) and also of the typical Charlotte Brontë situation of 'the lonely creature longing for its mate' both spiritually and erotically. Thus Humanity addresses Genius:

> 'My glorious Bridegroom! True Dayspring from on high! All I would have, at last I possess. I receive a revelation. The dark hint, the obscure whisper, which have haunted me from childhood, are interpreted. Thou art He I sought. God-born, take me, thy bride!'

This is what pure imagination, without 'truth', is like in Charlotte Brontë, and we must be thankful for her concern in the novels with realistic 'truth' as well. But the position of this curious essay as the thematic centre in *Shirley*, and its profound relation to the other novels, is indisputable. The phrase with which Genius answers the appeal of Humanity is worth noticing: 'Unhumbled, I can take what is mine.' In love, questions of superiority are ultimately meaningless.

In the Paul Emanuel part of *Villette* we return to the master–pupil relationship of *The Professor*, though Lucy Snowe and Paul Emanuel have at least a chance to get to know each other socially as well as educationally. True love for Lucy comes not from the gay and worldly friendship of the handsome Graham Bretton but from the half-sadistic bullying of the irate and ugly little professor. Their acquaintance starts inauspiciously, and as long as they are merely colleagues in the same teaching-establishment it does not develop very far. The turning-point comes in Chapter XXX, when the professor, finding Lucy deficient in some branch of knowledge, begins to instruct her. As long as she is ignorant and slow to learn, M. Paul is 'very kind, very good, very forbearing'.

> But, strange grief! when that heavy and overcast dawn began at last to yield to day; when my faculties began to struggle themselves free, and my time of energy and fulfilment came; when I voluntarily doubled, trebled, quadrupled the tasks he set, to please him as I thought, his kindness became sternness; the light changed in his eyes from a beam to a spark; he fretted, he opposed, he curbed me imperiously.

For a while here Paul Emanuel becomes the type of all those who resist female intellectual development, and Lucy, in her defiance, speaks with the voice of Charlotte Brontë herself:

> I was vaguely threatened with I know not what doom if I ever trespassed the limits proper to my sex, and conceived a contraband appetite for unfeminine knowledge . . . his injustice stirred in me ambitious wishes—it imparted a strong stimulus—it gave wings to aspiration.
>
>   In the beginning, before I had penetrated to motives, that un-comprehended sneer of his made my heart ache, but by-and-by it only warmed the blood in my veins, and sent added action to my pulses. Whatever my powers—feminine or the contrary—God had given them, and I felt resolute to be ashamed of no faculty of His bestowal.

Yet it is out of this very feminist struggle that their love grows: he can see in Lucy a lovable woman only after he has learnt to recognise her as an *individual*, with a mind and an intelligence of her own. On the other hand, Lucy does not end as a blue-stocking marrying her equal: she worships. Having learnt more about Paul Emanuel's real character she sees in him her 'Christian hero', and when he declares his love (characteristically by presenting her with a fully-equipped school), she kisses his hand:

> He was my king; royal for me had been that hand's bounty; to offer homage was both a joy and a duty.

And in the end she sees her whole identity transformed by him: 'penetrated by his influence and living by his affection, having his worth by intellect, and his goodness by heart'.

In Lucy Snowe we have come a long way not only from Caroline Vernon, but also from Jane Eyre, and yet Lucy embodies these two and all the other Charlotte Brontë heroines before her. In creating her, Charlotte achieved her ultimate reconciliation of 'realism' with 'poetry', into 'truth'; and that truth is a realisation of modern womanhood with its painfully paradoxical impulses: intellectual ambition and emotional hunger, drive towards independence and need for love.

For all this, it is not the hard-won love but the sufferings of loneliness that are at the centre of *Villette*, not the late and precarious fulfilment of hope, but the absence and thwarting of it for so long. It is the theme of deprivation that produces the most powerful passages in the novel— Lucy describing how 'a want of companionship maintained in my soul the cravings of a most deadly famine', or experiencing the agonies of waiting for Graham's letters thus:

> I suppose animals kept in cages, and so scantily fed as to be always upon the verge of famine, await their food as I awaited a letter.

And if we look for the imaginative climaxes in the novel, we are likely to find them in the two feverish and nightmarish scenes of desolation, first the one where Lucy wanders out in the city and ends up in the confessional, and secondly the night of the feast when she thinks Paul Emanuel lost to her for ever. Also, Charlotte Brontë would not allow Lucy a happy ending. She is left with her 'independency' and with the memory of a love barely discovered and never consummated. Theoretically Charlotte Brontë has left the ending of the novel open—and she jokes with her publishers about the merits of a do-it-yourself denouement: 'Drowning and Matrimony are the fearful alternatives'[1]—but the overall tone of the novel allows no alternative but drowning to Paul Emanuel, when the storm which has been Lucy Snowe's evil genius throughout the novel assails him. No wonder that Catherine Winkworth, in a letter which contains some of the best and most human criticism of this novel, should say that

> 'Villette' makes one feel an extreme reverence for any one capable of so much deep feeling and brave endurance and truth, but it makes one feel 'eerie', too, to be brought face to face with a life so wanting in *Versöhnung*.[1]

Also in a letter, Matthew Arnold asks 'Why is *Villette* disagreeable?', and goes on to answer his own question:

> Because the writer's mind contains nothing but hunger, rebellion, and rage, and therefore that is all she can, in fact, put into her book. No fine writing can hide this thoroughly, and it will be fatal to her in the long run.[2]

It is ironical that it should have been, not her unfeminine writing, not the 'truth' of her imagination, that became fatal to her in the end, but a real-life pregnancy toxaemia in combination with a Brontë constitution. In terms of the imaginative life of her novels, the marriage with the Reverend A. B. Nicholls seems so inappropriate; and in her own assessment of him—

> I believe him to be an affectionate, a conscientious, a high-principled man; and if, with all this, I should yield to regrets, that fine talents, congenial tastes and thoughts are not added, it seems to me I should be most presumptuous and thankless—[3]

he is so unlike the teacher-heroes of her novels. But we know that he was capable of passionate feeling—one remembers Charlotte's description of how, when he was leaving Haworth after she had refused his proposal, she found him 'in a paroxysm of anguish, sobbing as women never sob';[4] that she found wifehood a strangely pleasant mystery; that in her fatal illness she saw in him 'the best earthly comfort that ever woman had';[5] and that, according to Mrs. Gaskell, she fought death: 'He will not separate us, we have been so happy.'[6]

Inevitably Charlotte Brontë's art brings us back to her life, from which it drew its truth. Faced with the two, one must contradict the reviewer who found in her 'no sympathy or true insight into the really feminine nature'.[1] Highly personal as her vision is, her insight into 'the really feminine nature' surpasses not only that of either of her sisters, but also that of most other English novelists, of her own and any other period.

And so the art of Charlotte Brontë makes a natural end to my quest. It would be futile to attempt a summary and conclusion of a study which, from the nature of its material, has had to take the form of an exploration rather than a tight argument—an exploration which, I am keenly aware, still leaves many white areas on the Brontë map. But we have, I hope, seen how Charlotte, by being so much more conscious of the issues of feminism, in the widest sense, than either of her sisters and also so conscious of her own identity as a woman with a career to make and with a deep need to love and be loved, was in a unique position to bring to the English novel that 'precious speciality' of contribution which George Eliot speaks of when discussing female novelists. To Charlotte Brontë novel-writing became in a unique way a feminist activity: both a career and a necessary form of self-expression. Emily Brontë is the greater artist: the miracle of her imagination lies in her detachment from her actual situation, including her womanhood. Anne Brontë is the greater moralist: her artistry exists only as the product and vehicle of her morality. Of the three sisters, Charlotte Brontë is the one whose art, in its strengths as well as its weaknesses, is stamped through and through with evidence that she had made the woman question, in its least technical and most personal sense, her proper sphere.

Notes

TEXTS: All quotations from the Brontë novels in my text and notes are taken from the Shakespeare Head ed. (Oxford, 1931).

The poems of Anne Brontë are quoted from the Shakespeare Head ed.: *The Poems of Emily Jane Brontë and Anne Brontë*, ed. T. J. Wise and J. A. Symington (Oxford, 1934); those of Charlotte Brontë, from the Shakespeare Head ed.: *The Poems of Charlotte Brontë and Patrick Branwell Brontë*, ed. T. J. Wise and J. A. Symington (Oxford, 1934); and those of Emily Brontë, from *The Complete Poems of Emily Jane Brontë*, ed. C. W. Hatfield (N.Y., Columbia U.P., 1941).

ABBREVIATIONS USED IN THE NOTES

SHLL   *The Shakespeare Head Life and Letters* (*The Brontës: Their Lives, Friendships and Correspondence*, ed. T. J. Wise and J. A. Symington [Oxford, 1932], I-IV).

Life   Mrs. Gaskell's *Life of Charlotte Brontë* (Thornton ed., Edinburgh, 1924).

Hatfield   *The Complete Poems of Emily Jane Brontë*, ed. C. W. Hatfield (N.Y., Columbia U.P., 1941).

Tillotson   Kathleen Tillotson, *Novels of the Eighteen-Forties* (Oxford Paperback ed., 1961).

Young   G. M. Young, *Victorian England: Portrait of An Age* (Oxford Paperback ed., 1960).

Unless it is otherwise indicated, the place of publication of books referred to is London.

INTRODUCTION

page
xv 1 Letter to W. S. Williams, May 12, 1848 (*SHLL*, II, 215-6).
xv 2 *SHLL*, III, 150.
xvi 1 Young, 3.
xvi 2 Young, 91.
xvi 3 Letter to W. S. Williams, August 16, 1849 (*SHLL*, III, 11). The criticism referred to had appeared in the *North British Review*.
xvi 4 Ellen Nussey's description, quoted in *SHLL*, II, 273.
xvi 5 Hatfield, 205-6.

CHAPTER I

1 1 The pseudonym which Mrs. Gaskell used for some early magazine stories and for her collection, *Life in Manchester* (1848). In the same year, her first novel, *Mary Barton*, was published anonymously. Title-page anonymity was variously attempted: e.g., Mrs. Oliphant's first novel appeared as *Passages in the Life of Mrs. Margaret Maitland of Sunnyside. Written by herself* (1849).

2 1 *Fortnightly Review*, I (1865), 492.

2 2 *Life*, 373.

2 3 *Christian Remembrancer*, XV (April 1848), 396–409.

2 4 *SHLL*, III, 11.

3 1 *SHLL*, III, 31.

3 2 *Edinburgh Review*, XCI (January 1850), 153–73.

3 3 *SHLL*, III, 67.

3 4 *Blackwood's*, LXXVII (May 1855), 568.

3 5 *Athenaeum*, no. 1209 (December 28, 1850), 1369.

4 1 *Literary History of England* (1882), III, 168–9.

5 1 Samuel Richardson, *Sir Charles Grandison* (1754), II, Letter XXXII.

5 2 For an excellent discussion of the position of the woman novelist up to 1800, see J. M. S. Tompkins, *The Popular Novel in England, 1770–1800* (1932), Chapter IV. See also Joyce M. Horner, *The English Women Novelists and their Connection with the Feminist Movement (1688–1797)*, vol. XI, nos. 1–3, of *Smith College Studies in Modern Languages* (Northampton, Mass., 1930).

5 3 *SHLL*, I, 155.

6 1 'The Lady Novelists', *Westminster Review*, n.s. II (July 1852), 129–41.

6 2 'Novels with a Purpose', *Westminster Review*, n.s. XXVI (July 1864), 24–49. See esp. p. 49. An article, entitled 'English Novels' in *Fraser's Magazine*, XLIV (October 1851), 375–91, relates how one 'courageous lady' who set about translating George Sand into English 'felt it necessary to confine her labours to a careful selection, and, limited as that selection was, its failure as a speculation in our market brought it to a premature close' (p. 378). Charlotte Brontë was—though with some reservations—a devotee of George Sand, whom she saw as a greater novelist than Balzac.

6 3 'The Swedish Romances', *Fraser's Magazine*, XXVIII (November 1843), 505–25. Cf. George Eliot's review of Fredrika Bremer's novel *Hertha*, in *Westminster Review*, LXVI (October 1856), 571–8, where she praises Miss Bremer for trying to deal with contemporary problems (particularly the woman question), but regrets the 'pink haze of visions and romance' in which she envelops these problems. This review article, 'Three Novels', is reprinted in *Essays of George Eliot*, ed. Thomas Pinney (1963), 325–34.

6 4 *La Belle Assemblée*, XXVIII (March 1848), 158–62. This story, written

by 'M.A.Y.', has the usual pattern of improvident parents and poor daughter, making her way as a governess. Cf. the discussion of the governess theme in Chapter II, below. *La Belle Assemblée* in this period also frequently carried reviews of factual or fictional works on governesses, such as Augusta M. Wicks, *Education; or the Governesses' Advocate* (vol. XXVII, October 1847, 247), or Mrs. S. C. Hall's story 'The Old Governess' (vol. XXIX, August 1848, 119).

7 1 *The British Novelists;* with an Essay; and Prefaces, Biographical and Critical, by Mrs. Barbauld, I, (1810), 48.

7 2 *Westminster Review*, n.s. XXVI (July 1864), 25.

7 3 *Quarterly Review*, XIV (October 1815), 188–201. See esp. 189.

7 4 *Quarterly Review*, XXIV (January 1821), 352–76. See esp. 352–3.

8 1 *Fraser's Magazine*, XL (December 1849), 697.

8 2 *The Leader*, I (May 18, 1850), 189.

8 3 'Modern Novelists—Great and Small', *Blackwood's*, LXXVII (May 1855), 554–68; see 555.

9 1 *Westminster Review*, n.s. II (July, 1852), 133–4.

10 1 Letter to W. S. Williams, July 3, 1849 (*SHLL*, III, 6).

10 2 See Elizabeth Haldane, *Mrs. Gaskell and Her Friends* (1930), 35.

11 1 *Life*, 315–6.

11 2 'False Morality of Lady Novelists', *National Review*, VIII (January 1859), 144–67. The quotations are, respectively, from 147–8 and 144.

11 3 'Silly Novels by Lady Novelists', *Westminster Review*, n.s. X (October 1856), 442–61. Reprinted in Pinney (cf. note 6–3, above), 300–24.

12 1 Elizabeth Haldane, *George Eliot and Her Times* (1927), 107–8.

12 2 To Mrs. Peter Taylor, February 1, 1853. See *The George Eliot Letters*, ed. Gordon S. Haight (1954), II, 86. The lines quoted occur as part of an appraisal of Mrs. Gaskell's *Ruth*.

12 3 'Silly Novels', 460.

12 4 'Silly Novels', 460.

14 1 See Anthony Trollope, *An Autobiography* (1883), Chapters I–II, and also Eileen Bigland, *The Indomitable Mrs. Trollope* (1953). Her first novel, *The Refugee in America*, appeared later the same year (1832).

14 2 The most famous of these are in *Our Village*, which was published from 1824 onwards; there were further editions of *Belford Regis, or Sketches of a Country Town* (1835) in the 1840s; and her contributions to *The Edinburgh Tales* (1845–6) were popular.

15 1 *The Literary Chronicle*, no. 197 (February 22, 1823), 113–16. My attention was drawn to these reviews by Mrs. S. M. Salama (El-Shater), whose dissertation on 'The Novels of Mary Shelley' (1963) is in the Liverpool University Library.

15 2 *Blackwood's*, XIII (March 1823), 283–93. See esp. 283. Cf. also Appendix E, 318, in R. G. Grylls, *Mary Shelley* (1938).

16 1 Opening of Chapter XXXV (Premier World Classic ed., translated by Fayette Robinson [N.Y., 1961], 223).

page

16 2 *Athenaeum*, no. 1043 (October 23, 1847), 1101.

16 3 See Robert B. Heilman, 'Charlotte Brontë's "New" Gothic', reprinted in *Victorian Literature: Modern Essays in Criticism*, ed. Austin Wright (N.Y., O.U.P., Galaxy Paperback, 1961), 71–85.

17 1 See M. W. Rosa, *The Silver-Fork School: Novels of Fashion Preceding 'Vanity Fair'*, no. 123 of *Columbia University Studies in English and Comparative Literature* (N.Y., 1936).

17 2 *SHLL*, III, 150.

18 1 See, e.g., Friedrich Schubel, 'Literarhistorische Voraussetzungen für Thackerays *Vanity Fair*', *Sprache und Literatur Englands und Amerikas*, III, ed. G. Müller-Schwefe (Tübingen, 1959), 27–44; and Gordon N. Ray, '*Vanity Fair:* One Version of the Novelist's Responsibility', reprinted in *Victorian Literature*, ed. Austin Wright, 342–57.

19 1 *Blackwood's*, LXXVII (May 1855), 556.

19 2 In Thomas Morton's play, *Speed the Plough* (1798).

20 1 *The British Novelists*, I, 60.

21 1 Preface to *Belinda* (1801).

23 1 Review in *The New Weekly Messenger*, quoted on the dust-jacket of *Illustrations of Political Economy*, no. 5.

23 2 *Diary, Reminiscences, and Correspondence of Henry Crabb Robinson*, ed. Thomas Sadler (1872), II, 144.

25 1 'English Novels', *Fraser's Magazine*, XLIV (October 1851), 375–91. See esp. 375 and 380.

25 2 *La Belle Assemblée*, XXVII (December 1847), 373–5.

25 3 *Tait's Edinburgh Magazine*, XV (1848), 138.

25 4 *New Monthly Magazine*, LXXXII (January 1848), 140.

26 1 Raymond Williams, *Culture and Society, 1780–1950* (Penguin ed., 1961), 99.

27 1 Arnold Kettle, 'The Early Victorian Social-Problem Novel', *Pelican Guide to English Literature*, 6 (1960), 169–87. See esp. 171.

27 2 'The Old Governess', the first in a series of 'Sketches from Life', by Harriet Martineau, in *The Leader*, I (November 9, 1850), 788–9.

28 1 *Blackwood's*, LXXVII (May 1855), 556–7.

28 2 'Silly Novels', 449.

29 1 Young, 155.

29 2 Allibone's *Dictionary of English Literature and British and American Authors* (1870), gives a list of her works, as follows: *Hints on Reading: Addressed to a Young Lady* (1839); *Scriptural Poems for Children* (1840); *Every-Day Duties: in Letters to a Young Lady* (1840); *National Ballads, Patriotic and Protestant* (1841); *Female Writers* (1842); *Principles of Education practicably considered, with an especial reference to the present state of female education in England* (1844). The B.M. catalogue adds a selection of 'Christian Epigrams', 'translated from various Greek and Latin poems', which were added to the *Epitaphs from the Greek Anthology*, translated by Major R. G. Macgregor (?1857). Several of

her works appeared in new editions in the 40s and 50s. My attention was first drawn to Miss Stodart by a reference to her in Janet Dunbar, *The Early Victorian Woman* (1953), 117–8.

29 3 'A Few Words About Novels', *Blackwood's*, LXIV (October 1848) 459–74; see 462. On this point, see the interesting study by Margaret Maison, *Search Your Soul, Eustace: A Survey of the Religious Novel in the Victorian Age* (Stagbooks, 1961), esp. Chapter V, 'The Low Church Contribution'. Miss Stodart has a particular dislike of the religious novel, feeling that religion must inevitably suffer if contaminated by fiction: 'Does truth suffer no loss of dignity in availing herself of such a conveyance?' (p. 137). To illustrate this point, she uses the irresistable image of Queen Victoria riding in a wagon.

30 1 *Edinburgh Review*, XCI (January 1850), 155.

32 1 Tillotson, 58.

32 2 *Quarterly Review*, LXXXIV (December 1848), 173–4.

33 1 *Revue des Deux Mondes*, XXIV (1848), 471–94; the quotation is from 475.

33 2 Mrs. Oliphant, *Blackwood's*, LXXVII (May 1855), 558.

33 3 This essay is reprinted in *The Life and Letters of Sydney Dobell*, ed. 'E.J.' (1878), I, 163–86; see 178. He thinks *The Tenant* Charlotte's, too.

35 1 *SHLL*, II, 215–6.

37 1 'Woman, Her Duties, Education, and Position', *Oxford and Cambridge Magazine*, I (August 1856), 462–77. See esp. p. 463. The fullest discussion of feminist ideas in *The Princess* is to be found in John Killham's study of the poem, *Tennyson and 'The Princess': Reflections of an Age* (1958).

37 2 Charlotte Brontë to Mrs. Gaskell, September 20, 1851 (*SHLL*, III, 278). The article, on 'Enfranchisement of Women', had appeared in the July 1851 issue of the *Westminster Review* (289–311). At the time of writing, Charlotte believed it to be by John Stuart Mill; it was in fact by Mrs. John Taylor, who married Mill in 1851.

37 3 *Fraser's Magazine*, XLII (September 1850), 250.

39 1 *Quarterly Review*, XXIV (January 1821), 367.

39 2 There is an illuminating discussion of this conception in Walter E. Houghton, *The Victorian Frame of Mind, 1830–1870* (New Haven, Yale U.P., 1957), 348–53.

40 1 A review article on John W. Parker, *Woman's Mission*, 13th ed. [*sic!*] 1849, in *Westminster Review*, LII (January 1850), 352–78. The quotations are from, respectively, 354–5 and 378.

42 1 Cf. her letter to Mrs. Gaskell of April 26, 1852 (*SHLL*, III, 332). Cf. also Greg's discussion of the moral-artistic confusion in *Ruth*, in 'False Morality of Lady Novelists'.

42 2 *Blackwood's*, LXXVII (May 1855), 560.

43 1 *Blackwood's*, LXXVII (May 1855), 557–8.

43 2 *Christian Remembrancer*, XV (April 1848), 396.

page

44 1 See *SHLL*, IV, 43. Cf. *Villette* review, *Daily News*, February 3, 1853.

44 2 *Athenaeum*, no. 1320 (February 12, 1853), 186–8. See esp. 186.

45 1 *Christian Remembrancer*, XXV (June 1853), 401–43. Quotations from, respectively, 423, 442 and 443. The author of this review was Miss Anne Mozley (see *SHLL*, IV, 80).

45 2 *Christian Remembrancer*, XV (April 1848), 396.

46 1 *Edinburgh Review*, XCI (January 1850), 158. The reviewer is here referring to both *Jane Eyre* and *Shirley*.

46 2 *Fraser's Magazine*, XXXIX (April 1849), 417–32. See 424.

46 3 Letter to Mrs. Gaskell, May 14, 1857 (*SHLL*, IV, 222).

47 1 Letter to Emily Shaen, September 8, 1856 (*SHLL*, IV, 208).

47 2 *Fraser's Magazine*, LV (May 1857), 569–82. See esp. 578.

47 3 'Novels with a Purpose', *Westminster Review*, n.s. XXVI (July 1864), 24–49. Quotations from 48–9.

48 1 *Women Novelists of Queen Victoria's Reign* (1897), 26.

48 2 Reprinted, from *The Kenyon Review*, 1947, in *Forms of Modern Fiction*, ed. William Van O'Connor (Minneapolis, U. of Minnesota Press, 1948), 102–19.

48 3 Letter dated May 14, 1857. See *SHLL*, IV, 222. Kingsley's comments are the more significant as he was one of the leading exponents of the view of woman as, above all, a pure, moral, influence on man. Cf. Houghton, *The Victorian Frame of Mind*, 351, n. 27. Cf. also Kingsley's comment on *Shirley*, quoted on p. 46, above.

CHAPTER II

49 1 *Female Writers*, 67. Cf. Chapter I, above.

50 1 Shakespeare Head ed. of *The Poems of Emily Jane Brontë and Anne Brontë*, xxiv. The *Selections* of Emily's and Anne's poems were added by Charlotte to the 1850 ed. of *Wuthering Heights* and *Agnes Grey*.

52 1 'Thursday, July the 31st, 1845 . . . I have begun the third volume of Passages in the Life of an Individual'. The diary-type notes written by Anne and Emily Brontë on the occasion of Emily's birthday, July 30 (though in 1845 they were one day late), in 1841 and 1845, to be exchanged and opened four years later, have been much drawn on by Brontë biographers. They are reprinted, e.g., in Fannie E. Ratchford, *Gondal's Queen* (Austin, U. of Texas Press, 1955), Appendix II. On the identification of Anne's 'Passages' with *Agnes Grey*, see Winifred Gérin, *Anne Brontë* (1959), 225.

52 2 *New Statesman*, August 17, 1946, 119.

53 1 For two recent theories, see Daphne du Maurier, *The Infernal World of Branwell Brontë* (1960) and Winifred Gérin, *Branwell Brontë* (1961).

55 1 Compare the protracted death of one of the pupils which is the highlight of Miss Sewell's governess novel, *Amy Herbert*.

page

59 1 There is a useful survey of the governess in literature in Chapter II of
       Patricia Thomson, *The Victorian Heroine: A Changing Ideal, 1837–
       1873* (1956), but I disagree with the author's opinions on the social
       attitudes expressed in *Agnes Grey* and on the literary merits of this
       novel. An illuminating study of the social position of the governess
       is to be found in Wanda F. Neff, *Victorian Working Women: An
       Historical and Literary Study of Women in British Industries and Pro-
       fessions, 1832–1850* (1929), Chapter V, 'The Governess'.

59 2 The date of Mrs. Sherwood's novel is given by *C.B.E.L.*, conjecturally,
       as 1845, but the *English Catalogue* shows it to be 1835. Strictly speaking,
       Caroline Mordaunt is not a novel but a tale for the young. But, as I
       have suggested above on pp. 19–21, the borderline between didactic,
       even juvenile, fiction and the novel proper is very thin; and *Caroline
       Mordaunt* could easily be classed as a religious novel, with a strongly
       Evangelical tone and a moralistic intention. Similar to Lady Blessing-
       ton's *The Governess* in structure, it is diametrically opposed in tone
       and attitude. A comparison of the two, however, invites itself, if
       only because of the similarity in titles—*Caroline Mordaunt* is sub-
       titled 'The Governess'—and in heroines' names—the heroine of *The
       Governess* is called Clara Mordaunt. Mrs. Sherwood was known as
       the author of exceedingly pious works, not least through the many
       editions of her 'improved' version of Sarah Fielding's *The Governess*
       (initially published in 1749; Mrs. Sherwood's *The Governess; or, the
       Little Female Academy* first appeared in 1820), in which she replaced
       fairy-tales with 'such appropriate relations as seemed more likely to
       conduce to juvenile edification' (her Preface, iv). Charlotte M. Yonge,
       who includes Sarah Fielding's work, in its original form, in her
       collection of children's classics, *A Storehouse of Stories* (1870), I, 89–
       222, speaks (p. vii) of 'Mrs. Sherwood's adaptation to her own
       Evangelical style'.

60 1 Cf. Chapter I, above, esp. p. 27.

60 2 *Quarterly Review*, LXXXIV (December 1848), 176. These are, of
       course, some of the lines which Charlotte Brontë quotes in *Shirley*:
       cf. p. 34, above.

62 1 This, too, is the pattern of the *Belle Assemblée* story, 'The Young
       Governess', referred to above, p. 6 and n. 6–4, in which the heroine
       advances from a job as 'daily governess' with some very unpleasant
       people to one as 'in-door governess' in a good and kind family. It
       was probably the least revolutionary version of the success theme in
       the governess novel.

62 2 That this was due to the pressure of her reading public rather than to
       her own inclination, is indicated by her letter about *The Governess*,
       quoted in Michael Sadleir's study of her life and work, *Blessington-
       D'Orsay: A Masquerade* (1933), 275: 'It was my anxious wish to point
       attention and excite sympathy towards a class from which [more is]

expected and to whom less is accorded, than to any other. . . . I felt this so much that I wished to make my book a much more grave one; but the publisher, thinking only of the sale, bargained for its being interspersed with lively sketches, which in my opinion interfere sadly with the original intention.' Clearly her 'original intention' was one which, if fulfilled, would have anticipated the governess-novel-with-a-purpose of the 1840s; instead she had to live up to her reputation as a fashionable woman and a novelist of fashionable life and write a typical 'she-novel' (this is how the *Fraser* reviewer described her novel *The Two Friends* (1835)—see Sadleir, 250).

63 1 See note 59–2.

65 1 *Life*, 154–5. In the same context Mrs. Gaskell relates an occurrence which epitomises the reasons why the Brontës, and particularly Charlotte, so hated the life of a governess. In one of her situations Charlotte had managed, after many difficulties, to gain the respect and affection of her charges—so much so that one small boy, 'in a little demonstrative gush', put his hand in hers and said, 'I love 'ou, Miss Brontë'. But cold water was immediately poured on this display of unseemly feelings, by the children's mother exclaiming, before all the children, 'Love the *governess*, my dear!'

70 1 See, e.g., Winifred Gérin, *Anne Brontë*, and Ada Harrison and Derek Stanford, *Anne Brontë: Her Life and Work* (1959).

70 2 Roy Pascal, *Design and Truth in Autobiography* (1960).

70 3 George Moore, *Conversations in Ebury Street* (2nd ed. 1930), 219.

77 1 Patricia Thomson, *The Victorian Heroine*, 128.

84 1 Before the Marriage and Divorce Act of 1857 a divorce could be obtained only by an Act of Parliament, granted on the application of the husband and founded on the adultery of the wife. But even after the 1857 Act Helen Huntingdon would not have been likely to obtain a divorce.

CHAPTER III

86 1 *SHLL*, II, 274.

86 2 *Life*, 204.

86 3 Romer Wilson, *All Alone: The Life and Private History of Emily Jane Brontë* (1928), 115.

86 4 C. Day Lewis, 'Emily Brontë and Freedom', in *Notable Images of Virtue* (Toronto, 1954), 1–25; see esp. 19ff.

87 1 Ellen Nussey's words; see *SHLL*, II, 274.

87 2 See Ratchford, *Gondal's Queen*, 192–3. The tone of contentment in Emily's note contrasts markedly with that of depression in Anne's note of the same date: Anne, who has had 'some very unpleasant and undreamt-of experiences of human nature' feels that 'I for my part cannot well be flatter or older in mind than I am now'.

page

89 1 Cf. the poem 'All day I've toiled' (Spring, 1837; Hatfield, 35–6), and below, p. 110.

90 1 *The Leader*, I (December 28, 1850), 953.

90 2 *New Monthly Magazine*, LXXXII (January 1848), 140.

90 3 Peter Bayne, 'Ellis, Acton, and Currer Bell', in *Essays in Biography and Criticism*, 1st ser. (Boston, 1857), 398–402. Quoted in the excellent survey of *Wuthering Heights* criticism by Melvin R. Watson: '*Wuthering Heights* and the Critics', *The Trollopian*, III (March 1949), 243–63.

91 1 *Athenaeum*, no. 1052 (December 25, 1847), 1324.

91 2 *Tait's Edinburgh Magazine*, XV (1848), 138–40.

91 3 *Life and Letters of Sydney Dobell*, I, 175.

91 4 *The Spectator*, XX (1847), 1217; quoted by Melvin R. Watson.

91 5 *Quarterly Review*, LXXXIV (December 1848), 175.

91 6 *Athenaeum*, no. 1209 (December 28, 1850), 1369.

91 7 *Blackwood's*, CXLI (June, 1887), 758.

92 1 'Biographical Notice of Ellis and Acton Bell' (1850).

92 2 'Editor's Preface to the New Edition of *Wuthering Heights*' (1850).

92 3 Frederic Harrison, *Studies in Early Victorian Literature* (1895), 161.

92 4 Walter Pater, *Appreciations* (1904), 242. (In the essay, called 'Postcript', on 'classical' and 'romantic'.)

92 5 Swinburne, 'Emily Brontë', *Athenaeum*, no. 2903 (June 16, 1883), 762–3.

93 1 *Scrutiny*, XIV (September 1947), 269–86; see esp. 271.

93 2 *Early Victorian Novelists* (Penguin ed., 1948), 121.

93 3 *Essays in Criticism*, VIII (January 1958), 27–47.

96 1 *Early Victorian Novelists*, 119–20.

99 1 Cf. the account in Mario Praz, *The Romantic Agony* (Fontana Library ed., 1960), 91–2.

101 1 *Eugene Aram*, Bk. V, Chapter VII (Collins' Clear-type ed., n.d., 466, n. 1).

101 2 See Emily and Anne Brontë's joint note on Branwell's birthday, June 26, 1837: 'Charlotte working in Aunts room [,] Branwell reading Eugene Aram to her' (*Gondal's Queen*, 187).

101 3 Chase, 'The Brontës, or, Myth Domesticated', 114. (Cf. n. 48–2, above.)

102 1 Miriam Allott, 'The Rejection of Heathcliff', 47. (Cf. note 93–3, above.)

102 2 *Gondal's Queen*, 32. Cf. also Appendix I, 'Reconstructing Gondal', in Fannie E. Ratchford, *The Brontës' Web of Childhood* (N.Y., Columbia U.P., 1941).

102 3 Mary Visick, *The Genesis of Wuthering Heights* (Hong Kong, 1958), 5.

102 4 Edwin Morgan, 'Women and Poetry', *The Cambridge Journal*, III (August 1950), 643–73; see esp. 651–2.

103 1 *Notable Images of Virtue*, 4.

112 1 I am grateful to Dr. Fritz Wiener for letting me read his unpublished

essay on 'The Origins of the *Wuthering Heights* Story', in which he discusses similarities between *Wuthering Heights* and *Elective Affinities*. He confirms my own impression that Emily Brontë knew Goethe's novel, but that her memories of it, if she draws on them in *Wuthering Heights*, had undergone a thorough transmutation.

121   1   *Victory* (Penguin ed., 1963), 205.

130   1   C.P.S., *The Structure of Wuthering Heights* (The Hogarth Press, 1926).

141   1   Dorothy Van Ghent, 'The Window Figure and the Two-Children Figure in *Wuthering Heights*', *Nineteenth Century Fiction*, VII (1952), 189–97. See also the chapter on *Wuthering Heights* in Dorothy Van Ghent, *The English Novel: Form and Function* (Harper Torchbook ed., N.Y., 1961), 153–70.

142   1   Herbert Read, *Collected Essays in Literary Criticism* (1938), 283. (Essay on 'Charlotte and Emily Brontë'.)

146   1   Apart from his general popularity as a biographer, Lockhart seems to have been a special favourite of the Brontës. In 1834 Charlotte's list of recommended reading to Ellen Nussey includes his *Life of Burns* (*SHLL*, I, 122), and it is very probable that his *Life of Scott* was read in the parsonage some time after its publication in 1837–8. About a year after the appearance of *Poems, by Currer, Ellis and Acton Bell*, Charlotte Brontë sent presentation copies of the volume—which had had practically no sale at all—to Wordsworth, Tennyson, De Quincey and Lockhart (*SHLL*, II, 135–6); the company suggests how highly at least she (but presumably she would have consulted her sisters as to recipients) thought of Lockhart. His *Life of Scott* is in the list of volumes available in 1841 in the Keighley Mechanics' Institute Library (see Clifford Whone, 'Where the Brontës Borrowed Books', *Brontë Society Transactions*, XI, 5 (1950), 344–58). The quotation in my text is from *Memoirs of the Life of Sir Walter Scott*, VII (Edinburgh, 1838), 394.

149   1   *Blackwood's*, XLVIII (November 1840), 680–704. This story was suggested as a source for *Wuthering Heights* by Leicester Bradner, 'The Growth of *Wuthering Heights*', *P.M.L.A.*, XLVIII (1933), 129–46.

151   1   First published in *Romantic Tales* (1808), 'Monk' Lewis's adaptation of a German romance is now available in *Seven Masterpieces of Gothic Horror*, ed. R. D. Spector (Bantam Classic ed., N.Y., 1963). The quotation is from 245–6 in this edition.

152   1   First published, posthumously, in *Appleton's Journal*, 1877. Now in *Seven Masterpieces of Gothic Horror*. The quotation is from 336.

152   2   See Mark Schorer, 'Fiction and the "Matrix of Analogy"', *The Kenyon Review*, XI (1949), 539–60, esp. 549.

155   1   *Biographia Literaria*, Chapter XIV.

155   2   *SHLL*, II, 273.

155   3   *Athenaeum*, no. 2903 (June 16, 1883), 763.

CHAPTER IV

157 1 Letter dated August 27, 1850 (*SHLL*, III, 150).

158 1 Ian Watt, *The Rise of the Novel: Studies in Defoe, Richardson, and Fielding* (Penguin ed., 1963), esp. 62–77. On 147–51 Watt has an interesting discussion of the (im)possibility of female economic individualism in the eighteenth century.

159 1 'The Literature of the Last Fifty Years', *Blackwood's*, CXLI (June 1887), 737–61; see esp. 757. Mrs. Oliphant, in the same context, speaks perceptively of how Charlotte Brontë's work 'intensifies the sensations of solitude, and the vacancy of the heart, into a form of passion with which perhaps no woman, either before or since, has expressed that yearning of the woman towards the man which formed part of the primeval curse'; and ten years later, in the chapter on 'The Sisters Brontë' in her *Women Novelists of Queen Victoria's Reign*, she develops this theme more fully, speaking of Charlotte's articulation of 'the woman's grievance—that she should be left there unwooed, unloved, out of reach of the natural openings of life: without hope of motherhood: with the great instinct of her being unfulfilled'. At the same time, she is anxious to stress that there was nothing sensual in this longing of the lonely creature for its mate: 'I think it was the first time this cry had been heard out of the mouth of a perfectly modest and pure-minded woman, nay, out of the mouth of any woman; for it had nothing to do with the shriek of the Sapphos for love' (p. 24).

160 1 'Le Roman Contemporain en Angleterre', *Revue des Deux Mondes*, nouvelle période IV (1849), 714–35; see esp. 716.

160 2 Letter dated October 30, 1852 (*SHLL*, IV, 13–4).

160 3 She quotes her letter to Miss Martineau in one to George Smith, January 1, 1852 (*SHLL*, III, 303). Cf. *SHLL*, III, 42 and *SHLL*, IV, 34–5 for the letters to Ellen Nussey and Mrs. Gaskell, respectively.

161 1 Letter to W. S. Williams, September 1848 (*SHLL*, II, 255).

161 2 Letter dated July 9, 1853 (*SHLL*, IV, 76–7).

162 1 See the edition of selected Angrian material provided by Fannie E. Ratchford, in collaboration with W. C. DeVane, *Legends of Angria* (New Haven, Yale U.P., 1933); esp. 316.

162 2 Letter dated November 6, 1847 (*SHLL*, II, 152–3).

162 3 Letter to W. S. Williams, April 2, 1849 (*SHLL*, II, 319).

162 4 The defence of *Shirley* on the grounds of realism is in a letter to W. S. Williams, March 2, 1849 (*SHLL*, II, 313); that of *Villette* in a letter to George Smith, December 6, 1852 (*SHLL*, IV, 22–3). But cf. her criticism of *Henry Esmond* in a letter to George Smith very close in date to that on *Villette*: she finds that the first two volumes of Thackeray's novel have 'too much History—too little Story', and continues: 'I hold that a work of fiction ought to be a work of

creation: that the *real* should be sparingly introduced in pages dedicated to the *ideal*' (*SHLL*, IV, 17).

163 1 Cf. Franklin Gary, 'Charlotte Brontë and George Henry Lewes', *P.M.L.A.*, LI (1936), 518–42.

163 2 Letter dated January 12, 1848 (*SHLL*, II, 178–80).

164 1 G. H. Lewes, 'The Novels of Jane Austen', *Blackwood's*, LXXXVI (July 1859), 99–113; see esp. 107. Cf. Lewes's *Westminster Review* essay on 'The Lady Novelists' (LVIII, October 1852, 129–41; esp. 138).

164 2 Letter dated January 18, 1848 (*SHLL*, II, 180–1). For the comparison between George Sand and Balzac, see the letter to G. H. Lewes dated October 17, 1850 (*SHLL*, III, 172).

164 3 Letter dated April 12, 1850 (*SHLL*, III, 99).

169 1 *The Brontës' Web of Childhood*, 190–200.

170 1 Letter to W. S. Williams, December 14, 1847 (*SHLL*, II, 161).

173 1 Cf. n. 16–3, above.

177 1 Cf. her words to Lewes in January 1848: 'If I ever *do* write another book, I think I will have nothing of what you call "melodrama" . . . I *think*, too, I will endeavour to follow the counsel which shines out of Miss Austen's "mild eyes", "to finish more and be more subdued" ' (*SHLL*, II, 179).

177 2 'Emma' was published in *The Cornhill Magazine*, I (April 1860) 487–98, with an Introduction by Thackeray in which he sees Charlotte Brontë as a Jane Eyre figure: '. . . the trembling little frame, the little hand, the great honest eyes. . . . New to the London world, she entered it with an independent, indomitable spirit of her own . . . an austere little Joan of Arc marching in upon us, and rebuking our easy lives, our easy morals'. It is not easy to see just where Charlotte Brontë was going in this story of a little girl who is dumped in the Misses Wilcox's school, allegedly the daughter and heir of 'Conway Fitz-gibbon, Esq., May Park, Midland County', which gentleman, however, turns out to be a fraud. The Misses Wilcox are awarded 'some portion of that respect which seems the fair due of all women who face life bravely, and try to make their own way by their own efforts' (p. 488)—a typical Charlotte Brontë note thus sounded—but they are also ridiculed, for their manners, their dress and, above all, their making up to the aristocracy; and there is some shrewd observation of the society of country-gentry.

177 3 Letter dated January 28, 1848 (*SHLL*, II, 184).

177 4 Cf. Ivy Holgate, 'The Structure of *Shirley*', *Brontë Society Transactions*, XIV, 2 (1962), 27–35.

177 5 Letter to W. S. Williams, January 28, 1848. Cf. n. 177–3, above. On *Michael Armstrong*, cf. pp. 25–6, above.

177 6 See the letter to George Smith referred to in n. 160–2, above. On the other hand, Asa Briggs, in his valuable article on 'Private and

page

Social Themes in *Shirley*', *Brontë Society Transactions*, XIII, 3 (1958), 203–19, stresses Charlotte Brontë's genuine insight into the social situation. She did not, as she has sometimes been accused of doing, confuse the Luddites and the Chartists; not did she refrain out of ignorance or cowardice from providing a solution to the problems she deals with. She states the issues as seen from both sides and then points to 'the healing influence of time and experience' (Briggs, 215).

187   1   'Private and Social Themes in *Shirley*', 215.

191   1   *Legends of Angria*, 213.

192   1   *Legends of Angria*, 279–81.

193   1   *Legends of Angria*, 304–6.

198   1   Letter dated March 12, 1839 (*SHLL*, I, 174).

202   1   See letter to George Smith, March 26, 1853 (*SHLL*, IV, 55–6).

203   1   *SHLL*, IV, 53. Catherine Winkworth (1827–78) was a friend and pupil of the Gaskells; she later became an author and translator and was active in the movement for the promotion of higher education for women.

203   2   Letter to his sister, Mrs. Forster, April 1853. See *Letters of Matthew Arnold, 1848–1888*, ed. G. W. E. Russell (1895), I, 29.

203   3   Letter to Ellen Nussey, April 11, 1854 (*SHLL*, IV, 112–3).

203   4   Letter to Ellen Nussey, May 27, 1853 (*SHLL*, IV, 68).

203   5   One of her last letters to Ellen Nussey, February 21, 1855 (*SHLL*, IV, 175).

203   6   *Life*, 523.

204   1   *Christian Remembrancer*, XXV (June 1853), 443. Cf. pp. 44–5, above, and also Charlotte's letter to the Editor of the *Remembrancer*, July 18, 1853 (*SHLL*, IV, 79).

Index

The names of Anne, Charlotte and Emily Brontë are abbreviated as, respectively,
A.B., C.B., and E.B.

219

Index